THE
THRILL
OF THE
GRILL

THE
THRILL
OF THE
GRILL

Techniques, Recipes,
& Down-Home Barbecue

Chris Schlesinger

&

John Willoughby

WILLIAM MORROW
An Imprint of HarperCollins*Publishers*

Line drawings by Laura Hartman Maestro
Photography by Vincent Lee

First William Morrow paperback edition published 2002

The Library of Congress has catalogued the hardcover edition as follows:

Schlesinger, Chris.
    The thrill of the grill: techniques, recipes, & down-home
  barbecue / Chris Schlesinger and John Willoughby.
        p.   cm.
    ISBN 0-688-08832-5
1. Barbecue cookery. I. Willoughby, John. II. Title.
  TX840.B3S275   1990
  841.7'6—dc20   89-77522
                                                                      CIP

ISBN 0-06-008449-9 (pbk.)

03 04 05 06 /QW/ 10 9 8 7 6 5 4 3

To Cary, with love and respect

Acknowledgments

◆◆◆

First of all, thanks to my father, who took a strange kind of pride in a son who chose a career that, at the time, was offbeat and none too promising.

In the beginning of this career, there was Pat Ricks, owner of Blue Pete's restaurant in Virginia Beach, Virginia, who taught a young dishwasher what work was all about, and pulled, pushed, and shoved him into becoming a cook. Next came my pal and colleague Jim Burke, who showed me what it means to have passion for food, and Bob Kinkead, another pal and colleague, whose early confidence in me will always be a great source of pride.

These three inspired me to become the cook that I really wanted to be. But being a professional cook for fifteen years in no way prepared me to write a book. Fortunately, I had many talented people help me in the process. Without their assistance, this book would be only the subject of late-night dreaming. I can't name them all here, but I would like to give special thanks to some:

To Laura Bezel, Debbie Merriam, and Denise Landis for their recipe testing and development. Their comments and suggestions were a great help in making sure the recipes were easy to understand and use.

To the staff of the East Coast Grill, who have always worked hard, with pride and a sense of humor, and who helped create a situation in which a cookbook was a possibility for me. In particular, special thanks to Carl, Smiley, Tina, Boone, Elmer, Joanne, José, Marie, and Michelle.

To my sous-chefs, past and present: Bob Delbove, Paul O'Connell, and Joey Knauss. These are the guys I've spent the last five years with, working, developing, changing, laughing; guys who did most of the work and received little of the credit; guys who made it possible for me to take time to write this book without worrying about the food at the Grill. Most of the recipes in this book are a direct result of these people and our work together. Thanks, also, to Maurice and Cottonhead for filling in whenever they were needed.

A cook is only as good as the raw ingredients that he or she has to work with, so thanks go to Tony and Olgo Russo for their patience as they received my daily phone calls and educated me about the workings of the fresh produce trade; to John Dewar, for the consistent high quality of the meat he provided; and to Glenn and Terry at Rocky Neck Seafoods for their integrity and their dedication to acquiring the freshest possible fish.

Thanks to all my friends in the restaurant business in Boston for creating an excellent climate in which to work and play and eat excellent food.

To the customers of the East Coast Grill and Jake & Earl's Dixie Barbecue, who have been so supportive even under sometimes difficult conditions. To have people respond in a positive manner to my cooking has been one of the most rewarding experiences of my life.

Of course, the East Coast Grill would not be possible without my partner, Cary Wheaton, the brains of the operation, whose nonstop attention to detail has allowed me to cook and not have to deal with anything else. Our shared belief that work can be fun and rewarding if correctly appreciated continues to make my job seem easy.

When I started to work on this book, I spent most of my time reading and finding out how much I didn't know. Barbara Haber, the curator of the culinary wing of the Schlesinger Library at Harvard, was instrumental in pointing out where to find the very books that I needed to fill in the gaps. Also in that vein, I would like to give special thanks to Barbara Kafka who, in the early stages of the book, was generous enough to spend time talking to me and helping me clarify my ideas.

The photographs in this book are the result of the efforts of four very hard-working professionals who put their creative minds together: Vincent Lee, the photographer, whose steadiness and clarity of vision kept us on the right track, and who, in imminent danger of having his studio burn down, forged ahead in a dramatic session to produce the cover photo; his assistant, Eugene; Sarah Barbarise, whose sensibility provided the framework for the pictures, and who constantly amazed me with her ability to transform the spirit of my food into physical reality; and Grace Young, who had the knack of making adjustments on the run and always made the food look beautiful. Together, these four made me feel comfortable inside a process about which I knew nothing. I'd like to thank them for their company, and for that memorable day on the beach.

To my grandma, who has cooked more food that I have enjoyed than any other single person, and who taught me to appreciate food as food.

To my sister, Susan, her husband, Rick, and their children, Lizzie and Tommy, for being my family. Also, thanks to George and Jake for their intelligence, wit, and companionship.

Getting back to my lack of skills and the hours spent on the grind-it-out work of the book, to my co-author and friend, Doc, who bore the brunt of the work with nary a bad word. Through all the rough times, he was always there with his good humor and friendship. And, for those people who have actually read anything I wrote, you know what a monumental job he did in translating my ramblings into something readable. Thanks, Doc.

Chris Schlesinger

In addition to all of the people that Chris mentioned above, I'd like to thank Mark and Karen for all the dinners they fed me while I was working nights on the book. And, of course, special thanks to Susan, Rick, and Cary, for their unwavering support and friendship, and to Lizzie and Tommy, "the exsperts."

It may seem odd to thank my friend Chris for what is essentially his own book. However, it is not only his vision and skill with food, but also his friendship and his attitude toward life that has made this book possible. Without his sense of adventure, we would never have tried it. He has an uncanny ability to turn drudgery into fun, and has kept the whole project in perspective throughout. Besides, he had the confidence to take me on as his co-author. Thanks, Chris.

John Willoughby

Together, we would like to thank our agent, Robin Manna, who had the brilliant idea of writing this book in the first place. Her direction throughout the process was essential to making it happen, and she was at all times an excellent dinner companion.

Thanks, also, to the entire staff at Morrow for their precision and speed in putting the book together.

And, of course, special thanks to our editor, our guide and coach, Maria Guarnaschelli. Her expertise, capacity for work, and attention to detail were awe-inspiring. We thank her for her personal attention, her support, her easygoing style, and her sense of humor.

Contents

Introduction

◆◆

I'll try any kind of food at least once—particularly after a long day of surfing and a couple of rum drinks. Back in 1978, during my first stay in the tropics, this particular combination set me on a path that led to this book.

I had quit a humdrum cooking job and headed down to the Caribbean—Barbados to be exact—to spend the winter with the two great loves of my early life: overhead waves and low 80s temperatures. Being a misguided youth, I managed to exist on hamburgers, potato chips, and Cokes for the first month. Eventually, however, I bowed to financial needs and the entreaties of my newfound local friends and began to eat the food they ate. I started frequenting the same restaurants they did and cooking with ingredients from the open-air markets. This was the first time I had immersed myself in another culture and its food.

One fine Sunday afternoon shortly before I had to leave to come back stateside, my buddies and I were out back grilling some dolphinfish. Some of our Bajun friends showed up, among them my sometime culinary guide. He brought out some small, lantern-shaped red and yellow peppers. "Best in the world," he said. "Check 'em out." I trusted the guy, he had always come through before, and, like I said, I'll try any food once. So I chopped up the peppers, added some lime juice, mango, and herbs, and ended up with a yellow-orange relish. I whipped some of it on the fish, took a big bite, and . . . it practically blew my head off. Sweat poured down my face and every cavity in my head opened to twice its normal size as my mouth tasted a great, distinct, aromatic flavor. The culprit was the Scotch Bonnet, the World's Hottest Chile Pepper, and I loved it. Soon I was happily splashing this sauce and any other fiery hot condiment I could find on everything I ate. That was the beginning of my fascination with hot foods and tropical ingredients.

At the time, however, this fascination seemed to have little connection with my life as a professional cook. After starting out as a dishwasher, I had gone to the Culinary Institute of America, where my training had mostly been devoted to reproducing the classical recipes and techniques of Escoffier. Being a chef, it seemed, consisted of re-creating the past. I learned what my teachers had to teach me, but I can't say that I was inspired by food—until I returned from my Caribbean trip full of memories of spicy foods, exotic ingredients, and raw, strong flavors.

My timing was right. When I got back to the United States, the nouvelle cuisine movement, which had been under way in France for some time, was beginning to make its presence felt. In Boston, this was nowhere truer than at a Cambridge restaurant known at the time for being at the culinary vanguard. At the Harvest, the best expression of the emerging principles of nouvelle cuisine were in operation. For the first time, I found myself working with young, eager cooks who were inspired by the freedom this cuisine allowed.

The basis of this new cooking style was a rededication to the profession of cooking, in which integrity, freshness, and use of local ingredients replaced such irrelevancies as flaming dishes tableside. Cooks began to use the highest-quality ingredients and let them speak for themselves, rather than overpowering them with elaborate preparations. At the Harvest, curiosity and imagination were encouraged, and the kitchen staff was exposed to a vast array of new ingredients. This was the best training I could have had to complement my formal schooling, and it is from this time that I date my passion for food and my sense of culinary adventurousness.

All this innovation and ferment created a climate in which being a cook meant following principles, not recipes. As long as the principles were observed and the results were rewarding, each cook could bring his or her own background to bear on food. I began to look to my own background for inspiration.

I was weaned on grilled food, and that burned, crusty taste was one of my first taste memories. I grew up in Virginia and spent every possible minute at my parents' cottage near Virginia Beach. When we were there, we wanted cooking to be as easy as possible, which meant grilling. My dad taught me to appreciate food for itself, not the trappings that surrounded it. He always went to Woolworth's for hot dogs because they had the best grilled buns, and he would drive an hour out of his way for the perfect barbecue sandwich. He loved shad roe, oysters, and charred steak. When he cooked, which wasn't often, he'd grill a steak so that it was burned on the outside and raw on the inside. My sister and I would always tell him that it was both too burned and too raw, but he refused to cook steak any other way; and eventually we got to like it. Years later I would use this principle to create one of my favorite dishes: seared sushi-quality tuna, burned on the outside and raw on the inside.

Then of course, there was that great Southern specialty, barbecue. How can I do justice to this food, steeped in tradition, surrounded by myth and lore, subject of a million arguments and stubborn opinions—it is the most commonplace food around. The best barbecue is always found in a low-down dive that is as comfortable and easy as old clothes. I love barbecue for its taste and for the type of people who cook and eat it. Every year when I was a kid my folks would throw a "pig-picking" party. They always hired some local guys to come to our house the day before, dig a pit, and barbecue a whole pig. They would arrive just as I was going off to bed, pulling up in their trucks with their hats and their beers; they'd dig the pit and start the pig. When I got up in the morning I'd see them lounging around with that particular tired, satisfied slowness that comes from staying up all night drinking beer and tending the pit. I'd spend time with them, helping them cook and enjoying their easy camaraderie. So it is that I came to love the process of barbecuing and the atmosphere that surrounds it as much as the actual food. Barbecue taught me what I consider one of the cardinal principles of cooking: It's the cooking, not just the eating, that is to be enjoyed.

On holidays we would visit Grandma Wetzler's house in rural Pennsylvania. Her table was jammed with an incredible number of dishes—homemade applesauce, pickled eggs, corn pudding, ham salad, homemade baked beans. It always seemed like a picnic. She had developed an enormous repertoire of rural American dishes by cooking every meal for her large family since the age of sixteen. I still think of her table as the very essence of honest, bedrock American food.

I also drew on the memories of food I had eaten as I traveled around the world looking for the perfect wave. The Scotch Bonnet was followed by many such discoveries in tropical countries from Costa Rica to Thailand and points in between. I began to notice certain similarities and pieced together an understanding of why the food of hot climates captured my imagination. This style of cooking—highly spiced, usually grilled, and served in that informal, friendly fashion that goes with beaches and hot weather—defined my own feelings and ideas about food. For want of a more precise term, I call this food "equatorial cuisine." This doesn't mean that it is all found precisely midway between the Tropics of Cancer and Capricorn, but that it shares the characteristics of hot-weather food that I just described.

Running through all of my food memories and discoveries, from barbecue to the tropics, is my love of very distinct tastes. My food has strong flavors that are not blended into a single taste; instead they are combined without losing their individuality. My sauces are raw, with lots of herbs, spices, and garlic. I like to finish my relishes and sauces as close to serving time as possible so the individual flavors stand out rather than blend together during cooking. So I add something at the last minute—a squeeze of lime, some fresh herbs, a chunk of spicy butter. I like my sauces to reach as many parts of the palate as possible simultaneously. In general, my food has an earthy simplicity, a casual style, with the emphasis on the clarity and dimension of the taste. I pay more attention to the proper preparation of particular ingredients than to flourish and presentation.

Since 1985, I have been the co-owner and chef of the East Coast Grill in Cambridge, Massachusetts. There I have a custom-designed open-pit wood-fired grill, which in its five years of constant use has been a testing ground for my own brand of culinary adventurousness. A menu that changes monthly, combined with my frequent research-and-development field trips, has given the kitchen staff the opportunity to creatively explore the relationship among spices, grilled food, and hot-weather staples. On any given night, a rather complex Thai-inspired dish like Steamed Clams with Lemongrass and Chiles de Árbol may share the menu with a straightforward Grilled Big Black-and-Blue Steak for Two as we try to encourage our customers to explore new food experiences in an atmosphere that doesn't intimidate.

One constant menu item, though, is barbecue. My fascination with the intricacies of the craft of barbecue has led me to crisscross the country sampling other people's versions of this classic, taken me to the Memphis in May International Barbecue Championship three years running, and eventually found me at the doorstep of John Willingham, two-time National Barbecue Champion. With a little work, I talked him into building me a barbecue pit that incorporated his infinite knowledge of the method. Satisfied that we finally had the understanding, experience, and equipment necessary to do it justice, in 1988 my partner and I opened our own version of that unique American phenomenon, the barbecue joint. We called it Jake and Earl's, after my one-eyed dog and my partner's two-eyed father.

I love food but I think of it as part of the celebration of life, rather than the centerpiece. *The Thrill of the Grill* presents no-fuss food, meant for people who like to explore new and interesting tastes but don't want to be burdened by intricate preparations. Strong equatorial flavors and spices, the barbecue of the South, and the excitement and informality of cooking over live fire are what this book is all about.

Chris Schlesinger
Boston, Massachusetts

Grills Just Wanna Have Fun

Grilling is described by Auguste Escoffier, the father of classical cuisine, as "the remote starting point, the very genesis of our art." He wasn't kidding. In fact, humans have been cooking with fire since before they were humans: There is good evidence that *homo erectus* types like the Peking man and Java man were grilling just after dinosaurs had checked out. Through the years, the basic principles they observed have not really changed much, a fact you should keep in mind as you read this chapter. I want to give you the benefit of my fifteen years of professional grilling, but at the same time I want you to preserve the notion that it is one of the simplest and purest of cooking forms.

What exactly is grilling, and how is it distinguished from other cooking methods? Well, in grilling, the food to be cooked is placed within a few inches of the direct heat of a fire and is cooked by conduction, the goal being to concentrate the juices in the middle while searing the outside. During the searing process, the reaction of the food to the high heat of the fire produces a browning and a concentration of flavor on the exterior. This is what we mean when we talk about that indefinable "grilled" flavor.

The physical process that takes place during searing is known as the Maillard reaction, after the French scientist who discovered it. In layman's terms, this complex reaction can be summarized easily: "Brown food tastes better." Think of the difference between the taste of golden-brown bread crust versus the rest of the bread, or the aroma of roasted versus unroasted coffee beans, and you will understand the process that gives grilled foods their intensity of flavor. So now that you know all about the Maillard reaction, you'll have an answer to the favorite rhetorical question of backyard cookouts, "How come grilled food tastes so good?"

A cooking process can also be defined partially by looking at the characteristics of the food best suited for it. In general, grilling is suitable for ingredients that are tender and cook relatively quickly, since the intense heat needed for grilling makes it impossible for any food to remain on the fire for very long without being cremated. For example, when grilling meat, only cuts such as steaks or chops, which are relatively small and free of connective tissues, are suitable.

It is good to know these things about grilling, because they increase our appreciation of the technique as a serious and time-honored culinary method. It is also important to note that it is a very healthful method of cooking, since you very rarely use butter, cream, or fats in grilling. The most important aspect of grilling, however, is still the indisputable fact that cooking outdoors with fire is fun.

To me, grilling lends itself to the invitation "Let's eat and drink and enjoy some time together." In the words of James Beard, one of the first to fully appreciate the American grilling tradition, "What fun is there to a picnic or a barbecue if there is present the feeling of discipline or restraint? Whether your first task is to be grilling two lamb chops or barbecuing a couple of pigs . . . do either with a heart and spirit and have a good time doing it. Otherwise there is no point to this business at all."

To me, that's the gospel from the mountain.

The Grill

There are grills of all types on the market. They range from inexpensive hibachis you can buy in the Seasonal Items aisle of any supermarket or discount drugstore to megaexpensive, architecturally beautiful covered grills. Covered grills such as the Webber kettle are probably the most versatile, since they allow you to do covered as well as conventional grilling. Many experts, however, do not recommend these types of grills since their grill surfaces cannot be adjusted up and down, a feature that allows you to regulate the temperature of your fire more closely.

I don't recommend any particular type of grill for cooking the food in this book, nor do the recipes assume that you need to own any one piece of equipment. All you really need is a fire and a grill surface that is fixed above that fire. Whether you are grilling on a tiny hibachi on a city fire escape or on a giant brick grill with a four-foot firebox in a new age restaurant, the essential determinant is not the grill but the griller—as long as you watch your fire, check your food frequently, and keep yourself in the proper relaxed frame of mind, you are all set. You will learn to use your own piece of equipment.

If I am asked for my recommendation about equipment, however, I always say that the design of the grill is not as important as its size. This is because when cooking, a large grill offers you maximum flexibility in terms of moving your food around to different areas of the fire where there are hotter and cooler spots, depending on how fast you want to cook the food. What I am encouraging you to do here is give yourself as much room to move as you can afford.

Fuel
♦ ♦ ♦

There's a lot of hoo-ha going around about the fuel to use for open-fire cooking, but I wouldn't take any of it all that seriously. In my opinion, there are three basic types of fuel, and anything else is a variation of one of them. Your choices are (1) your basic charcoal briquettes, (2) hardwood lump charcoal, and (3) hardwood itself. In addition, there are such exotica as grapevines, dried herbs, and as many different types of wood chips as Howard Johnson had ice creams, but I consider these to be flavoring agents, not fuels.

Again, I don't want to try to dictate what you should use, but there are a few general principles I think you should know about, and that do lead to certain conclusions about which type of fuel is most suitable for the grilling you plan to do.

The most important of these principles is that grilling is conducted at a very high heat and is therefore a very quick method of cooking. Because of this, the fuel you use is not a major factor in the flavor of the product. A chicken breast that stays on the fire for ten minutes is simply not going to absorb that much flavor from the fuel. The use of vine cuttings, herb stems, or aromatic wood chips is fine, so long as you understand that they are useful more for atmosphere than for taste.

Having said this, I have to follow it up by saying that the type of fuel you use, while not a major factor in the taste of the food you grill, will have some impact on it. (Also, the fuel used is of prime importance when barbecuing: see Woods as Fuels, page 264.) This is true not only because of the particularities of the smoke, which after all is partially composed of unburned particles of fuel, but also because of the characteristic ways in which different fuels burn. Because it does make some difference what you use, you should understand the qualities of the three basic types of fuel available.

STANDARD CHARCOAL BRIQUETTES: Briquettes are adequate. They start easily; create a fire with a regular, steady heat; and have the additional advantage of being readily available in every supermarket, twenty-four-hour store, bait and gun shop in America. However, you might want to pay some attention to the process by which these briquettes are made. Like all charcoal, the raw material for your basic briquettes is made by burning a wood product in the absence of oxygen until the wood is reduced to carbon. The wood product used for standard briquettes is sawdust and scrap wood. (In fact, the process of making briquettes was an invention of Henry Ford, who was looking for a way to profit from the leftover wood from his Model T frames.) After the material has been turned to carbon, it is compressed into briquettes along with starch binders and ground coal. Many manufacturers add other chemicals, such as sodium nitrite, which give off oxygen to make the briquettes get started more easily. The chemicals in the briquettes, as well as the coal itself, do contribute to the smoke given off by briquettes and consequently can affect the taste of the food you are grilling.

HARDWOOD LUMP CHARCOAL: The fuel I most highly recommend, hardwood lump charcoal is made by burning hardwood in a closed container with no oxygen until it is turned to carbon. Since it is left in the "lump" form of the individual wood pieces rather than shaped into briquettes, it contains no additives. Hardwood lump charcoal is more convenient than wood itself, starts easily, and gives you a regular fire that burns very cleanly and is long-lasting. It creates a somewhat hotter fire than briquettes do, which is an advantage in that you get a quicker and more complete sear on the exterior of your food. In addition, lump charcoal is becoming more readily available all the time.

HARDWOOD: In its natural form hardwood is fun to use for grilling and certainly an acceptable fuel, since it was the original and only fuel used for grilling for tens of thousands of years. Any hardwood will do. Oak, hickory, mesquite, and various fruitwoods are the easiest to locate. However, wood does have drawbacks as a fuel, and in general I would recommend it only if you are an expert or if you are not too uptight about the results of your grilling. The main difficulty is that wood does not burn consistently because of irregularities in the size, consistency, and moisture content of various logs or even various parts of the same log. Thus it is much harder to get a uniform bed of coals when using wood, and the process requires a tremendous amount of patience. Wood also takes considerably longer to reach the coal stage at which you should begin cooking, so you need to allow a longer precooking start-up time. When making the recipes in this book and using wood, allow approximately ten minutes more for start-up time than the recipes call for. Despite all this, though, cooking with wood is challenging. After a few sessions with hardwood charcoal, you might want to try the original.

The Fire

Laying Your Fire

My first rule when laying a fire is not to skimp on the fuel. The extra buck you may spend to use the correct amount of fuel will be well worth it in the end. Like having a large grill, having plenty of coals allows you that extra maneuverability that makes grilling easier.

Keeping this in mind, lay a fire with a slightly larger surface area than that of the food you are going to cook, and make it about four inches thick. Then lay a section next to it about half that area—two inches thick. This will give you fairly large surface areas with differing temperatures. (It should now be obvious why I recommended that you get the largest possible grill that suits your budget and your cooking location.) Then you will have plenty of room to move food around when it is cooking too fast or too slow, as well as to avoid the frequent flare-ups that occur during grilling.

Remember, this suggestion is a general guideline. If your grill is too small to allow you to build a fire of this size, just build a fire that is at least as large in area as the surface area of the food you are cooking, and make sure that a good portion of the fire—let's say a third—has considerably less fuel than the rest.

Starting Your Fire

Here again, convenience is the key word, but only if the fuel you use does not interfere with the taste of the food. I will assume that you are using charcoal briquettes or hardwood charcoal for your fuel. If you are using wood, I assume that you were in some type of scouting group and learned the basic paper-underneath-twigs-neatly-arranged-in-a-teepee-with-bigger-logs-on-top method. So, in order of least to most recommended, these are your basic options.

PRESOAKED CHARCOAL BRIQUETTES: Forget it. Unlike using lighter fluid by itself, grilling with presoaked briquettes, which are soaked through with fluid and release chemical fumes throughout much of the cooking process, is taking convenience one step too far.

LIGHTER FLUID: Many people believe that lighter fluid imparts a "chemical" taste to the food. I don't buy this. The fluid cooks off in the first five or ten minutes after the fire is lit, and the intense heat of a proper grilling fire makes sure that no residue sticks to the grilling surface. So unless you plan to reapply fluid just before cooking, splash it on and light away. For the best results, pile your fuel in a loose pyramid shape, soak it with fluid, and allow a minute or two for the fluid to soak in before lighting. Just be careful, and never apply lighter fluid to a fire that has already been lit.

KINDLING: Satisfying to those who are unhappy with the continuing encroachment of technology on our lives, the kindling method works—but not always. It consists of building a small fire of kindling, then gradually placing more and more coals on top as the fire gains full strength. This method has the twin disadvantages of requiring a ready supply of kindling and constant attention to the fire over the initial period. On the other hand, this is the method my brother-in-law uses—largely because he forgets to buy lighter fluid at the store and is a contractor with a ready supply of wood trimmings—and he builds excellent fires in a relatively short period of time. I suspect he also enjoys the required fiddling with the fire during the start-up period, as some of you might, too.

ELECTRIC STARTER: If you have a long extension cord or an outside outlet, an electric starter is probably the easiest method of starting a fire. It is inexpensive, totally reliable, and so consistent that you always know how long it is going to take to get your fuel properly ignited. Although it is unappealing to many people because it retains an aura of "gadgetry," it is really much more useful and less silly than the electric can opener or the automatic fruit ripener. To prolong the life of this handy device, take it out of the coals as soon as they are properly lit, unplug it, and set it aside on a fireproof surface until it is cool.

METAL FLUE: Second only to the electric starter in ease and reliability, a metal flue is even less expensive. Basically it is a sheet metal cylinder, open at both ends, with ventilation holes around the bottom and a grid about two inches from the bottom. You simply put crumpled newspaper in the bottom section, then fill the top section with charcoal and light the newspaper. This device relies on a simple principle of physics: Hot air rises and creates a draft. This sweeps the fire up from the newspaper through the charcoal, which then ignites readily. I know it doesn't sound all that promising, but then neither does the airplane when you hear the explanation of how it works.

My dad used to make a simple version of this by taking the ends off a coffee can and punching holes around the bottom with a church key, but the commercial version has the advantage of being more durable and having a wooden handle which makes it easier to remove after the coals are fully ignited, so I recommend you invest a couple of bucks and buy one rather than making your own.

Is It Ready Yet?

Whichever method you use to light the fire, you should not start cooking until the coals are all uniformly gray. If you want a low-temperature fire, it is better to catch the fire on the way down rather than on the way up. Smoke is basically unburned particles of fuel, and therefore the more completely your fuel is ignited, the cleaner a flame you will have. Escoffier himself (there he is, again) called for a clean flame for grilling, and that means you want to burn over coals rather than flames.

In any case, once the coals are covered with a fine layer of gray ash, you need to check to make sure that the fire is the temperature needed to cook whatever you are making that day. A good way to test is by holding your hand about five inches above the cooking surface and seeing how long you can hold it there. If you can hold it there for five to six seconds, you have a low fire; three to four seconds is a medium fire; and one to two seconds means you have a hot fire. If you need some help in estimating how long a second is, try saying the number followed by a word or phrase of about two or three syllables. I do it by counting, "One-one-thousand, two-one-thousand."

Another factor you should be very aware of is that it takes a fair amount of time for the coals to reach the gray ash stage. You should light your coals about thirty-five to forty minutes before you start cooking if you want a hot fire; forty to forty-five minutes before cooking if you want a medium fire; and forty-five to fifty minutes before cooking if you want a low fire.

Tools
◆ ◆ ◆ ◆ ◆

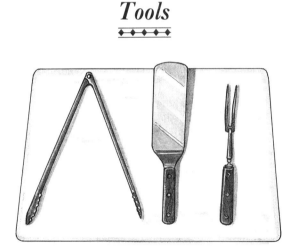

In addition to the grill and the fuel, you will need a few simple tools for grilling. None of them is expensive or difficult to procure, but each is essential. All can be found at your local restaurant supply store, and I recommend that you get them there, since you are more likely to find the heavy-duty type of equipment that makes grilling easier and more carefree. You don't want to be worrying about your tools giving out on you while you're in the middle of grilling.

HEAVY-DUTY, LONG-HANDLED, SPRING-LOADED TONGS: Absolutely the most essential grilling tool, tongs are to the griller what brushes are to a painter. With them, you can manage almost any product on the grill from a skewer of shrimp to a thick steak to a tiny scallop. Each adjective in the description of this tool is important. They must be heavy-duty so they don't give or bend when you are lifting heavy items on and off the grill. Tongs that are long-handled allow you to work over a hot fire—essential for grilling many items—without burning your hands and forearms. And being spring-loaded makes them infinitely easier to use than the scissor types found in many kitchen stores, which require you to manually open and close the tongs every time you want to use them.

You may have noticed that I am reluctant to make many absolute statements in this book, preferring to give general guidelines and let people find the method or tool that is right for them. This is an exception. These tongs will make your grilling life much easier. Get them.

OFFSET SPATULA: In the restaurant business, an offset spatula is also known as a dogleg spatula. As you can see, it is basically a spatula with a bent neck, which allows you to easily get under and lift an item on the grill that is not easily handled with tongs—such as a hamburger or a fish fillet. Try to get the large professional size, which is about 7½ inches long by 3 inches wide. This size gives you the capability to lift more delicate items like fish fillets and is also sturdier than the smaller home models.

HEAVY-DUTY, LONG-HANDLED FORK: You don't want to use this fork to move food around on the grill, since piercing things allows juices to escape. However, it is a very handy tool for any number of uses: probing the flesh of chicken or fish to check for doneness; moving the grill surface when you need to add more fuel; stirring up the coals when you want a hotter fire; even fending off a too-inquisitive neighborhood dog. Again, the long handle allows you to work safely and comfortably over a very hot fire, and the sturdier a fork you can find, the better.

SKEWERS: You can use either disposable wooden or bamboo skewers or metal ones, depending upon whether you are most concerned with convenience, ecology, or sturdiness. The bamboo and wooden types come in small and large sizes, but even the larger ones are not as sturdy as the metal varieties. Here I make no particular recommendation other than that you decide what makes the most sense for you—or what you can find in the kitchen drawer. If you are using the metal ones, though, try to get ones that are twisted or flat-sided, either of which ensures that when you move the skewers the food does not twist around and end up with the same side down.

WIRE BRUSH: You will need a wire brush, an unfortunate necessity for the one slightly unpleasant part of grilling: cleaning the grill surface. Nothing can ruin the taste of an excellent portion of grilled food faster than the added taste of the food previously cooked on that grill. The best time to clean a grill is immediately after you have finished cooking but before the fire has died. That way, any residue from cooking will fall into the fire and disintegrate, and any grease on the grill will not have had time to congeal and become difficult to clean. Never use soap on your grill, just brush it vigorously with the wire brush and it will come clean easily. As always, try to get the longest-handled version of this tool you can find. I recommend that you buy it in a hardware store, since hardware stores usually have a wide selection and tend to carry heavy-duty models. And, if you find yourself thinking that cleaning off the grill is a real drag, think about cleaning pots and pans and your burden will lighten immediately.

Going About Grilling

Since grilling over live fire is not an exact science, the cooking times given in my recipes are guidelines, not gospel, and must be backed up by your own observations. There are different methods for telling when various foods are properly done, and I have included these methods in the introductions to the appropriate chapters as well as in the recipes. Keep in mind that there is nothing magical about knowing when something you're grilling is done—it is the result of experience. A professional cook may grill two thousand steaks before he or she knows with a quick look and a poke of the finger that a particular steak is perfectly medium rare. So don't expect instant expertise. Take a reasonable approach, learning a little bit each time you grill, and after a season of grilling you will be pretty accurate.

SAFETY: Remember Mrs. O'Leary and her barn. You are working with live fire, which entails certain risks and therefore calls for certain precautions. Set up your grill in the largest available open space in case it tips over; check to be sure there are no tree branches or other objects above the grill; and never light your coals with gasoline. Be sure to have a fire extinguisher handy. A bucket of sand or a garden hose will do if you don't have a commercial extinguisher. Also, keep toddlers well away from the grilling area, and don't let older children play around a portable grill.

GRILL SPACE: A mistake that novice grillers make is to crowd the grill. This makes it very difficult to turn the things you are cooking, or to move them to hotter or cooler areas when they are either cooking too fast or need a little boost. Give yourself plenty of room to work.

THE MISE-EN-PLACE: Most important of all, however, is your grilling mise-en-place. More than half the work of any professional is done before he or she begins to cook. The process of setting up, gathering ingredients and tools, arranging the cooking area, etc., is known as preparing your mise-en-place, which translates roughly as "everything in its place." In order to enjoy yourself while you are grilling—which, after all, is the whole point—you have to create the proper setup, adhering to the invaluable premise "Work smarter, not harder." The general idea here is to take a certain pride in your grilling area. You want to be organized and efficient so you can approach the grill with confidence and calm. Before you start, clear your area of any bystanders so you will have the mental room to set the framework for the activity ahead. You need to be of single mind for a few minutes.

Now . . . make sure that you have a large table; there's nothing more annoying than constantly having to shift the hot pepper sauce in order to get to the limes. Once you've set the table in place, assemble everything you will need for the day's grilling, which should include the following:

- a couple of folded kitchen towels, indispensable for everything from handling hot pans to cleaning up spills to wiping your hands after you mix something;
- a small bowl of coarse salt;
- a loaded pepper grinder or a bowl of freshly ground pepper, which makes it even easier;
- a number of disposable foil pans, which you can wash and rinse, and which are incredibly useful for mixing and transporting raw or cooked ingredients;
- a pan of salad oil to rub whatever you are going to be grilling;
- a cutting board and a couple of sharp knives;
- all the ingredients that you will need for whatever you are planning to grill;
- your tongs, spatula, fork, and wire brush;
- a bountiful supply of your favorite libation.

Make sure the area stays clean and superorganized. This way you won't have to be interrupting your cooking to run back into the house for this or that. Sit back, pour yourself a cool one, and get ready for an afternoon of relaxation.

Enough of These Will Make a Meal

The recipes in this chapter are not appetizers in the traditional sense. I prefer to think of them as small courses that can make cooking and eating a more integrated process in which everyone can participate. They will help you avoid the "Thanksgiving Day syndrome," in which one or two people cook for four days, the meal gets eaten in about fifteen minutes, and then everyone falls asleep. For example, if I had guests coming by at 7:00, I might have my fire ready by then and cook up some Basque Wings to chew on while everybody is relaxing. I would then refuel my fire and be ready for the next course. This gives everyone a chance to munch on some wings and have a couple of cocktails while I cook. I like to continue this process throughout the meal: Cook something, eat it, refuel the fire; cook something else, eat it, refuel the fire.

The basic idea here is to enjoy the process. The longer a dinner lasts, the more enjoyable I find it. A slow, comfortable pace is best. I think that this style may have some health benefits to it, but to me the main attraction is that it is relaxing and allows for time to be spent enjoying the company.

There is also a growing trend in restaurant dining toward combining two or more appetizers to make a meal, rather than following the traditional progression of appetizer, entrée, and dessert. This way diners can enjoy a number of different tastes and preparations without eating more than they want to. Many people also claim that appetizers are more appealing and varied in flavor than entrées on restaurant menus, an opinion with which I tend to agree. For some reason I have yet to figure out, cooks find it easier to create an imaginative interplay of ingredients in an appetizer than in a main course. So, for a really interesting dinner, string together four or five of the recipes in this chapter, serving them all together or one after the other, as you and your guests prefer.

Chilled Grilled Tomato Soup with Fresh Basil

◆◆◆◆◆◆◆◆◆◆◆◆◆◆◆◆◆◆◆◆◆◆◆◆◆◆◆◆◆◆◆◆◆◆◆◆◆◆◆

4 pounds ripe tomatoes
Olive oil
Salt and freshly cracked black
   pepper to taste
1 large onion
3 garlic cloves
¼ cup white vinegar
2 tablespoons sugar
2 cups chicken broth
   (approximately)
8 tablespoons lemon juice
   (about 2 lemons)
2 tablespoons balsamic vinegar
4 tablespoons chopped fresh
   basil

1. Remove the stems from the tomatoes, split them in half, rub them lightly with oil, salt, and pepper to taste, and throw them on a grill with a low fire. What you are trying to achieve here is a charred surface and a smoky flavor, so the tomatoes are done when there is some color. Depending on your flame, this could be 3 to 10 minutes. I suggest a lower fire here because the longer the tomatoes stay on the grill, the smokier the flavor.

2. Peel and quarter the onion, oil it slightly, and place it on the grill. Grill until browned, about 5 to 7 minutes.

I came up with this dish one September when a friend dropped off a bushel of magnificent garden tomatoes. It seems a crime to use luscious, ripe, red tomatoes this way since a lot of a tomato's best qualities are lost in cooking. But if you have an abundance, a soup made from vine-ripened tomatoes is an exciting experience. ◆ *Serves 4 to 6*

SERVING SUGGESTIONS: This is great served with hunks of bread sprinkled with extra virgin olive oil, or as an accompaniment to Cold Orzo Salad (page 316). For a pleasant summer lunch, serve this with Grilled Hearthbread with Sopressata, Melon, and Torta Basil (page 182) and Celeriac and Fennel Slaw (page 81).

3. Chop the grilled onions and tomatoes coarsely, and place them in a pot with the garlic, white vinegar, sugar, and 1 cup of the chicken broth, and simmer uncovered for 1 hour.

4. Purée the cooked mixture and let it cool. Use whatever you need of the second cup of chicken broth to adjust the consistency to approximate the thickness of a chowder or cream soup.

5. Cover and chill the mixture completely, and finish the preparation by adding the lemon juice, balsamic vinegar, and basil. Season with salt and pepper to taste, and serve chilled or at room temperature. This soup will keep for about 5 days, covered and refrigerated.

PREHISTORIC GREENS

Evidence suggests that kale has been around since the days of the dinosaurs, and it certainly has a fair claim to being the first of the cultivated greens. In ancient Egypt, for example, it was considered an antidote to hangovers. Today, it is very popular in Scotland, Denmark, Germany, and Portugal, as well as the American South. In Portugal, in fact, soups made with liberal amounts of kale, called *caldo verde,* approach the stature of a national dish.

When you buy kale, it is important to avoid leaves that are yellowed or wilted, as they have a harsh, bitter taste. And if you can't find fresh kale, don't bother—frozen is an entirely different animal.

Grilled Chorizo Soup with Kale and Sweet Potatoes

◆◆◆

1½ pounds chorizo (you may substitute linguica)
8 tablespoons olive oil
4 large Spanish onions, finely chopped
3 tablespoons minced garlic
2 bay leaves
4 large sweet potatoes, peeled and cut into eighths
1 head green kale, washed and coarsely chopped
4 ripe tomatoes, quartered (use canned Italian plum tomatoes if fresh are not available)
2 quarts chicken stock (homemade if you have it, although canned is acceptable)
1 tablespoon fresh thyme
1 teaspoon red pepper flakes
Salt and freshly cracked black pepper to taste

In this hearty Portuguese-inspired dish, I grill the chorizo to add a little smoky flavor and add sweet potatoes for a hint of the American South. If you live in the Northeast, try Portuguese sweet bread with this. Any crusty white bread is a fine substitute. Either way, this is a great cold day warmer. ◆ *Serves 8*

SERVING SUGGESTIONS: This makes a nice, light meal in combination with Romaine-Feta Salad with Lemon–Olive Oil Dressing (page 286), or an excellent first course in front of Grilled Turkey Steaks with White Grape–Cranberry Relish (page 174).

1. Over a medium fire, grill the chorizo until it has some color, about 5 minutes per side.

2. In a heavy-bottomed 4-quart stockpot, heat the olive oil over medium heat. Add the onions and sauté until clear, about 5 to 7 minutes. Add the garlic and bay leaves, and cook an additional 2 minutes.

3. Add the sweet potatoes, kale, tomatoes, chicken stock, thyme, pepper flakes, and salt and pepper to taste. Bring the soup to a boil, and use a ladle to skim off any foamy substance or grease that comes to the surface. Reduce the heat and simmer for 30 minutes.

4. Cut the chorizo into bite-size chunks, add them to the soup, and serve.

Exotic Caribbean Root and Tuber Soup with Curried Scallion Butter

◆ ◆

3 pounds of any or all of the following roots and tubers: malanga (see Pantry, page 372), yuca root (see Pantry, page 373), sweet potatoes, and boniato (see Pantry, page 371) (you may substitute baking potatoes for boniato)
4 tablespoons butter
2 medium yellow onions, diced
2 tablespoons curry powder
2 quarts chicken stock
Salt and freshly cracked black pepper to taste
½ teaspoon allspice
½ teaspoon nutmeg
½ cup heavy cream

A potage-style soup featuring a virtual "Who's Who in Caribbean Tubers." Although these may seem like wild ingredients, walk into any Latin or Caribbean store and you will soon discover that the largest aisle is taken up by root vegetables. Feel free to substitute if you can't find these particular ones—check in the Pantry for a description of the characteristics of each ingredient, but don't worry about exactly matching the taste and texture of the original when you substitute. The main point is to use a variety of Caribbean roots and tubers, whatever is available. ◆ *Serves 8*

1. Peel and dice the roots and tubers and set aside.

2. In a large stockpot, melt the butter and cook the onion over medium heat until clear, 5 to 7 minutes. Add the curry powder and cook an additional 1 minute.

3. Add the chicken stock, turn the heat to high, and bring to a boil. Add the diced roots and tubers. Reduce the heat and simmer gently, uncovered, until the roots and tubers are very easily pierced with a fork, about 1 hour.

4. Remove from the heat and purée in small batches in a food processor or blender.

5. Stir in the salt and pepper to taste, allspice, and nutmeg. Return to a low heat, add the heavy cream, and cook until just heated through, about 5 minutes. Taste and adjust seasonings as you desire. Top each serving with a slice of Curried Scallion Butter.

SERVING SUGGESTIONS: Try this with Grilled Swordfish Steaks with Yucatán Orange-Herb Paste (page 100) and Salad of Green Mango, Coconut, and Hot Chile Peppers (page 295).

Curried Scallion Butter

❖❖❖❖❖❖❖❖❖❖❖❖❖❖❖❖❖❖

½ pound unsalted butter, softened
1 bunch of scallions, chopped
2 tablespoons curry powder
1 tablespoon lemon juice (about ¼ lemon)
1 tablespoon raisins, coarsely chopped

1. Place all the ingredients in a food processor or blender and purée until smooth.

2. Form the butter into a cylinder, wrap it in plastic wrap, and chill well.

Tropical Gazpacho

◆◆◆

6 cups canned tomato juice
1 cup canned papaya juice (you
    may substitute pineapple)
2 medium green or underripe
    mangoes *or* papayas, diced
    small
½ medium pineapple, peeled,
    cored, and diced small
½ red bell pepper, diced small
½ green bell pepper, diced small
½ cup lime juice (about 4 limes)
4 dashes of Tabasco sauce
½ cup chopped cilantro
Salt and freshly cracked black
    pepper to taste

Combine the tomato and papaya juice in a large bowl. Add the remaining ingredients, stir a few times, cover, and allow to stand in the refrigerator for at least 2 hours—4 to 6 is best—before serving.

Just kind of fooling around one day with some underripe mango and pineapple, I came up with this recipe, one of my all-time favorites. It uses a principle common in tropical regions, treating underripe fruits as vegetables. Here I combine tomato juice with papaya and lime juice for a unique and crisp summer soup. ◆ *Serves 6*

SERVING SUGGESTIONS: Try this with West Indies Breadfruit Salad (page 312) and Lime-Marinated Grilled Kingfish with Red Onion and Mango Relish (page 91) for an island-theme dinner.

---

96 Degrees in the Shade —A Summer Lunch

◆◆◆◆◆◆◆◆◆◆◆◆◆◆◆◆◆

Tropical Gazpacho
Above

Avocado Stuffed with Seared
Tuna Estilio Seviche
Page 54

Sweet Potato–Peanut Pie
Page 348

Grilled Vegetable Gazpacho

◆·◆

4 tablespoons olive oil
Salt and freshly cracked black
  pepper to taste
1 red bell pepper, halved and
  seeded
1 green bell pepper, halved and
  seeded
1 small red onion, peeled and
  halved
½ small eggplant, cut into ½-
  inch-thick circles

3 garlic cloves
2 slices day-old bread
Salt and freshly cracked black
  pepper to taste
5 tablespoons olive oil
2 tablespoons balsamic vinegar
1 quart Clamato juice
2 tablespoons chopped fresh
  basil
4 tablespoons lemon juice
  (about 1 lemon)

In its original days, gazpacho was a bread porridge and not the tomato-vegetable preparation that goes by that name today. Here I restored a little bread for texture, and grilled the vegetables. I like to leave the vegetables in larger pieces rather than chopping them fine, since this gives the soup more textural and taste variety. The char flavor spreads throughout the soup for a very interesting light lunch on a hot day. This is also a good way to use up last night's leftover grilled antipasto. ◆ *Serves 6*

SERVING SUGGESTIONS: I would serve this with Grilled Lamb Steaks with Rosemary, Garlic, and Red Wine (page 150) and Romaine-Feta Salad with Lemon–Olive Oil Dressing (page 286).

1. Rub the vegetables with 4 tablespoons of olive oil and salt and pepper to taste, and grill them over a medium-hot fire. Grill the peppers and onion for 2 to 3 minutes, turning once or twice, until slightly charred. Then remove them, slice thinly, and set aside. Grill the eggplant circles 2 to 3 minutes per side, until brown, then remove them, cool, and dice small.

2. In a food processor or blender, purée the garlic and bread until fine. Add salt and pepper to taste.

With the processor or blender still going, slowly add 5 tablespoons of the oil. Add the balsamic vinegar and blend or process for an additional 15 seconds.

3. Pour the Clamato juice into a large bowl and gradually whisk in the bread mixture.

4. Add the grilled vegetables to the Clamato mixture and refrigerate, covered, for 2 to 4 hours.

5. Just before serving, adjust the seasoning with salt and pepper and add the chopped basil and lemon. Mix briefly and serve. Will keep, covered and refrigerated, for 2 to 3 days.

Clam Posole

◆◆

2 quarts bottled clam juice
1 smoked pig's foot, approximately 1 pound
1 medium Spanish onion, diced small
3 tablespoons minced garlic
Salt and freshly cracked black pepper to taste
2 tablespoons chili powder
2 tablespoons ground cumin
1 pound fresh, raw clams, chopped (you may substitute frozen)
1 cup hominy, rinsed
3 tablespoons chopped fresh oregano
½ green cabbage, shredded, for garnish
1 medium red onion, finely diced, for garnish

A different version of the posole of the American Southwest, this preparation substitutes seafood, in the person of clams, for the traditional pork. ◆ *Serves 8*

SERVING SUGGESTIONS: Serve this with Quesadilla Bread (page 326) and a Salad of Green Mango, Coconut, and Hot Chile Peppers (page 295).

1. Bring the clam juice to a boil in a large stockpot. Add the pig's foot and simmer gently, uncovered, for 1 hour. Remove the pot from the stove, strain the stock, and return it to the pot, discarding the pig's foot.

2. Add the onion, garlic, salt and pepper to taste, chili powder, and cumin to the stock, and bring to a boil. Reduce the heat and simmer for 10 minutes.

3. Add the clams and hominy and simmer slowly for an additional 20 minutes. Season with more salt and pepper if needed. Just before serving, add the oregano, and serve garnished with the cabbage and red onion.

POSOLE POSOLE

The word "posole" has two different meanings: It may refer either to a dried corn kernel (also called hominy) or to a Mexican/Native American stew made with this corn. A traditional menu dish on holiday tables, the stew combines the dried corn with a rich pork broth and red or green chile peppers.

HOMINY

As the major crop of early Native Americans, corn was used in many different ways during Colonial times. One of the more popular preparations was hominy, which is made from whole kernels of hard corn (Indian corn) cooked in water with ashes (lye) to remove the tough outer shells. Today hominy is available either canned or dried, but its lengthy cooking time and the difficulty of processing it have caused it to lose popularity dramatically. It is in fact very interesting to work with, and lends itself to a wide variety of preparations.

Grilled Tripe and Hominy Stew

◆◆◆◆◆◆◆◆◆◆◆◆◆◆◆◆◆◆◆◆◆◆◆◆◆◆◆◆◆◆◆◆◆◆◆◆◆◆◆

1 cup kosher salt
1 cup white vinegar
2 pounds honeycomb tripe
Salt and freshly cracked pepper
  to taste

4 tablespoons peanut oil
3 large onions, diced small
2 tablespoons dried leaf oregano
3 tablespoons minced garlic
2 quarts chicken stock (canned
  will do)
1 small ham hock (8 to 10
  ounces)
1 16-ounce can hominy
4 tablespoons finely chopped
  fresh red *or* green serrano
  chile peppers

6 limes, halved, for garnish

To deal with the tripe

1. Mix the salt and vinegar together well. Pour a third of the salt-vinegar mixture into a large bowl, and scrub the tripe in this mixture vigorously, for 5 minutes, with a brush, as if the tripe were a dirty shirt collar. Rinse in cold water and repeat two more times.

2. Place the tripe in a bowl of cold water to cover, and place it in the refrigerator, covered, for at least 12 hours. Change the water once or twice during this period.

This is my version of *menudo*, the Mexican stew that has become a cultlike dish in some circles due to its alleged ability to relieve hangover symptoms. I've altered the classic method by searing the tripe, imparting a smoky flavoring. Cleaning the tripe is semitedious, but thoroughly necessary to transform its taste to marvelously distinct. In combination with hominy, this makes an excellent stew. The heat called for here is the medium-hot serrano, but you can substitute any fresh chile pepper from the mild jalapeño to the volcanic Scotch Bonnet. ◆ *Serves 6*

SERVING SUGGESTIONS: Serve this in front of Grilled Pork Loin with Indonesian Chile-Coconut Sauce (page 156), or along with Avocado Stuffed with Seared Tuna Estilio Seviche (page 54).

3. Remove the tripe from the water and place it in a large pot with fresh water to cover. Bring it to a boil and simmer for 1 hour. Remove it and drain.

4. Sprinkle the tripe with salt and pepper to taste and grill it over very low heat for 10 to 15 minutes or until the exterior is evenly crusty golden brown.

5. Remove the tripe from the grill, cool, and slice very thinly. Set aside.

To make the stew

6. Heat the oil in a soup pot and add the onion. Sauté over medium heat until the onion is clear, 5 to 7 minutes. Add the oregano and garlic, and cook an additional 2 minutes.

7. Add the chicken stock, bring to a simmer, and add the ham hock, hominy, and grilled tripe. Simmer, uncovered, for 2 hours.

8. Just before serving, stir in the serranos and add the juice of a halved lime to each individual serving bowl. Garnish with a lime half. Will keep, covered and refrigerated, 1 week.

AN EXPERT SPEAKS OF TRIPE

"I don't like tripe, but after many years of research, I have finally decided that its presence on the menu of a Mexican restaurant is a badge representing seriousness of intention."

—CALVIN TRILLIN,
Alice, Let's Eat

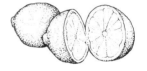

Grilled Toast Canapé Variations

◆◆

1 cup olive oil
2 tablespoons minced garlic
1 fresh baguette, cut into ¼-inch
　slices (about 40)

Olive oil
Balsamic vinegar

1. Combine the 1 cup olive oil and the garlic and, using a brush, paint both sides of each slice of bread with this mixture.

2. Over a low fire, grill the bread slices on both sides until golden brown and crisp, about 1 minute per side.

3. Arrange items from last night's grilled feast or your favorite local store on top of the bread slices. You might use grilled mushrooms with parsley; roasted red peppers with fresh mozzarella; goat cheese and sun-dried tomatoes; cucumbers chopped with tomatoes, lemon, and herbs; grilled eggplant with grated pecorino cheese; anchovies chopped with bread crumbs and capers; prosciutto with olive oil; grilled onions and chopped fresh oregano. Arrange the canapés on a large platter, and drizzle olive oil and balsamic vinegar over all.

These canapés are perfect for cocktail parties. The grilled bread makes them rather special, and when you put them on a platter together they look like a huge sea of different colors, shapes, and textures. I have given some ideas here, but these canapés are an excellent vehicle for using leftovers. Use your imagination. The only principle is that each one should have a strong flavor. I bring all the food I'm going to use for the canapés, go to the grill with my bread, and start putting them together as the fancy strikes me. ◆ *About 40 canapés*

SERVING SUGGESTIONS: Serve with Raw Bar Variations (page 48) for an elaborate cocktail hour.

Grilled Vegetable Antipasto with Braised Garlic Bread

◆ ◆

8 tablespoons good olive oil
2 garlic cloves, unpeeled
1 summer squash
1 zucchini
1 yellow onion
1 red onion
1 red bell pepper
1 green bell pepper
10 medium mushrooms
Salad oil for rub
Salt and freshly cracked pepper
  to taste
2 tablespoons balsamic vinegar
8 sun-dried tomatoes
1 cup black olives
2 tablespoons capers
4 tablespoons lemon juice
  (about 1 lemon)
French *or* Italian bread

To braise the garlic:

Put 3 tablespoons of the olive oil with the garlic, wrap in foil, and cook in a medium oven (300°F) for ½ hour. The garlic should easily squeeze out of its skin, after which you mix it with the oil in which it was cooked to make a paste. Now you are ready to grill the vegetables.

To prepare the vegetables

1. Slice the squash and zucchini into ¼-inch rounds.

This dish—the result of my early experiments with the "grillability" of different vegetables at a time when vegetables were not used for grilling—is largely responsible for my reputation for grilling anything and everything. I encourage you to experiment with your favorite vegetables. Make sure they are ultrafresh.

Assembling this antipasto is a lot of fun. Braise the garlic ahead of time, then plan to start cooking this as your guests arrive and let them view all the colors, shapes, and sizes on the grill. It really looks beautiful. Fresh mozzarella or hard provolone makes a smart addition, and adding prosciutto can transform it into a great summer entrée. It's a dish that can sit on a table where people help themselves, and it also makes great leftovers. ◆ *1 large appetizer plate for 4 to 6 people*

SERVING SUGGESTIONS: Team this up with another appetizer for a light dinner. Try Grilled Tripe and Hominy Stew (page 38), Seared Sirloin, Sushi Style (page 76), or Wilted Greens with Grilled Lamb and Blue Cheese (page 72).

2. Cut the onions into quarters.

3. Cut the peppers in half and clean out the seeds and membranes.

4. Rub all the vegetables lightly with the salad oil, sprinkle them lightly with salt and pepper to taste, and grill over high heat. What you are looking for here is color. With the exception of the onion, all of the vegetables will be cooked properly when the color is right. It's actually fine to have some black parts, because that's the sugar in the vegetables caramelizing, but what you are looking for is really a dark golden brown. Don't overcook them, since you'll want to retain some crispness/rawness in the vegetables to provide texture. The onions require special care: Keep them in quarters and grill them well on the cut sides so that when they are removed from the grill and separated, each piece will have some edges with color and grilled flavor.

5. When the vegetables have achieved the desired state, toss them in balsamic vinegar and 5 tablespoons of the olive oil and arrange them on a platter along with the tomatoes, olives, and capers. Just before serving, squeeze the lemon juice over everything.

6. Cut 4 to 6 chunks of Italian or French bread. If the grill is hot, toast lightly. Be careful, as bread burns easily over an open grill. If the grill is not hot, use the oven to toast the bread. Spread with garlic paste, add to the platter with vegetables, and chomp.

Midsummer Cocktail Party

◆ ◆ ◆ ◆ ◆ ◆ ◆ ◆ ◆ ◆ ◆

Smithfield Ham Hush Puppies with Fresh Corn

••

¾ cup yellow cornmeal
¼ cup all-purpose flour
½ teaspoon salt
1 tablespoon baking powder
1 teaspoon cayenne pepper
To 1 egg add enough buttermilk
    to make ¾ cup total
1 tablespoon melted bacon fat *or*
    vegetable oil
½ cup Smithfield ham, diced
    small
¾ cup fresh corn kernels *or*
    drained canned kernel corn
½ cup chopped scallion
Vegetable oil for frying (about 2
    tablespoons)

1. Sift together all the dry ingredients, including the cayenne, into a bowl.

2. In a small bowl, whisk the egg and buttermilk until well mixed.

3. Stir the melted bacon fat or oil into the egg-milk mixture.

4. Gently stir the egg-milk mixture into the sifted dry ingredients until completely blended, but do not overmix.

5. Fold in the diced ham, corn kernels, and chopped scallion.

Growing up in Williamsburg, Virginia, we were very close to Smithfield, the Virginia town that produces the famous ham, which was present at every holiday function. Although I was turned off by its acute saltiness as a kid, I later championed it by insisting to all my Yankee friends that a Smithfield ham could match a prosciutto any day. In fact, the processes the two hams undergo are very similar. The chief difference is simply that the Smithfield ham is traditionally eaten cooked and sliced thick, whereas prosciutto is cured but served uncooked and sliced paper thin.

In this recipe any type of ham can be used, but I prefer the salty Smithfield because its homeland is the same as the hush puppy's. Use it raw or cooked, as you wish. You'll find that it tastes much the same either way, but it is slightly saltier when raw, less dense and more mealy when cooked.

Hush puppies are basically deep-fried balls of corn bread which originated as a means of keeping hounds quiet around the campfire. Now they are served in the South as an alternative to dinner rolls. The addition of fresh corn here gives the puppies a bit of a fritter look. Serve them with lots of butter and Georgia Peach Chutney (page 218) for an appetizer course; the sweetness of the chutney complements the saltiness of the ham beautifully. ♦ *Makes 1 big litter: about 2 dozen pups*

6. To cook, heat the vegetable oil in a skillet over medium heat until a drop of water crackles when dropped into the oil. The amount of oil you use will depend on the size of the skillet, since you want to use only enough to come halfway up the sides of the puppies.

7. Drop heaping teaspoons of batter into the hot oil and cook until golden brown on all sides, 2 to 3 minutes. The interior texture should be dense but not damp. Be careful not to overcook or they become dry and slightly bitter.

8. Serve hot with plenty of butter.

SERVING SUGGESTIONS: Serve these with Tidewater Coleslaw (page 274) and Barbecued Whole Chicken (page 263) for a full Southern meal.

Y'all Come on Over— Down-home Feed for a Crowd

◆◆◆◆◆◆◆◆◆◆◆◆◆◆

Grilled Chicken and Black-eyed Pea Salad with Chipotle Vinaigrette
Page 70

Smithfield Ham Hush Puppies with Fresh Corn and Georgia Peach Chutney
Pages 43 and 218

Grilled Country Ham and Applesauce
Page 154

Grilled Turkey Steaks with White Grape–Cranberry Relish
Page 174

Doc's Cheddar Biscuits
Page 309

Sweet Potato Salad
Page 302

East Coast Grill Maple-Pecan Bread Pudding
Page 335

Huevos del Diablo

The Devil's Own Deviled Eggs

12 eggs
¼ cup Homemade Mayonnaise
  (page 248)
1 tablespoon Dijon mustard
1 tablespoon Thai-Style All-
  purpose Hot Mixed Curry
  Paste (page 255)
2 tablespoons chopped fresh red
  or green jalapeño chile
  peppers
2 tablespoons chopped scallion
2 tablespoons chopped cilantro
Salt and freshly cracked black
  pepper to taste

Pickled ginger (see Pantry, page
  370) for garnish
Chutney for garnish

1. Fill a large mixing bowl half full
of cold water, and add a tray of
ice cubes.

2. Place the eggs in a pan of cold
water to cover and bring to a boil.
Boil for 10 minutes, remove the
eggs from the water, and plunge
them into the ice-water bath.

3. Cut the eggs in half and scoop
out the yolks. In a medium bowl,
mash the yolks together with the
mayonnaise, mustard, and curry
paste.

4. Add the jalapeños, scallion, cilantro, salt, and pepper to taste,
and mix well.

Whenever my folks would have people over in the summer, my mom would serve deviled eggs. For that reason, no summer function seems really complete to me without them. I always insist on serving this, my own peculiar version, at all such affairs. It is a quick preparation, as much a novelty as a serious food item, and dates from a stage in my cooking career when people would dare me to make everything hot. They thought they had me with this one, but I turned it on them.

I'd break this out for the chile heads, but probably wouldn't serve it if Grandma were coming over. ◆ *24 halves*

SERVING SUGGESTIONS: This should be the first course of a long day of barbecuing, featuring Barbecued Ribs, Missouri Style (page 269), The Only Real Barbecue Sandwich (page 271), or Texas Barbecued Beef Brisket (page 275).

5. Scoop the yolk mixture back into the whites and garnish with a piece of pickled ginger or a bit of your favorite chutney. Try Raisin-Ginger Chutney (page 217) or Very Aromatic Tomato-Ginger Jam (page 231).

Chili Auténtico con Mucha Cerveza

◆◆

Real Chili with Lots of Beer

4 tablespoons peanut oil
2 pounds pork butt, cut into
  ¼-inch cubes
5 large yellow onions, diced
  small
2 tablespoons minced garlic
6 bottles beer
4 tablespoons chili powder
4 tablespoons ground cumin
2 tablespoons dried oregano
1 teaspoon cinnamon
½ cup red wine
¼ cup white vinegar
2 to 4 tablespoons finely
  chopped fresh green *or* red
  jalapeño chile peppers

For the garnishes

1 cup sour cream
½ cup chopped cilantro
½ pound Jack cheese, shredded
½ onion, diced small
6 lime halves

It's fairly common knowledge today that "real" chili has no tomatoes and that if you served a chili with beans, those whose culture first produced the dish wouldn't even recognize it. Well, back when I wasn't too smart my roommate Jorge was always bragging about his chili, which he learned to make in Corpus Christi, Texas, and which he made with no beans, no tomatoes, and cubed pork instead of ground beef. I thought that was pretty strange. On the other hand, he also put a lot of beer into his chili. This was something my mom never did, but I thought maybe he was working on something good. Indeed he was, and here it is. You can make this dish spicy or not, as you please. This chili is a little soupier than what you might be used to. Garnish each bowl with sour cream and raw onions, and serve it with beans, rice, and East Coast Grill Corn Bread (page 324) on the side. Grab a couple of beers, turn the game on, you're all set. ◆ *Serves 6*

1. In a large pot, heat the oil until very hot and brown the pork very well over high heat in 2 or 3 batches.

2. Turn the heat down to medium, add the onions, and cook until clear, 5 to 7 minutes. Add the garlic and cook and stir for 1 minute.

3. Add the beer, chili powder, cumin, oregano, cinnamon, wine, vinegar, and jalapeño, and bring to a slow simmer. Simmer, uncovered, until the pork is tender, about 2½ to 3 hours. The chili should have the texture of a thickish stew.

4. Serve each bowl garnished with a dollop of sour cream, a sprinkling of cilantro, Jack cheese, diced onion, and a lime half.

YOUR FAVORITE GRILLED CHILE PEPPER SALSA

Grilling chile peppers adds a pleasant smoky dimension to any salsa that you make with them. Just grill the peppers over a hot fire, turning occasionally, until they attain a slight char on all sides, about 2 to 3 minutes, then follow the recipe for the salsa as usual.

This is a very popular Mexico salsa: Grill five of your favorite chile peppers, then let them steep for a few minutes in a mixture of 4 tablespoons lime juice (from about 2 limes), 1 teaspoon of minced garlic, and 1 tablespoon chopped fresh cilantro. Simple as can be, and it results in a very aromatic salsa that's great with fish.

Raw Bar Variations

4 dozen clams
4 dozen oysters
1 bottle Tabasco sauce
3 cups Tommy's Hot Cocktail Sauce (page 50)
½ cup Fresh Horseradish (page 254)

½ dozen lemons, quartered

These days when my friends and family have a raw bar, we still stick pretty close to home as far as the sauce is concerned. Most of us veer toward straight horseradish, but it may take a lifetime to achieve that level of understanding. Through my travels to beaches in different countries, I have found that each place seems to have its own special raw bar sauce, so I am offering some general guidelines and some adaptations. For each sauce, the preparation consists of just putting all the ingredients together in a bowl and mixing well. No sense making it complicated. The amount of shellfish above calls for about 3 cups of sauce, so either use 1 full recipe Tommy's Hot Cocktail Sauce or a variety of different sauces.

Growing up near the mouth of the Chesapeake Bay, I was lucky to have the raw bar as a part of my childhood. Of course, my early memories were of my parents' parties, and I couldn't imagine what perversity would make people eat raw clams and oysters. In those days the raw bar was a simple affair consisting of a large table, bushel baskets full of clams and oysters, a bunch of lemons, a couple of bottles of Tabasco, cocktail sauce, and a bowl of plain fresh horseradish. The latter was used by only a few people, and while it seemed to me that their reaction to it was part pain and part joy, the horseradish fanciers did seem to enjoy the whole experience more than the other guests.

Eventually my friends and I started earning extra dollars shucking at these affairs. Since the older kids goaded the younger ones into shucking, peer pressure was the only way to learn the technique, and the idea of wearing protective gloves was too shameful to even consider. My hands still show the many knicks and scrapes gained while working upward on that particular learning curve, but it is a great source of pride for me to open clams and oysters cleanly and quickly. ◆ *Serves 10*

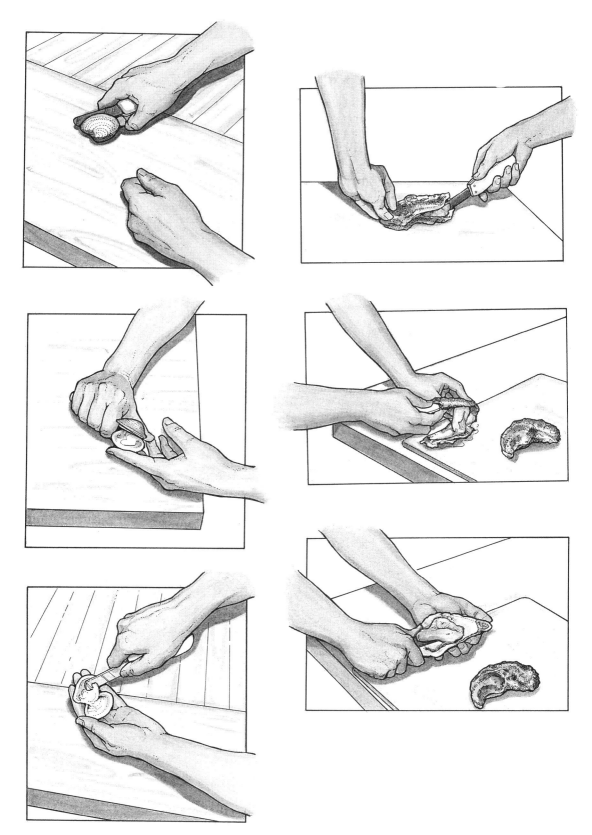

Tommy's Hot Cocktail Sauce

2 cups ketchup
1 cup Fresh Horseradish (page 254)
8 tablespoons lemon juice (about 2 lemons)
4 tablespoons lime juice (about 2 limes)
Dash of Tabasco sauce
7 dashes of Worcestershire sauce

In line with a particular Tidewater tradition of handing down recipes from uncle to nephew, this cocktail sauce is now being perfected for the next generation by my nephew Tommy. ◆ *About 3 cups*

Central American Variety

1 small red onion, chopped small
10 radishes, chopped small
¼ cup chopped cilantro
4 tablespoons lime juice (about 2 limes)
1 tablespoon minced hot red *or* green chile pepper

About ½ cup

Mignonette Sauce

½ cup red wine vinegar
1 tablespoon minced garlic
2 tablespoons chopped parsley
1 tablespoon black pepper
Salt and freshly cracked black pepper to taste

About ½ cup

Balsamic and Basil Sauce

½ cup balsamic vinegar
8 tablespoons lemon juice
  (about 2 lemons)
¼ cup chopped basil
1 tablespoon minced garlic
Salt and freshly cracked black
  pepper to taste

About 1 cup

Lemon-Herb Sauce

8 tablespoons lemon juice
  (about 2 lemons)
1 tablespoon fresh thyme
1 tablespoon fresh oregano
1 tablespoon chopped parsley
2 tablespoons chopped shallots

About ½ cup

Chile-Garlic Sauce

½ cup red wine vinegar
6 tablespoons lime juice (about
  3 limes)
1 tablespoon Vietnamese chili
  garlic paste (you may
  substitute 1 tablespoon of a
  mixture of: 1 tablespoon of
  your favorite fresh hot chile
  peppers finely chopped, 1
  tablespoon minced garlic, 1
  teaspoon sugar, and 1
  tablespoon ketchup)
1 tablespoon minced fresh
  lemongrass (see Pantry, page
  372) *or* 1 teaspoon dried

About ¾ cup

Mango-Lime Chile Sauce

◆◆

1¼ cup lime juice (about 10
   limes)
1 mango, diced small
2 tablespoons minced fresh red
   or green chile peppers
2 tablespoons chopped cilantro
Salt and freshly cracked black
   pepper to taste

About 2 cups

Steamed Clams with Lemongrass and Chiles de Árbol

◆◆

2 dozen littleneck clams
2 tablespoons minced fresh
   lemongrass, *or* 2 teaspoons
   dried (see Pantry, page 372)
½ head Chinese (Napa)
   cabbage, thinly sliced
1 cup dry white wine
1 cup bottled clam juice
½ tablespoon minced garlic
2 tablespoons dried chiles de
   árbol (see Pantry, page 375)
   (you may substitute red
   pepper flakes)
8 tablespoons lime juice (about
   4 limes)
¼ cup chopped cilantro
2 tablespoons chopped fresh
   mint
Salt and freshly cracked black
   pepper to taste

Thailand has some of the best seafood I've ever tasted, which may partially be due to the fact that in Bangkok restaurants the seafood is kept alive in tanks until the moment of preparation. While I think that seafood usually calls for rather subtle flavor combinations that will not overburden the fish, in Thailand I found cooks who could apply highly aromatic, hot preparations to seafood without burying the flavor. (I should note, however, that what is subtle heat to some Thai folks might seem like molten lava to some Western diners.) I think that this combination soup/clam dish works in that way. The broth is great, and I would garnish it with some chopped peanuts and fresh mint. ◆ *Serves 4 as appetizers*

Coarsely chopped roasted,
  unsalted peanuts for garnish
Mint leaves for garnish

1. Wash the clams and place them in a large stockpot with the lemongrass, cabbage, wine, clam juice, garlic, and chile pepper.

2. Cover and cook over medium heat until the clams have opened, about 10 minutes.

3. Remove them from the heat and add the lime juice, cilantro, chopped mint, and salt and pepper to taste. Swirl around to mix all the ingredients, then serve, garnished with peanuts and mint leaves, in bowls with chunks of bread to soak up the juice.

SERVING SUGGESTIONS: Serve this with Grilled Pork Loin with Indonesian Chile-Coconut Sauce (page 156) or Grilled Pork Skewers with Green Mango (page 158).

Some Like It Hot
♦ ♦ ♦ ♦ ♦ ♦ ♦ ♦ ♦ ♦ ♦ ♦

Equatorial Fruit Cocktail with
Lime Juice and Jalapeños
Page 85

Huevos del Diablo
(The Devil's Own Deviled Eggs)
Page 45

Pasta from Hell
Page 73

Steamed Clams with
Lemongrass and Chiles de Árbol
Page 52

Sweet Potato Salad
Page 302

Your Basic Black Beans
Page 318

Herman's Margarita
Number Three
Page 364

Avocado Stuffed with Seared Tuna Estilio Seviche

VERY HIGH

◆ ◆

1 pound 2-inch-thick tuna steak
8 tablespoons lime juice (about 4 limes)
1 tomato, chopped into large chunks
1 medium red onion, diced small
1 red bell pepper, finely chopped
2 tablespoons chopped cilantro
2 tablespoons extra virgin olive oil
Salt and freshly cracked black pepper to taste
2 ripe avocados, halved, pitted, and peeled
½ medium head green cabbage, very thinly sliced

3 radishes, finely sliced, for garnish
1 lime, cut into rounds, for garnish

1. Over an extra-hot fire, sear the tuna until well browned on both sides. Make sure your fire is very hot, and grill the tuna very quickly, maximum 2 to 3 minutes per side. You're looking for very high color on the outside, but with the tuna still raw on the inside.

2. Remove the tuna from the grill, let it cool, then slice it into ¼-inch slices.

This dish was inspired by an evening in Isla Mujeres, an island off the Yucatán in Mexico. I had been shopping for a Panama hat, which I discovered was available in a number of different styles, or *estilios*—Estilio Al Capone, Estilio Gary Cooper, etc. While wearing my hat Estilio Hoagy Carmichael, I went to a beachfront stand, a *palapa*, and had some great seviche.

Classically, the seviche method—using the acidity of lime or lemon juice to cook fish—is used with raw seafood. Here the tuna is half cooked first. This gives you a concentration of grilled flavor on the cooked side, then the remaining raw part of the fish cooks in the lime juice. I like the contrast of the sharpness of the acid-marinated tuna with the mellowness of the avocado. ◆ *Serves 4 as an appetizer*

SERVING SUGGESTIONS: Serve this with a side of Hot Pepper Corn Bread (page 325) for lunch, or with Grilled Chicken Breast with Fresh Herbs and Lemon (page 167) for dinner.

3. Lay the sliced tuna in a shallow pan, cover it with the lime juice, and allow it to sit for 2 to 3 hours.

4. Sprinkle the tomato, onion, pepper, cilantro, and olive oil over the tuna. Season it with salt and black pepper to taste, and toss lightly.

5. Place the avocado halves on a bed of the sliced cabbage. Put 2 to 3 slices of tuna on each avocado half, and spoon any remaining tomato-pepper mixture on top.

6. Sprinkle the radish slices over the tuna, and garnish the platter with the lime rounds.

AVOCADOS

Let's face it, avocados are rather strange. For one thing, assuming that its outer skin remains unbroken, an avocado will not ripen as long as it is left on the tree. Avocados also have a fat content which is about twenty times that of most other fruit, which gives them the buttery flavor and smooth, almost oily texture that makes them so wonderful.

Then, too, they are one of those "acquired tastes," something that children almost invariably despise and then as adults grow to love. Perhaps this has some connection with the persistent notion that these rough-skinned green fruit have aphrodisiac properties. I guess the only way to check that out is by personal experience.

Grilled Shrimp with Sweet Asian Carrot Relish and Pancakes

◆◆◆

For the relish

2 cups shredded carrots
½ cup rice wine vinegar
2 tablespoons sugar

24 16/20 count (medium-size) shrimp
Salt and freshly cracked pepper (white is best if you have it)

For garnishes

½ cup coarsely chopped roasted, unsalted peanuts
¼ cup chopped cilantro
¼ cup chopped fresh basil
¼ cup chopped fresh mint
2 tablespoons Vietnamese chili garlic paste (you may substitute 2 tablespoons of a mixture of: 1 tablespoon of your favorite fresh hot chile peppers, finely chopped, 1 tablespoon minced garlic, 1 teaspoon sugar, and 1 tablespoon ketchup)

12 8-inch store-bought rice flour pancakes *or* flour tortillas, warmed slightly in the oven

1. Combine all the carrot relish ingredients, mix well, and allow the mixture to stand for at least 1

This dish is loosely based on a Vietnamese-style spring roll. The combination of herbs and peanuts with a sweet carrot relish makes an interesting array of tastes and textures. If you are near an Asian market you will be able to find the rice flour pancakes called for here, but flour tortillas, which are easier to find, are fine.

This is a dish in which your guests get to assemble their own shrimp rolls. I would set everything up in small bowls and let them go at it. Be careful of the chili-garlic condiment—it's superhot.
◆ *Serves 6 as an appetizer*

SERVING SUGGESTIONS: Serve this as an appetizer in front of Grilled Pork Loin with Indonesian Chile-Coconut Sauce (page 156) or Grilled Pork Skewers with Green Mango (page 158).

hour before serving. (This relish can easily be made ahead, and will keep, covered and refrigerated, for 2 to 3 days.)

2. Peel and devein the shrimp, and remove the tails. Thread them on skewers, season them with salt and pepper to taste, and grill them over medium heat, 3 to 4 minutes per side. Remove and set them aside.

3. When the shrimp are cool, chop them coarsely in 2 or 3 pieces each.

4. Put the shrimp, relish, garnishes, and warm pancakes or tortillas out in the middle of the table, and let your guests make their own little spring rolls.

Southeast Asian Style

Grilled Shrimp with Sweet Asian
Carrot Relish and Pancakes
Page 56

Spicy Green Bean Salad
with Grilled Pork and Peanuts
Page 288

Grilled Sea Scallops
with Coconut-Chile Sauce
Page 115

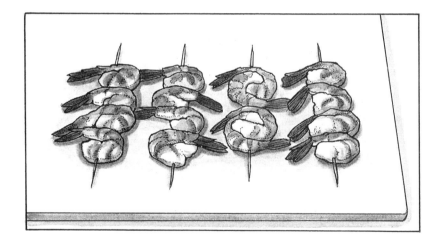

Grilled Shrimp with Pineapple–Ancho Chile Salsa and Tortillas

◆◆

24 16/20 count (medium-size) shrimp
Salt and freshly cracked black pepper to taste

For the salsa

½ ripe medium pineapple
½ red bell pepper
½ large red onion
4 ancho chile peppers, soaked in water for 12 hours, drained, and puréed
1 tablespoon chopped fresh oregano
1 teaspoon ground cumin
6 tablespoons lime juice (about 3 limes)
¼ cup pineapple juice
16 soft tortillas (flour or corn), warmed slightly in the oven

For the garnishes

½ head green *or* red cabbage, shredded
½ cup sour cream
¼ cup chopped fresh red *or* green jalapeño chile peppers

1. Peel and devein the shrimp and remove their tails.

This is one of your basic guest participation dishes, calling for folks to create according to their own taste.

I first tasted pineapple and cilantro in a salsa in San Blas, on the west coast of Mexico, which possesses some of the best shrimp I ever ate, as well as the longest rideable wave in Mexico. Taking breathers from many hours in the water, we would come up to a *palapa* (a beachfront stand) to eat bowlfuls of shrimp and drink beer.

You can serve the shrimp in a heap with piles of chopped onion and thinly sliced cabbage. You have to have fresh, soft tortillas and just slap them on the grill for a second to warm them up.
◆ *Serves 4 as an appetizer*

SERVING SUGGESTIONS: Serve this with Grilled Pork Birdies with Tangerine-Rosemary Glaze (page 161) or Grilled Lime-Marinated Flank Steak with Chipotle-Honey Sauce (page 141). It would also make a nice, light summer dinner in combination with Caribbean-Style Grilled Seafood Soup (page 122).

2. Thread the shrimp on skewers, salt and pepper them to taste, and grill over medium heat, 3 to 4 minutes per side, until they are opaque.

3. Remove the shrimp from the skewers and chop each shrimp into 3 or 4 pieces. Set aside.

4. Make the salsa: Dice the pineapple, red pepper, and red onion. Add the puréed ancho chile peppers, and mix together in a medium bowl with the oregano, cumin, and lime and pineapple juices.

5. Warm the tortillas slightly on the grill.

6. Put the shrimp, salsa, and tortillas out on a table, along with the shredded cabbage, sour cream, and jalapeños as garnishes, and let people make their own rolled tortillas.

Shrimp are sold in counts per pound, starting as low as "7 and under," which means seven or fewer shrimp to the pound. These are huge and extremely expensive. Or you can get shrimp as small as 68 to 70 per pound, which are really tiny. I use 16/20 count shrimp, which are big enough so you don't get tired of peeling them before you get full, but are not outrageously priced. When buying shrimp, look for head-off, unpeeled, raw shrimp, as opposed to cooked and peeled, which is an inferior product. If you are fortunate enough to live close to the ocean you might be able to find fresh shrimp, but most shrimp sold in the United States is caught in the Gulf of Mexico and off the coast of South America, processed on the boat, and quick-frozen. The usually fully justifiable disdain for frozen fish doesn't apply here, because shrimp meat does not alter much when frozen. So don't feel bad buying frozen shrimp. A lot of markets, as a matter of fact, buy frozen shrimp, thaw it, and sell it as fresh.

Grilled Shrimp with Sopressata, Fresh Mozzarella, and Basil

◆◆◆

½ pound fresh mozzarella
3 tablespoons extra virgin olive oil
1 tablespoon balsamic vinegar
Salt and freshly cracked black pepper to taste
16 16/20 count (medium-size) shrimp
½ pound sopressata
2 tablespoons chopped fresh basil

1. Slice the mozzarella thinly and arrange it in a single layer on a platter. Sprinkle it with the olive oil, vinegar, and salt and pepper to taste.

2. Peel and devein the shrimp, but leave their tails on. Cut the sopressata into 8 pieces, then cut each of these pieces in half. Thread the shrimp and sopressata on skewers alternately.

3. Season the skewers with salt and pepper to taste and grill over a medium-hot fire for 3 to 4 minutes per side.

4. Remove the shrimp and sopressata from the skewers and arrange them on top of the mozzarella. Sprinkle the chopped basil over the whole platter and serve with crusty bread.

Sopressata is a hard Italian cured sausage that has great flavor. If you can't get it you may substitute your favorite pepperoni or salami. This dish is a contrast in flavors and textures, with the firm spiciness of the sausage playing off the mellow creaminess of the mozzarella. It makes for a light antipasto-style first course on a warm summer evening. It is good hot, warm, or cold, so you needn't fuss about when it gets served. Have another glass of red wine, set out the crusty bread, and add some lemon wedges and black olives for color.
◆ *Serves 4 as an appetizer*

SERVING SUGGESTIONS: Serve this in front of Grilled Duck Breast with Kumquat-Sugarcane-Basil Glaze (page 198) or Grilled Poussin with Grilled Leeks, Garlic, and Rosemary (page 196).

Grilled and Chilled Shrimp with Cabbage and Peanuts

MED

◆◆

16 16/20 count (medium-size) shrimp

Salt and freshly cracked pepper to taste (white is best, if you have it)

1 small head green cabbage

½ cup rice wine vinegar

¼ cup roasted, unsalted peanuts, coarsely ground

2 tablespoons chopped fresh basil

2 tablespoons chopped cilantro

2 tablespoons very finely minced fresh lemongrass *or* 2 teaspoons dried lemongrass (see Pantry, page 372)

1 teaspoon sugar

2 tablespoons sesame oil

1 teaspoon Vietnamese chili garlic paste (you may substitute 1 teaspoon of a mixture of: 1 tablespoon of your favorite fresh hot chile peppers, finely chopped, mixed with 1 tablespoon minced garlic, 1 teaspoon sugar, and 1 tablespoon ketchup)

4 tablespoons lime juice (about 2 limes)

1. Peel and devein the shrimp and remove their tails.

2. Season the shrimp with salt and pepper to taste, thread them on a

This is perfect for a lunch entrée on a hot summer day or a first course at dinner. The lightness, freshness, and aromaticity of the typical Thai/Southeast Asian herb combination go very well with the shrimp. ◆ *Serves 4 as an appetizer*

SERVING SUGGESTIONS: Serve this as an appetizer followed by Roasted Then Grilled Half Duck (page 175) or Simple Grilled Whole Beef Tenderloin (page 146). If you're serving it as a lunch entrée, accompany it with a bowl of Spicy Cucumber Relish (page 232).

skewer, and grill them over medium heat until opaque, about 3 to 4 minutes per side.

3. Remove the skewered shrimp from the heat and allow to cool.

4. While the shrimp are cooling, slice the head of cabbage very thin and, in a large bowl, combine the cabbage with all the remaining ingredients and mix well.

5. Remove the cooled shrimp from the skewers and chop each one into 5 to 6 pieces.

6. Add the chopped shrimp to the other ingredients, toss lightly, and serve at once.

Grilled Salmon, Lomi Lomi Style

◆◆

1½-pound center-cut salmon fillet, in 1 or 2 pieces
2 tablespoons vegetable oil
Salt and freshly cracked black pepper to taste
¾ cup lime juice (about 6 limes)
½ cup pineapple juice
1 medium red onion, diced small
3 scallions, diced small
2 tablespoons chopped parsley
½ teaspoon Tabasco sauce
½ teaspoon sugar
3 fresh tomatoes, diced small

This is a takeoff of sorts on the Hawaiian luau salmon preparation called *lomi lomi*. The difference is that in this preparation, the salmon is not salt-cured, but instead is half cooked on the grill before cooking is completed by the acidity of the lime juice.

This dish illustrates my observation that the natural cuisine of Hawaii is unique among tropical cuisines in its absence of spicy ingredients and preparations. Serve it chilled as a first course on a bed of thinly sliced cabbage with pineapple slices and lime wedges.

◆ *Serves 6 as an appetizer*

1. Skin the salmon and, if you have bought one fillet, cut it into 2 pieces. Brush the tops with vegetable oil, sprinkle them with salt and pepper to taste, and place the salmon top down (the side you skinned up) on a very hot grill. Cook for 4 to 5 minutes, until brown and crusty.

2. Remove the salmon from the grill. It should be well cooked on one side, but still raw on the other. Allow it to cool to room temperature.

3. Meanwhile, combine all the other ingredients except the tomato in a large mixing bowl and mix well.

4. When the salmon is cool, break it into bite-size pieces and add them to the lime juice mixture, cooked-side up. Stir lightly to make sure that all the pieces are well coated, then cover tightly and refrigerate for 4 to 5 hours.

5. Remove the bowl from the refrigerator and add the chopped tomatoes. You can serve this chilled or at room temperature.

SERVING SUGGESTIONS: Try this in front of Seared Sirloin, Sushi Style (page 76), or in combination with West Indies Breadfruit Salad (page 312) and Grilled Baby Eggplant with Miso-Soy Vinaigrette (page 296).

TRADITIONAL HAWAIIAN LUAU MENU

Kalua pig (pig wrapped in banana leaves, stuffed full of hot rocks, and baked in an *imu,* or pit)
Sweet potatoes
Squid in coconut milk
Salmon, Lomi Lomi Style (salt-cured salmon)
Poi (mashed taro root)
Pipkaula (jerked beef)
Haupia (coconut pudding)

Grilled Chicken Drumsticks Berberé

MED-LOW

◆◆◆

1 teaspoon powdered ginger
1 tablespoon red pepper flakes
1 teaspoon ground cardamom
2 teaspoons ground coriander
1 tablespoon star anise, crushed
1 teaspoon turmeric
1 tablespoon dry mustard
1 teaspoon fenugreek seeds,
   crushed (optional)
1 teaspoon nutmeg
1 teaspoon cinnamon
1 teaspoon allspice
2 tablespoons cayenne pepper
1 tablespoon freshly cracked
   black pepper
2 tablespoons salt
½ cup paprika
½ cup dry red wine
4 tablespoons peanut oil
¼ cup fresh orange juice

16 chicken drumsticks

Lemons for squeezing

1. Combine all the dry spices, from the ginger through paprika, in a bowl and mix well.

2. In a large sauté pan, cook the combined spices over medium heat for 2 to 3 minutes, until they are heated completely through. Be careful of the fumes—the spice aroma is very strong and quite bizarre. Your house will smell like

Berberé is the name of a peppery spice paste that is a staple in Ethiopian cooking. It can contain any number of spices, and I'm sure that in Ethiopia cooks argue the merits of their own particular blend. My recipe is one of many variations but retains the classic Ethiopian method of pan-cooking the spices to bring out their flavor, and of course I would not be true to the dish if I made it any less hot than the original. File this one under "Wicked Hot" and make sure to have some cold ones on ice. ◆ *Serves 8 as an appetizer*

SERVING SUGGESTIONS: Try these with Grilled Squid with Asian Slaw and Hoisin Barbecue Sauce (page 107) as a two-appetizer meal, or in front of Grilled Peppered Wolffish (page 89).

a Moroccan *souk* (market) even if you use the fan.

3. Add the red wine to the spice mixture and cook 2 to 3 minutes, stirring constantly, until a uniform paste is formed.

4. Remove the spice paste from the heat and allow it to cool. Add the peanut oil and orange juice and mix well. The paste should have the consistency of wet sand.

5. Rub the drumsticks all over with the *berberé* mixture and allow them to stand, covered, in the refrigerator for 2 hours.

6. Grill the drumsticks over medium-low heat for 10 to 12 minutes, rolling them around to ensure even coloring. Check for doneness by nicking the largest one at its thickest point. The meat should be fully opaque with no traces of red.

7. Remove the drumsticks from the heat and serve them at once with lemons for squeezing and plenty of cold beer.

THE KETCHUP OF ETHIOPIA

It may be stretching it to call *berberé* the ketchup of Ethiopian cuisine, but there the uses for this atomic paste are as varied as ours are for ketchup. It is used as

a dip for *kitfo*, raw beef
a seasoning paste in *watt* (stews)
a cure for dried meats
in *dabo kolo*, a biscuitlike cracker
in *yehimbra assa*, a fish stew

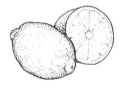

Grilled Basque Wings

◆◆

3 large garlic cloves, chopped
8 tablespoons lemon juice
 (about 2 lemons)
2 tablespoons virgin olive oil
5 to 15 dashes of Tabasco
 sauce, depending on your
 taste
3 tablespoons chopped fresh
 herbs (whatever you've got:
 basil, parsley, sage, thyme,
 oregano, or rosemary)
20 chicken wings (you can
 usually get a pack of wings at
 the market very cheap)
Salt and freshly cracked black
 pepper to taste

1. In a large serving bowl, mix together all the ingredients except the chicken wings.

2. You will notice that the wing has two joints. Cut through both joints, separating the wing into three pieces (see the diagram). The wing tip is not usable here, so either toss it out or freeze it and throw it into your next stock, a purpose for which it is excellent.

3. Salt and pepper the wing pieces to taste and whip them onto a medium-hot grill. Turn them occasionally until golden brown, about 5 minutes. To see if they're done, take a big one off the grill and bite into it.

These wings are great to gnaw on while you're diligently grilling the main course and sipping a cold one, as my Basque friend Juan Riesco often demonstrated to me. The level of heat is up to you—the Tabasco is your fuel. ◆ *Serves 4 to 6 as an appetizer*

SERVING SUGGESTIONS: These are excellent "tapas"-style appetizers. Serve them at a large cocktail party along with some other Mediterranean-inspired appetizers such as Grilled Figs with Prosciutto and Provolone (page 178) and Grilled Steamed Littlenecks Johnson (page 113).

4. When the wings are cooked through, add them to the bowl with the dressing and mix to thoroughly cover. Set them on a platter, open a cold beer, and enjoy yourself.

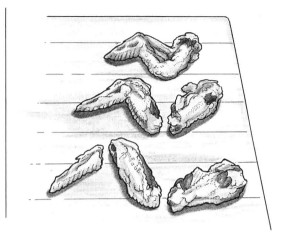

When separating chicken wings, at first you will probably want to use a cleaver. With a little practice, however, you will easily find the weak spot in the joint every time and can graduate to using a sharp knife.

Grilled Chicken Thighs with Peach, Black Olive, and Red Onion Relish

MED-LOW

3 ripe peaches
½ cup fresh black Kalamata
    olives (you may substitute any
    fresh black olives, but do not
    use canned)
1 small red onion, diced small
1 roasted red pepper, diced
    small (see Pantry, page 368)
4 tablespoons extra virgin olive
    oil
2 tablespoons balsamic vinegar
1 teaspoon minced garlic
1 tablespoon fresh thyme
Salt and freshly cracked black
    pepper to taste
4 tablespoons lemon juice
    (about 1 lemon)
8 chicken thighs

I think the contrasting flavors of ripe fruit and black olives meld together very well. The earthy Kalamatas add just a trace of bitterness against the sweetness of the fruit. Combine these tastes with the distinctive flavor of grilled chicken, and you have a dish simple to prepare with a wide range of flavors competing for your attention but not getting out of hand. Sort of like having dinner with a well-behaved family group. I use chicken thighs here because the meat has more flavor than a breast does and the pieces are smaller and therefore easier to grill without burning. ◆ *Serves 8 as an appetizer*

1. Pit the peaches and cut them into pieces about the size of sugar cubes. Pit the olives and cut them in half.

2. Combine the peaches, olives, onion, and red pepper in a mixing bowl.

3. Add the olive oil, vinegar, garlic, and thyme, and toss lightly. Add salt and pepper to taste.

4. Cover the mixture and allow it to stand at room temperature for at least 1 hour. It will keep, cov-

SERVING SUGGESTIONS: Serve this in front of a simple grilled seafood dish such as Plain Grilled Lobster (page 132), or try it as a main course with Your Basic Grilled Corn (page 317) and Rice Salad with Wasabi-Miso Dressing (page 315).

ered in the refrigerator, for up to 3 days, if you want to make it ahead, although this additional time won't change the flavor for better or worse.

5. Just before serving, add the lemon juice and mix lightly.

6. Season the chicken thighs with salt and pepper to taste. Grill skin-side down over medium-low heat, 8 to 10 minutes, or until the skin is crispy. Flip them over and cook an additional 4 to 6 minutes. To make sure they are fully done, make an incision close to the bone and look for redness, which you don't want. Serve them warm or cold with peach relish.

Grilled Chicken and Black-eyed Pea Salad with Chipotle Vinaigrette

◆ ◆

1 boneless, skinless chicken
   breast
Salt and freshly cracked black
   pepper to taste
2 cups black-eyed peas (do not
   soak overnight)
6 cups water
1 tablespoon salt

For the vinaigrette

Juice of 1 orange
8 tablespoons lime juice (about
   4 limes)
2 tablespoons molasses
2 tablespoons cider vinegar
2 tablespoons canned chipotles
1 tablespoon ground cumin
2 tablespoons tomato purée
¼ cup chopped cilantro
1 red bell pepper, cored, seeded,
   and chopped
½ red onion, chopped

1. Rub the chicken with salt and pepper to taste and grill it skin-side down over a medium fire for 10 to 12 minutes. The skin should be quite crisp. Turn it and grill for an additional 5 to 6 minutes. Remove it from the grill and set aside.

2. Put the black-eyed peas into a saucepan with the water and salt. Bring them to a boil, lower the

Chipotle vinaigrette meshes well with the smokiness of grilled chicken and contrasts perfectly with the mellowness of black-eyed peas. This is a neat way to use any leftovers from the Grilled Chicken Breasts with Fresh Herbs and Lemon (page 167). ◆ *Serves 4 as an appetizer*

SERVING SUGGESTIONS: This makes a good double-appetizer meal with Chilled Grilled Tomato Soup with Fresh Basil (page 29), or a good appetizer in front of Grilled Pork Loin with Indonesian Chile-Coconut Sauce (page 156).

heat, and simmer them for 20 to 30 minutes or until tender. Drain the peas and set aside.

3. Make the dressing: In a blender or food processor, combine the orange and lime juice, molasses, vinegar, chipotles, cumin, and tomato purée. Mix until the ingredients are thoroughly combined and smooth. (The vinaigrette will keep 1 week, covered, in the refrigerator.)

4. Mix the peas with the dressing, then stir in the chopped cilantro, red pepper, onion and black pepper to taste.

5. Remove the bones from the chicken breast and cut the meat into 1-inch pieces. Stir the chicken into the salad, taste for seasoning, adding more salt if necessary, and cover the bowl tightly with plastic wrap. Refrigerate the salad for at least 2 hours, or up to 2 days. Allow the salad to sit at room temperature for 30 minutes before serving so it will not be too cold.

THE PEA THAT'S NOT A PEA

Black-eyed peas are part of a family of legumes brought to the American South by slaves from Africa. Actually more of a bean than a pea, they grow in odd-shaped pods that can become over a foot long and are related to mung beans and other Asian legumes. Field peas, crowder peas, and cow peas are among the other members of the family, and all are securely ensconced in traditional Southern cooking. Hoppin' John, a traditional Southern New Year's dish, contains black-eyed peas to ensure a continuous supply of pocket change in the year to come.

Wilted Greens with Grilled Lamb and Blue Cheese

◆◆◆

1 pound lamb from the leg, cut
  into ½-inch cubes
Salt and freshly cracked black
  pepper to taste
4 tablespoons olive oil
2 pounds dandelion greens,
  separated, washed, and dried
4 tablespoons balsamic vinegar
Pinch of sugar
6 ounces blue cheese, crumbled

1. Season the lamb cubes with salt and pepper to taste, thread them on skewers, and grill over high heat for 3 to 4 minutes per side. The lamb should remain pink inside.

2. In a large sauté pan, heat the oil until very hot but not smoking, then add the greens. Turn them furiously with tongs while you count to five, being sure to coat them all with oil.

3. Remove the greens from the heat to a bowl, and continue mixing until they are bright green or wilted. Add the vinegar and sugar, salt and pepper to taste, and toss well.

4. Spoon out the greens mixture onto 4 individual plates, place the cubes of grilled lamb on top, and sprinkle generously with the crumbled blue cheese.

Although this dish may seem a little "out there," I encourage you to try it. The combination of bitter greens and blue cheese is outstanding, and the grilled lamb provides a distinct texture and flavor. I like to use dandelion greens, but others will suffice. Avoid kale or collard greens, though, because you won't have enough time to tenderize them. Use a combination of 3 parts spinach greens to 1 part mustard, beet, or turnip greens if no dandelions are available. ◆ *Serves 4 as an appetizer*

SERVING SUGGESTIONS: Serve this with Grilled Scallops with Rocotillo-Mango Relish (page 117) as a two-appetizer dinner, or in front of Grilled Peppered Wolffish (page 89).

Pasta from Hell

+ +

2 tablespoons olive oil
1 yellow onion, diced small
1 red bell pepper, diced small
2 bananas, sliced
¼ cup pineapple juice
Juice of 3 oranges
4 tablespoons lime juice (about
   2 limes)
¼ cup chopped cilantro
3 to 4 tablespoons finely
   chopped fresh red *or* green
   hot chile peppers (Scotch
   Bonnet or Habañero are best)
   or 4 to 6 ounces Inner Beauty
   Hot Sauce (see Sources, page
   380)
About ¼ cup grated Parmesan
   cheese
2 teaspoons unsalted butter
1 pound fettuccine
Salt and freshly cracked black
   pepper to taste

Constantly challenged by my fire-eating customers to create hotter and hotter food, I decided to put a stop to it once and for all by developing a dish that would satisfy their desires and quiet their demands. A dish so hot that there was no hotter; so hot that never again would I have to take a ribbing from the heat freaks.

This is it. Your heat source here is the Scotch Bonnet chile pepper, widely accepted as the hottest commercially cultivated chile pepper in the world. Many of my customers think this dish is just a bit too much, Kitchen Out of Control. But a handful of others, with sweat coming off the tops of their heads, eyes as big as saucers, bathed in satanic ecstasy, tell me that it's the best thing I've ever created. The truth lies somewhere in the middle, and in fact the heat in this dish can be controlled by using far fewer peppers without impairing the flavor of the dish. But . . . every once in a while, when the really hard case sits down and insists on something that has a "real kick" to it, whip the full-bore Pasta from Hell on him. We're talking culinary respect here. ♦ *Serves 4 as an appetizer*

1. In a large saucepan, heat the oil and sauté the onion and red pepper in it over medium heat for about 4 minutes.

2. Add the bananas and pineapple and orange juice. Simmer over medium heat for 5 minutes, until the bananas are soft.

3. Remove from the heat, add the lime juice, cilantro, chile peppers or Inner Beauty sauce, and 3 tablespoons of the Parmesan cheese, and mix well.

SERVING SUGGESTIONS: Serve this with a Last Resort (page 363) and East Coast Grill Corn Bread (page 324) to serve as a fire extinguisher.

4. In 4 quarts of boiling salted water, cook the fettuccine until al dente, about 8 to 10 minutes for dried pasta, 3 to 4 for fresh. Drain and put it into a stainless steel bowl.

5. Add the spicy mixture, butter, and mix well. Season with salt and pepper to taste and garnish with the remaining grated Parmesan.

HOW HOT IS HOT?

(Relative Heat Measurements of Chile Peppers)

Our individual reaction to the heat in a particular chile pepper is a subjective experience. However, the incendiary properties of chile peppers can be rated scientifically. This is done by measuring the amount of capsaicin (the heat-causing property) in each chile pepper using a standard called Scoville units. A Scoville unit is the number of units of water it takes to make a unit of chile pepper lose all traces of heat. For example, it takes between 2,500 and 5,000 units of water to neutralize the heat from one unit of jalapeño. My favorite *capsicum*, the Scotch Bonnet, aka habañero, checks in at a scorching 150,000 to 300,000 Scoville units.

Below is a relative heat scale that was prepared by chile pepper expert Dave DeWitt, editor of the *Whole Chile Pepper* magazine.

Chile	Scoville Units
Bell Pepper/Pimiento/Sweet Banana	0
Cherry/Mexican Bell	100–500
Big Jim/Anaheim/New Mexican #6	500–1,000
Ancho/Pasilla/Poblano	1,000–1,500
Cascabel/Rocotillo	1,500–2,500
Jalapeño	2,500–5,000
Serrano	5,000–15,000
De Árbol	15,000–30,000
Piquin/Cayenne/Tabasco	30,000–50,000
Aji/Chiltepin/Thai	50,000–100,000
Habañero or Scotch Bonnet	150,000–300,000

Pasta with Grilled Tomato-Basil Sauce

MED

◆ ◆

12 ripe tomatoes, destemmed and halved
3 yellow onions, peeled and halved
12 to 16 ounces of your favorite pasta (I use fettuccine)
½ cup chopped fresh basil
½ cup chopped parsley
4 tablespoons extra virgin olive oil
1 tablespoon minced garlic
1 teaspoon red pepper flakes
1 cup grated Parmesan cheese

1. Over medium heat, grill the tomato and onion halves until nicely browned, about 8 to 10 minutes. Remove them from the grill and chop them coarsely.

2. In 4 quarts of boiling salted water, cook the pasta until al dente, about 8 to 10 minutes for dried pasta, 3 to 4 minutes for fresh.

3. Drain the pasta and place it in a large bowl. Add the basil, parsley, olive oil, garlic, and pepper flakes, and toss well.

4. Add the tomatoes and onions to the pasta, toss again, and pass the grated Parmesan.

This is a recipe for late August when your bumper tomato crop is coming in, and they are bright red, big, and sweet. I'd have this with fettuccine, a loaf of garlic bread, a salad, and a big red wine. The sauce is also good on fish or grilled chicken. ◆ *Serves 6 to 8 as an appetizer*

SERVING SUGGESTIONS: Serve this with Grilled Eggplant with Olive Oil, Parsley, and Capers (page 298) or Grandma Wetzler's Sweet-and-Sour Wilted Chicory (page 285).

Seared Sirloin, Sushi Style

Spice rub for the steak

1 tablespoon freshly cracked
  white pepper
1 tablespoon freshly cracked
  black pepper
1 tablespoon kosher salt
1 tablespoon Five Spice Powder
  (available in Asian markets)
1 tablespoon paprika
1 teaspoon powdered ginger

16- to 20-ounce sirloin steak, 2
  inches thick, trimmed of all
  the fat (let your butcher
  prepare it)

Accompaniments

½ cup soy sauce
6 ounces pickled ginger (see
  Pantry, page 370)
4 tablespoons wasabi, mixed
  thoroughly with 4 tablespoons
  water (see Pantry, page 371)

1. Mix the white and black peppers, salt, Five Spice Powder, paprika, and ginger, and rub the steak on all sides with the spice mixture. Allow it to stand, uncovered, at room temperature for 1 hour.

2. Over a very hot fire, heavily sear the steak on all its surfaces, 2 minutes per surface. (You will have four surfaces on a steak this thick: top, bottom, and two sides.) You are looking for a well-

For those who like steak tartare and carpaccio, an Asian-inspired addition to the raw beef dish line. Rubbed with spices, the steak is then cooked quickly at a high heat, concentrating flavor on the seared surface while leaving the interior basically raw. It is served with the traditional Japanese raw fish accompaniments of soy sauce, pickled ginger, and wasabi, a Japanese green horseradish. I always like the combination of rare/raw meat and horseradish, and the sweet ginger smoothes it all out. I rub wasabi on the meat with a little ginger, then roll it up and dunk it in the soy sauce. ♦ *Serves 4 as an appetizer*

SERVING SUGGESTIONS: I would serve this in front of Grilled Bluefish with Chipotle Vinaigrette (page 94) or Grilled Pompano with Lime and Olive Oil (page 95).

browned, thoroughly seared surface, but since you want the heat to penetrate only the outer layer of the meat, you must be sure to do it at a very high heat.

3. Remove the meat from the grill and allow it to cool at least 20 minutes before serving. If you want, you can refrigerate it, covered, for up to 2 days, and bring it out an hour before serving to remove the chill.

4. Slice the meat paper-thin across the grain and arrange it on a platter with the accompaniments.

Surf 'n' Turf
◆ ◆ ◆ ◆ ◆ ◆ ◆ ◆ ◆

Grilled Chicken Liver Satay with Indonesian Hot Peanut Sauce

HIGH

◆ ◆

Indonesian Hot Peanut Sauce
(page 80)

¾ pound chicken livers (about
15 livers)
1 cup milk
4 tablespoons lime juice (about
2 limes)
2 tablespoons sugar
1 tablespoon minced garlic
2 tablespoons soy sauce
2 tablespoons chopped cilantro
1 teaspoon red pepper flakes
2 tablespoons peanut oil

1. Make the Indonesian Hot Peanut Sauce (page 80).

2. Rinse the livers well, pat them dry, and place them in a large shallow pan.

3. In a large bowl, combine all the remaining ingredients except the peanut oil and mix well. Pour over the livers, cover, and let stand for 3 to 4 hours.

4. Drain the livers and pat them dry. Discard the marinade.

5. In a large sauté pan, heat the peanut oil until very hot but not smoking. Place the livers in a single layer in the oil and cook until

If you're talking about grilled food in Indonesia, you're talking about satay, which basically means skewered meat. The difference between satays from various Indonesian islands is as pronounced as the difference between "barbecue" from different regions of the United States. The satay recipe here is said to be most popular on Java and includes the unusual combination of lime juice and milk in the marinade. It is said that the milk draws out impurities from the liver, while the lime adds a tartness to counteract the milk's smooth richness. The peanut sauce, of course, is the barbecue sauce of Indonesia. ◆ *Serves 6 as an appetizer*

SERVING SUGGESTIONS: To make a full meal, serve this with Grilled Chorizo Soup with Kale and Sweet Potatoes (page 31), or serve it as an appetizer in front of Grilled Sausage and Scallops with Peppers, Lemon, Basil, and Garlic (page 116).

brown and crisp, turning once. This should take 2 to 3 minutes. Be careful not to crowd the livers together, since that will keep them from browning. You might have to cook them in batches, depending on the size of your sauté pan.

6. Remove the livers from the pan and dry them on paper towels.

7. Thread the livers on 6 skewers and grill over high heat for 2 to 3 minutes, until crusty brown.

8. Serve with Indonesian Hot Peanut Sauce for dipping.

SATAY NIGHT FEVER

Throughout Indonesia, satays are eaten at any time of day and at almost every meal. They come in an endless variety, the only common denominator being that they are skewered and cooked over charcoal. The most popular time to eat satays, though, seems to be late in the evening. At that time, vendors, each having his own unique basting sauce, open up stands selling beef, goat, and chicken satays along every roadside.

Indonesian Hot Peanut Sauce

½ cup rice wine vinegar
½ cup water
¼ cup sugar
1 cup roasted, unsalted peanuts
2 tablespoons grated fresh
  ginger
1 tablespoon minced garlic
2 tablespoons chopped cilantro
Pinch of red pepper flakes
½ teaspoon salt
3 tablespoons soy sauce
1 tablespoon sesame oil

About 2 cups

1. In a small saucepan, combine the vinegar, water, and sugar. Bring to a boil and boil for 5 minutes, stirring occasionally to make sure the sugar is dissolved. Remove from the heat and allow the mixture to cool.

2. Put the peanuts and vinegar-sugar mixture into a food processor or blender and purée until smooth.

3. Add the ginger, garlic, cilantro, red pepper flakes, and salt, and mix well.

4. Add the soy sauce and sesame oil, and beat until well integrated into the peanut mixture. This sauce will keep up to 10 days, covered, in the refrigerator. Warm slightly before serving.

Grilled Sausage Patties with Celeriac and Fennel Slaw

◆◆◆◆◆◆◆◆◆◆◆◆◆◆◆◆◆◆◆◆◆◆◆◆◆◆◆◆◆◆◆◆◆◆◆◆◆

For the sausage patties

1 pound fresh Italian sweet link
  sausages
1 tablespoon minced garlic
1 tablespoon finely chopped
  fresh basil
1 tablespoon finely chopped
  fresh rosemary
Salt and freshly cracked black
  pepper to taste

When I grew up we had sausage patties only for breakfast. Now, happily, they turn up on lunch and dinner menus. To make these patties, use fresh Italian sweet link sausages, slash the casing, and squeeze the meat out. Or, if you prefer, you can simply grill the links. The celeriac and fennel slaw provides a hearty, earthy companion to the Italian theme of the dish. ◆ *Serves 4 as an appetizer*

1. Slash the casings of the sausages and squeeze the meat out into a large bowl. Add all the remaining ingredients, mix very well, and shape into 4 flat patties.

2. Make a hot fire under half of the grill. Place the sausage patties over the side without the fire (to avoid constant flare-ups from the high fat content of the sausages) and cook about 10 minutes per side. Check doneness by slicing one of the patties in half like a bun. The meat should be cooked through, a uniform juicy gray. If not done, slice all the patties in this manner and grill raw-side down for 3 more minutes to finish.

3. Remove them from the grill and serve with the slaw.

SERVING SUGGESTIONS: I would serve this dish in front of Spice-Rubbed Grilled Monkfish (page 90), or with World-Famous Fried Soft-shell Crab Sandwich with Tartar Sauce (page 121).

For the slaw (about 4 cups)

½ bulb fresh fennel (about ½
    pound), julienned
1 pound celeriac, julienned
1 tablespoon celery seed
2 tablespoons Dijon mustard
½ cup olive oil
¾ cup lemon juice (about
    3 lemons)
2 tablespoons chopped parsley
Salt and freshly cracked black
    pepper to taste

1. In a large bowl, combine the
fennel, celeriac, celery seed, mustard, and olive oil, and mix very
well.

2. Add the lemon juice, parsley,
and salt and pepper to taste, and
toss well. Grilled Hearthbread
with Sopressata, Melon, and Torta
Basil (page 182) is a great accompaniment to this dish.

MARINADES AND GRILLING

Many people advise you to marinate meat and fish before grilling,
but I don't usually recommend it.

There are two reasons that people give for marinating—to impart
flavor, and to aid in tenderizing. Now,
I might occasionally use a marinade
to impart flavor, but only when using
cuts with a very large surface area,
such as flank steak. This is because,
in a twenty-four-hour marinating
period, the actual penetration of the
marinade into the food is minimal,
so you really gain nothing but surface flavor. In general, I prefer a dry
rub, which not only imparts surface
flavor more efficiently, but also aids
in the formation of a flavorful crust
or sear. Of course, a rub is not prac-
tical for all situations. When it isn't,
I prefer to take the flavors I would
be adding by marinating, and instead add them after cooking, in the
form of a dressing or relish.

As far as tenderizing goes, most
meat that is suitable for grilling is
tender to begin with, so there is no
need for tenderizing. Also, if you are
using an acid-based marinade, you
actually break down the cell struc-
ture of the protein in meat, with the
result that the outside of the meat
becomes slightly mushy while the
interior is unaffected. I suppose this
makes the meat more palatable to
some, but I think the term "tenderizing" in the case of marinades is a
bit of a misnomer—"surface soft-
ening" might be more accurate.

Grilled Marinated Beef Heart in the Peruvian Style

◆ ◆

1 small beef heart (3 to 3½ pounds)
1 cup plus 1 tablespoon red wine vinegar
½ cup vegetable oil
2 tablespoons minced garlic
1 tablespoon ground cumin
1 tablespoon red pepper flakes
1 tablespoon ground achiote seeds (see Pantry, page 369) (you may substitute paprika)
4 minced fresh red *or* green jalapeño chile peppers
1 large red onion, minced
¼ cup chopped parsley
Salt and freshly cracked black pepper to taste

2 limes, quartered, for garnish

This is typical Peruvian street food, which you will find served with boiled sweet potatoes and grilled corn in any marketplace in Peru. Or at least I did when I was there. In fact, I ate this dish throughout my stay, thinking it was just plain old tough beef. On the last day, I found out it was actually beef heart. I still like it because it's authentic food of the people, and an interesting eating experience. It's a good thing to serve when that wild man who will eat anything and thinks he's seen it all is coming over. Surprisingly tasty, this dish is very meaty with a hint of liver. ◆ *Serves 10 as an appetizer*

1. Remove the fat from the beef heart and cut the beef into ½-inch chunks. Place them in a shallow bowl.

2. In a large bowl, combine 1 cup of the vinegar, the vegetable oil, 1 tablespoon of the minced garlic, and the cumin, red pepper flakes, and achiote. Mix well and pour over the beef heart. Let sit, covered, overnight.

3. Remove the meat from the marinade, dry it well with paper towels, and thread it on a skewer. Discard the marinade.

SERVING SUGGESTIONS: This is enough red meat taste for one meal. Serve it with a straightforward fish or poultry dish, like Grilled Pompano with Lime and Olive Oil (page 95) or Grilled Chicken Breast with Fresh Herbs and Lemon (page 167).

4. Over a hot fire, grill the meat until the outside is brown and crisp, 2 to 3 minutes per side.

5. In a small bowl combine the minced jalapeños, onion, the other tablespoon of garlic, the parsley, the tablespoon of vinegar, and salt and pepper to taste.

6. Place the grilled meat on a platter, pour the sauce over it, and garnish with lime quarters.

Wild, Quixotic Dinner

◆◆◆◆◆◆◆◆◆◆◆◆◆◆◆◆◆◆

Grilled Marinated Beef Heart
in the Peruvian Style
Page 83

Sake-Marinated Grilled Frogs'
Legs with Japanese-Flavored
Barbecue Sauce
Page 188

West Indies Breadfruit Salad
Page 312

Chilled Spinach
with Soy and Ginger
Page 287

Equatorial Fruit Cocktail with Lime Juice and Jalapeños

◆◆◆

1 ripe mango
1 ripe banana
1 ripe papaya
½ pineapple
6 tablespoons lime juice (about
   3 limes)
3 diced fresh red *or* green
   jalapeño chile peppers

1. Peel all the fruits and cut them into ½ -inch cubes.

2. In a large, decorative bowl, combine all the fruits with the lime juice and jalapeños and mix well. For a little jolt, add a splash of dark rum.

Fruit with hot chile peppers may seem a little weird to our American palates, but it is a common combination in tropical regions, particularly Africa and India. A friend of mine discovered this difference in approach when, traveling in India and tiring of spicy food, he found fresh-squeezed orange juice on a menu. He ordered it, but when it arrived it was laced with ground black pepper. I use the fruit-hot combination quite a bit because it's an excellent accompaniment to grilled food. This dish makes a unique first course or salad on a hot day and goes particularly well with rice dishes.
♦ *Serves 6 as an appetizer*

SERVING SUGGESTIONS: Serve this in front of Chicken Hobo Pack (page 171) or Grilled Pork Tenderloin with Roasted Corn–Bacon Relish (page 163), or as a double appetizer with Grilled Chicken Drumsticks Berberé (page 64). Serve it with Clam Posole (page 36) for a pleasant lunch or light dinner.

Fish and Other Water Dwellers

Although seafood is more delicate and a bit less durable than meat and poultry, you need look no further than the beaches of the tropics to discover the long-standing relationship between water-dwelling creatures and grilling. Some of my most memorable meals have resulted from this relationship.

Seafood generally calls for a fire that is not as hot as one needed to grill other things, since you don't want to produce as heavy a sear or crust. A sear as thick as you look for on a steak would simply overpower the more delicate flavor of seafood, and you want to allow the natural fish flavor to emerge.

Not all types of fish are appropriate for grilling. Delicate fish such as cod or flounder cannot stand up to grilling and simply fall apart. Similarly, fish with a lot of bones are not as suitable for grilling as are fish cut into fillets. In this chapter, I have used recipes that showcase the wide range of fish and shellfish I think work best on the grill. As you will see, I am a big fan of shrimp. I think the larger sea scallops are also exceptionally good for grilling, and the high temperature and quick cooking time of grilling make it perfect for squid.

It is particularly important to make sure that your grill rack is very clean when cooking fish so that there is no residue to interfere with the delicate flavor. A superclean grill also helps prevent the most common problem that occurs when grilling fish: the fish sticking to the grill.

There are a number of other precautions you can take to help prevent sticking. Since a very hot grill surface is a key to keeping fish from sticking, and since most fish call for a medium fire, you should keep the grill rack on top of the fire throughout the whole fire-starting process, thus allowing the metal to get sufficiently hot. Coating the fish very lightly with vegetable oil before cooking is somewhat helpful—but don't use too much oil, or it will drip into the fire and cause flare-ups, which create a greasy smoke that affects the flavor of the fish. You want the fish moistened with oil, not dripping with it. I have also seen fishermen on the beach in Costa Rica putting salt water on the grill before cooking fish as a means of preventing sticking. Finally, you should let the fish remain in its original position on the grill for at least 2 to 3 minutes before you try to move it. This will allow for a sear to develop between the metal and flesh, which again prevents the flesh from sticking to the grill.

To check fish for doneness, I recommend that you gently pick up the fish and bend, twist, or fondle it—whatever technique will afford a view of the interior. Fish is generally quite pliable, so this should be no problem. If necessary, however, use the "Nick, Peek, and Cheat" Method, in which you actually cut into the meat of the fish in order to get a good view. Properly cooked fish will show a consistent opacity, while undercooked fish will appear translucent. Personally, I like fresh fish slightly undercooked. Some fish of sushi quality, such as tuna (page 193) and perhaps yellowtail (page 101), is also very good almost raw. Most, however, are better cooked almost completely. Remember that with thicker fish there will be a slight amount of carry-over cooking after you have removed it from the grill, so do leave a trace of translucency near the center to avoid overcooking. Shrimp and lobster should be cooked completely through, and, in their cases, probing the flesh should reveal a consistent opacity with no remaining translucent areas.

Perhaps the most important aspect of grilling fish is its quality when you buy it. I would try to locate a fishmonger of high standards, build a relationship with him or her, and be flexible enough in your buying habits to take advantage of the freshest fish available.

Grilled Peppered Wolffish

HIGH

◆ ◆

4 8- to 10-ounce wolffish fillets
4 tablespoons olive oil
½ cup freshly cracked black
   pepper

1. Rub the fillets all over with the oil, then coat them evenly and heavily with the pepper.

2. Over a hot fire, grill the fillets 5 to 6 minutes per side, until uniformly crusty. Probe the flesh to check for a consistently opaque center which indicates that the fish is properly cooked. If a proper crust has been obtained but the flesh is underdone, leave the fillets on the grill but move them over to the side so they are not over the flames. Continue to cook them until completely opaque.

The wolffish spends most of its time in the North Atlantic just north of Cape Cod, and its season is from fall to spring. Its name comes from its nasty wolflike appearance. It also goes under the more salable name of ocean catfish, because its face vaguely resembles the freshwater catfish, and because it is more marketable that way, and anyway, what's in a name? This is not a super-popular fish, although I'm not sure why. It is a lean, mild-tasting white fish with a very firm texture similar to that of monkfish, making it excellent for grilling. It is usually reasonably priced and has the texture and consistency to go well with strong preparations. Here I rub it with freshly cracked black pepper and grill it over high heat to get a flavor-intensive crusty coating that still leaves the inside moist. You can serve this with a fresh mustard or mayonnaise, or with just a squeeze of lemon and a hunk of butter on top. ◆ *Serves 4 as a main course*

SERVING SUGGESTIONS: In the fall, serve this preceded by Clam Posole (page 36). In the summer, serve it accompanied by Your Basic Grilled Corn (page 317), Basil Tabbouleh (page 313), and Roasted Eggplant and Pepper-Garlic Purée with Lemon and Thyme (page 297).

Monkfish goes under many names: anglerfish, sea devil, goosefish, and, in Europe, lotte or rape. It runs from St. George's Bay in Newfoundland to North Carolina but has only recently taken its just place on American menus. Being in the shark family, its appetite is legendary, and it has very discriminating taste, dining on such gourmet items as lobster and crabs. It will also eat seagoing birds like cormorants and ducks, as well as the not-so-gourmet wooden buoys and, from time to time, the feet of bathers. For years considered a trash fish by U.S. fishermen, it has always been treasured in Europe. Americans returning from Paris would clamor for the beautiful lotte, which they had eaten in fancy Parisian restaurants, and slowly monk-fish started to gain cachet. It took a while for people to catch on, and they were not aided by the incredibly ugly look of the fish. Seriously. If you ever saw one of these fish whole, you would be tempted to throw it away. It looks like your worst nightmare with fins. Only the meat in the tail section is edible, but its firm texture has earned it another of its many names: poor man's lobster. Monkfish is perfect for grilling, as it is in no danger of falling apart.

MED‑HIGH

Spice-Rubbed Grilled Monkfish

◆ ◆

For the spice rub

¼ cup ground cumin
2 tablespoons paprika
2 tablespoons chili powder
1 tablespoon light brown sugar
1 tablespoon freshly cracked
   black pepper
1 tablespoon cayenne pepper
2 tablespoons dried oregano

1 2½-pound monkfish fillet

The slightly sweet, mild monkfish is a fantastic foil for strong preparations, which it can stand up to because of its meaty consistency. This is wonderful with Chipotle Pepper Mayonnaise (page 249) served on the side. When you buy monkfish, make sure the tough outer membrane is removed, or you will have some trouble with it. ◆ *Serves 4 as a main course*

1. Combine all the spice rub ingredients in a bowl, then rub the fillet thoroughly with the mixture.

2. Over a medium-hot fire, grill the monkfish on both sides for a total of about 15 minutes. The fillet will be sort of round, so roll it as opposed to flipping it in order to cook it evenly. Don't worry when the exterior of the fish gets dark brown: This is the result of the spice rub and just indicates that the fish is properly done.

SERVING SUGGESTIONS: Serve this with Rice Salad with Wasabi-Miso Dressing (page 315) or Spicy Green Bean Salad with Grilled Pork and Peanuts (page 288).

Lime-Marinated Grilled Kingfish with Red Onion and Mango Relish

MED

◆◆

2 pounds kingfish fillets, cut into 8-ounce portions
Salt and freshly cracked black pepper to taste
6 tablespoons lime juice (about 3 limes)
2 tablespoons vegetable oil

1. Place the kingfish skin-side down in a small, flat plastic container or shallow baking pan. You need a container in which the fillets can be packed tightly together, but with their surfaces exposed.

2. Season the fillets with salt and pepper to taste, and pour the lime juice over them. Cover and place

The kingfish, the largest member of the mackerel family, runs in the summer as far north as the Chesapeake Bay, but it mostly resides on the east coast of Florida and the West Indies—smart fish. It is similar to the bluefish in its oily content, but to me has a much more subtle taste. Don't be turned off by either the "oily" quality—think of it as "buttery" and you'll like it a lot better —or by its membership in the mackerel clan. More than one person has thanked me for forcing him to try this fish. Obviously a favorite of mine, this firm-textured fellow is well suited for grilling and has enough taste to stand up to spicy sauces. Putting a pie pan over the fish creates an oven effect that helps cook it through before it burns. ◆ *Serves 4 as a main course*

them in the refrigerator for 4 to 6 hours.

3. Remove the fillets, pat them dry, and brush them with the oil.

4. Place the fillets skin-side up on the grill over medium heat. Cover them with a pie pan and cook 8 to 10 minutes.

5. Remove the pie pan, flip the fillets, and cook them an additional 5 to 7 minutes. Check to see if they are properly cooked by probing the flesh, looking for a consistent opacity.

6. Serve the fish accompanied by Red Onion and Mango Relish.

SERVING SUGGESTIONS: Serve this with Green Bean Salad with Tomatoes and Jicama (page 290), West Indies Breadfruit Salad (page 312), or Basil Tabbouleh (page 313).

Red Onion and Mango Relish

◆ ◆

1 ripe mango, diced
2 tablespoons chopped cilantro
1 small red onion, diced
1 tablespoon chopped red *or* green jalapeño chile peppers
3 tablespoons lime juice (about 1½ limes)
2 dashes of Tabasco sauce
Salt and freshly cracked black pepper to taste

About 1½ cups

1. Mix all the ingredients together. This relish will keep up to 3 days, covered, in the refrigerator.

Grilled Halibut Steaks with Fresh Tomato Sauce

MED-HIGH

◆◆◆

2 large ripe tomatoes, diced
¼ cup fresh basil, chopped
3 tablespoons extra virgin olive oil
1 tablespoon balsamic vinegar
4 8-ounce halibut steaks
3 tablespoons vegetable oil
Salt and freshly cracked black pepper to taste
4 tablespoons lemon juice (about 1 lemon)
1 teaspoon minced garlic

1. Put the diced tomato into a mixing bowl.

2. Add the basil, olive oil, and vinegar, mix well, and set aside.

3. Rub the fish with vegetable oil and season with salt and pepper to taste. Grill the fish over a medium-hot fire for 5 to 6 minutes per side, until the flesh is opaque all the way through.

4. Add the lemon juice and garlic to the tomato mixture, and mix well. Spoon some sauce on a plate and place a fillet on top of the sauce.

The halibut is the largest member of the flounder family, sometimes weighing as much as seven hundred pounds. This means that, although it is a flat fish, its body is thick enough to cut steaks from, with the bone in. When grilling, I always prefer fish or meat with bones, since they hold together better, are tenderer, and retain more juice and flavor. The halibut's firm flesh and delicate flavor also make it particularly suitable for grilling.

I would be reluctant to serve this fish with a strong relish for fear it would be too overpowering. Here I serve it with a fresh raw tomato sauce that provides a subtle background for the main attraction, the high-quality, delicately flavored fish. ◆ *Serves 4 as a main course*

SERVING SUGGESTIONS: Serve this with Your Basic Grilled Corn (page 317) and Rice Salad with Wasabi-Miso Dressing (page 315).

Grilled Bluefish with Chipotle Vinaigrette

◆◆◆

4 tablespoons cider vinegar
1 tablespoon brown prepared
  mustard
1 tablespoon puréed chipotle
  pepper
1 teaspoon chopped cilantro
4 tablespoons lime juice (about
  2 limes)
1 teaspoon sugar
½ cup extra virgin olive oil
Salt and freshly cracked black
  pepper to taste
4 8-ounce bluefish fillets
2 tablespoons vegetable oil

Lime halves for garnish
Chopped cilantro for garnish
Chopped red onion for garnish

1. In a small bowl, whisk together the vinegar, mustard, puréed pepper, cilantro, lime juice, and sugar. Add the olive oil, still whisking, until the mixture is well mixed. Add salt and pepper to taste.

2. Season the fillets with salt and pepper to taste and rub them with the vegetable oil.

3. Over medium-low heat, place the fillets skin-side up on the grill, and cover them with a pie pan. Cook 10 to 12 minutes, remove the pie pan, and flip the fillets with a spatula. Cook them an additional 5 minutes. Check to see if

Here you're talking strength against strength. A very strong, distinct-tasting, oily fish versus a hot, smoky, highly acidic vinaigrette. A great combination, as both flavors will definitely be heard from. I like to use chipotles a lot with grilled food because the tastes complement each other very well, and because it is always available canned.

This dish can be served warm or cold and is a good item for buffets because the cooling-down process doesn't affect the flavors. If you want to make a more colorful presentation, throw a couple of lime halves on the platter and sprinkle chopped cilantro and red onion on top. ◆ *Serves 4 as a main course*

SERVING SUGGESTIONS: Serve this with Sweet Potato Salad (page 302) and Grandma Wetzler's Sweet-and-Sour Wilted Chicory (page 285).

they're completely done by probing the flesh, looking for consistent opacity.

4. Remove the fillets from the grill, place them on a platter, and pour the vinaigrette over them. Garnish with lime halves, chopped cilantro, and red onion.

Grilled Pompano with Lime and Olive Oil

MED-HIGH

◆ ◆

4 8-ounce pompano fillets
3 tablespoons vegetable oil
Salt and freshly cracked black
    pepper to taste
¼ cup extra virgin olive oil
2 limes, halved
2 tablespoons chopped parsley

1. Rub the fillets with vegetable oil and season with salt and pepper to taste.

2. Grill the fillets skin-side up over a medium-hot fire for 3 to 4 minutes. Flip them and cook an additional 2 to 3 minutes, until the fish is opaque all the way through.

3. Remove the fillets from the fire, drizzle them with the olive oil, squeeze a half lime over each, and sprinkle them with the parsley.

The pompano is an East Coast fish that runs from New England to South America. I know a lot of people in Florida who claim this is the best-eating saltwater fish around. I'm not sure I would say the best, but its flesh combines firmness, sweetness, and tenderness in a way that makes it perfect for grilling. I would never try to impose a lot of spice action on this fish, because its strongest characteristic is its subtlety. Because of its thinness, this is a short cooker, and olive oil and lime juice work well with the slight grill flavor that it takes on. If you can get ahold of this fish fresh, buy it and cook it. ◆ *Serves 4 as a main course*

SERVING SUGGESTIONS: Serve this preceded by Grilled Sweetbreads with Smithfield Ham and Parsley-Caper Dipping Sauce (page 204), or along with Sweet Potato Salad (page 302) and Chilled Spinach with Soy and Ginger (page 287).

Red Snapper Fiesta al Carbón con Dos Salsas

MED-HIGH

Grilled Whole Red Party Snapper with Two Sauces

4 1½-pound whole red snappers,
  scaled and gutted
4 tablespoons vegetable oil
Salt and freshly cracked black
  pepper to taste

1. On each fish, make 3 cuts with a knife diagonally along each side, down to the bone (see the diagram). This is done to facilitate cooking and also because it is easier to peek into these gaps to determine doneness.

2. Brush each fish with vegetable oil and season with salt and pepper to taste.

3. Take special care with the fire here, since a whole fish is somewhat tricky to cook all the way through without torching its exterior. Wait until your fire is medium-hot but on the way down to low. This way, the first side of the fish to be cooked will get a nice color coating, while the flip side can stay on the grill long enough to finish cooking at a lower temperature.

The red snapper is the king of the tropical sea-dwelling snapper family. This fish runs from the east coast of the United States all the way down to Brazil, and spends a lot of time off the shores of Florida in the Gulf of Mexico. Its distinctive red skin makes a beautiful presentation, and the delicately sweet small flake belies its firm texture. Eminently suitable for grilling, this is a signature dish in the beach shacks of the Yucatán. The impressive sight of a whole red snapper cooking on the grill is surpassed only by the sight of that same fish on the plate in front of you, looking festive and delicious. I serve it here with two salsas, Hot Red Salsa (page 98), a very spicy version of the standard red salsa, and José's Tomatillo-Pineapple Salsa (page 99).

Don't be intimidated by the imagined difficulty of grilling a whole fish. Take it slow and be patient and you won't have any problems. The bones in the fish help keep it moist, and they are not a serious pain to remove. ◆ *Serves 4 as a main course*

4. Okay, so here we go. Place the fish on the grill and cook them on the first side for 10 to 12 minutes, until well charred. Using your dogleg spatula, flip the fish and continue cooking an additional 12 to 15 minutes. Probe in the slashes to check for doneness—the flesh should be uniformly white. Remove the fish from grill and serve, accompanied by the two salsas.

5. Instruct your guests to remove the top fillet of each fish, then yank the spine from the tail up, removing all bones.

Mexican-Flavored Seafood Dinner

◆◆◆◆◆◆◆◆◆◆◆◆◆

Clam Posole
Page 36

Quesadilla Bread
Page 326

Salad of Green Mango,
Coconut, and Hot Chile Peppers
Page 295

Red Snapper Fiesta
al Carbón con Dos Salsas
(Grilled Whole Red Party Snapper
with Two Sauces)
Page 96

Your Basic Black Beans
Page 318

Your Basic Grilled Corn
Page 317

Hot Red Salsa

◆ ◆

4 large ripe tomatoes (about 1½ pounds), cored and coarsely chopped
½ cup lime juice (about 4 limes)
¼ cup chopped cilantro
1 medium red onion, diced small
4 small fresh red *or* green jalapeño chile peppers, finely chopped
Salt and freshly cracked black pepper to taste

About 2 cups

1. Put all the ingredients in a mixing bowl, and mix well. Salsa will keep up to 3 days, covered, in the refrigerator.

José's Tomatilla-Pineapple Salsa

1 10-ounce can tomatillos *or*
    about 12 fresh (see Pantry,
    page 371)
½ pineapple, diced small
½ red bell pepper, diced small
½ green bell pepper, diced small
1 medium red onion, diced small
2 tablespoons canned chipotles
    (see Pantry, page 369),
    minced
½ cup chopped cilantro
1 tablespoon minced garlic
¼ cup white vinegar
6 tablespoons lime juice (about
    3 limes)
Juice of 2 oranges
Salt and freshly cracked black
    pepper to taste

1. If using canned tomatillos, purée them in a food processor or blender. If using fresh, chop them fine.

2. To the tomatillos, add the pineapple, red and green bell peppers, and onions.

3. In another bowl, combine the chipotles, cilantro, garlic, vinegar, and lime and orange juice. Stir well.

4. Combine the chipotle mixture with the tomatillo mixture. Stir well and season with salt and pepper to taste. This salsa improves after sitting in the refrigerator for a few hours, and it will keep for 1 week covered and refrigerated.

Tomatillos provide the base for the common green table sauces used throughout South and Central America, with each country, even each region, adding its own ingredients to make its version unique. This combination turns up in more than one place, I'm sure, although I saw it most often in the Yucatán. This particular recipe was developed by my talented day chef at the East Coast Grill, José Velasquez.

♦ *About 6 cups*

SERVING SUGGESTIONS: I suggest that you serve this with Sweet Potato Hash Browns with Bacon and Onions (page 300) and Salad of Green Mango, Coconut, and Hot Chile Peppers (page 295).

Grilled Swordfish Steaks with Yucatán Orange-Herb Paste

◆◆

For the paste

1 teaspoon minced garlic
1 teaspoon ground cumin
1 teaspoon chili powder
2 tablespoons chopped fresh oregano
2 tablespoons chopped cilantro
6 tablespoons orange juice combined with 2 tablespoons lime juice
4 dashes of Tabasco sauce
2 tablespoons extra virgin olive oil

4 10-ounce swordfish steaks, cut ½ to 1 inch thick
Vegetable oil for brushing

1. Make the paste: In a food processor or blender, combine all the ingredients, purée, and set aside.

2. Brush the swordfish steaks with vegetable oil. Over a medium fire, grill the swordfish steaks, 4 to 5 minutes per side, or until they are almost completely opaque.

3. Brush three quarters of the paste onto both sides of the swordfish steaks and cook an additional 1 minute per side.

4. Remove the swordfish steaks from the grill, brush on the remaining paste, and serve.

In this preparation it is important to cut the swordfish steaks thinly so the paste doesn't burn before the fish is cooked. Pastes like the one used here are common in tropical countries, since they lend intensity and complexity to simple grilled foods. This approach is similar to the Cajun "blackening" technique.
♦ *Serves 4 as a main course*

SERVING SUGGESTIONS: Serve this with Black Bean Salad (page 319), Hot Pepper Corn Bread (page 325), and/or Green Bean Salad with Tomatoes and Jicama (page 290).

Grilled Yellowtail with Water Chestnut–Scallion Relish

✦✦✦✦✦✦✦✦✦✦✦✦✦✦✦✦✦✦✦✦✦✦✦✦✦✦✦✦✦✦✦✦✦✦

4 8- to 10-ounce yellowtail fillets
4 tablespoons vegetable oil
Salt and freshly cracked black
    pepper to taste

1. Rub the fillets with the vegetable oil, salt and pepper to taste, and grill them over a medium fire, skin-side up, until the top surface has a light golden crust, 5 to 7 minutes.

2. Flip to skin-side down and grill them another 5 to 7 minutes, observing closely and checking often so the fillets don't overcook.

3. Remove the fillets from the grill, and serve accompanied by Water Chestnut–Scallion Relish.

Not to be confused with yellowfin tuna, the yellowtail is a member of the jack family which is present in all tropic and subtropical waters. It spends its days in the Southern Pacific, and the best fishing grounds for it are off the southern California coast. This mild-tasting, large-flaked fish has a firm texture that makes it a natural for grilling. It is definitely one of the top three on my list of fabulous undiscovered food fish. In Mexico, however, it is a very popular fish, and in Japan it is used in sushi known as *hamachi*.

This fish is similar to tuna in that it is appropriate to severely undercook it on the interior while charring it on the exterior. Because of its density, it has a tendency to dry out if overcooked, so check it often and try it a little rare.

The subtly flavored, crunchy Water Chestnut–Scallion Relish with which I accompany the yellowtail is perfect for fish, but it can also be served by itself as a Japanese-style salad. Because of the scallion, this relish won't keep more than a day or two in the refrigerator— best used the day it is made. ◆ *Serves 4 as a main course*

SERVING SUGGESTIONS: Accompany this with Very Aromatic Tomato-Ginger Jam (page 231), José's Jicama Slaw (page 294), or Chilled Spinach with Soy and Ginger (page 287).

Water Chestnut–Scallion Relish

•••

1 cup canned water chestnuts, sliced

1½ cups very thinly sliced scallion (both green and white parts)

1 tablespoon sugar

2 tablespoons sesame seeds, toasted in a single layer in a 350°F oven for 25 minutes

3 tablespoons soy sauce

2 tablespoons sesame oil

3 tablespoons rice wine vinegar

About 2 cups

1. In a bowl, combine the sliced water chestnut and scallion. Add the sugar and sesame seeds, and toss well.

2. Add the soy sauce, sesame oil, and vinegar, and toss once again.

3. Serve at once. Will keep covered and refrigerated for only 1 or 2 days.

Grilled Tuna Steak with Nectarine–Red Onion Relish

◆◆

4 8- to 10-ounce boneless tuna
　steaks, 1 inch thick
4 tablespoons salad oil
Salt and freshly ground pepper
　(white is best) to taste

Lightly rub the tuna steaks with oil and season with salt and pepper. Grill the tuna steaks 4 to 5 minutes per side over a medium-hot fire, being careful not to overcook them. Check for doneness by bending a steak gently and peering inside it, looking for a slight translucence in the center. Remove the steaks from the grill and place them on top of the relish.

I don't think many cooks will disagree when I say grilling is the best cooking method for tuna—its strong character and distinct flavor allow it to take the grill without being overpowered, and its sturdy texture is extremely durable.

I like to leave the fish a little underdone in the center, as it dries out rapidly if overcooked. The combination here of the sweet and sour taste of the relish against the willful grilled flavor of the tuna is a strong contrast that I find successful. ◆ *Serves 4 as a main course*

SERVING SUGGESTIONS: Serve this with Green Bean Salad with Tomatoes and Jicama (page 290), Salad of Green Mango, Coconut, and Hot Chile Peppers (page 295), or, my personal favorite, Your Basic Grilled Corn (page 317).

NECTARINE–RED ONION RELISH

1 red bell pepper, seeded and
  cut into thin strips
6 ripe but firm nectarines,
  peeled and cut into 8 slices
  each
1 medium red onion, sliced into
  long, thin pieces
1 teaspoon minced garlic
¼ cup julienned fresh basil
¼ cup red wine vinegar
¼ cup fresh orange juice
2 tablespoons lime juice (about
  1 lime)
¼ cup virgin olive oil
Salt and freshly cracked black
  pepper to taste

Combine all the ingredients in a bowl, and toss them gently. It works best if you use a stainless steel bowl much larger than you would think you need for this recipe so you get some real mixing action as you toss. This will be a slightly runny relish, as the solids and liquids mix but do not combine. Keep chilled until ready to serve. This relish will keep, covered and refrigerated, up to 2 weeks.

I often serve fruit relishes with grilled fish, since the bright, fresh taste of the relishes is excellent against the rather subtle, smoky fish flavors. In tropical climates, fruits like mangoes and papayas are often served in salad form with lime or vinegar. This is a similar treatment, but I've given it an Italian/Mediterranean slant by combining the fruit with red wine vinegar, olive oil, garlic, and basil.

Peaches or plums can be used in place of nectarines in this relish, although the color is not quite as attractive. Whatever fruit you use, it should be firm rather than superripe. Underripe fruit can also be used, but in that case add 1 teaspoon of sugar to the relish to compensate for the lack of sugar in the fruit. ◆ *About 3 cups*

Grilled Salmon Steak with Watercress, Ginger, and Sesame

◆◆

4 12-ounce salmon steaks (1 to 1½ inches thick)
2 tablespoons peanut oil
Salt and freshly cracked black pepper to taste

2 bunches watercress, separated, washed, and dried
½ medium red onion, thinly sliced

For the vinaigrette

2 tablespoons sesame oil
1 teaspoon sugar
2 tablespoons soy sauce
1 tablespoon minced fresh ginger
2 tablespoons rice wine vinegar
2 tablespoons red wine vinegar
¼ cup olive oil
Salt and freshly cracked white pepper to taste

4 tablespoons sesame seeds, toasted in a single layer in a 350°F oven for 25 minutes

1. Rub the salmon steaks on both sides with the peanut oil and sprinkle them with salt and pepper to taste. Over a medium-hot fire, grill the steaks 5 to 6 minutes

The Indians of the Pacific Northwest were said to revere the salmon as a god. You might think that is going a bit too far, but if you get some superfresh salmon, have your fishmonger cut it into steaks for you, and grill it up, you just might want to join the congregation.

In any case, I agree with Escoffier's precept that salmon should be served as simply as possible. Here a saladlike accompaniment of watercress in a ginger vinaigrette complements the fish's natural flavor. This dish is outstanding served cold the next day, but I would suggest removing the bones from the salmon before refrigerating. ◆ *Serves 4 as a main course*

SERVING SUGGESTIONS: On a cool day, I would serve this with Grilled Tripe and Hominy Stew (page 38) or Grilled Chorizo Soup with Kale and Sweet Potatoes (page 31). On a hot day, serve it after Grilled Vegetable Antipasto with Braised Garlic Bread (page 41).

per side. Remove them from the grill.

2. Meanwhile in a salad bowl, combine the watercress and sliced onion. In another bowl, combine all the vinaigrette ingredients and mix well. Pour the vinaigrette onto the watercress-onion mixture and toss lightly.

3. Arrange the dressed watercress on a platter and place the salmon steaks on top. Sprinkle the steaks liberally with the toasted sesame seeds.

What is the difference between a fish steak and a fish fillet? A steak is cut vertically from the body and includes the backbone, while a fillet is removed horizontally and avoids the bone. Some fish like swordfish are always cut into steaks because of their size and skin texture, while others such as bluefish, snapper, and sole are usually filleted. Yet others, including salmon as well as halibut and striped bass, can be cut in either fashion. In the case of salmon, I prefer the steak because it is slightly less fragile than the fillet and the backbone makes the fish a bit sturdier for grilling. Also, the meat that lies up next to the bone in a steak tastes sweeter to me and seems tenderer than the meat of a fillet.

Grilled Squid with Asian Slaw and Hoisin Barbecue Sauce

◆◆◆◆◆◆◆◆◆◆◆◆◆◆◆◆◆◆◆◆◆◆◆◆◆◆◆◆◆◆◆◆◆◆◆◆◆◆◆

PRAISE FOR THE SQUID

The squid, in my opinion, holds the undisputed title as most under-utilized edible sea creature in the world. Although very popular in Asian and Mediterranean cuisines, the annual catch of this mollusk falls far short of the potential catch of some 2½ million pounds.

The squid's lean meat is high in protein, and over 75 percent of its total body weight consists of edible meat. In addition, its intense texture enables squid to stand up to powerful flavors and still retain its character—a trait that makes it eminently suitable for a whole range of uses and preparations.

Many people consider squid to be a member of the rubber family. This is because squid very often is not cooked properly. There are two basic methods that are acceptable for cooking squid: one is to stew it for a long period of time; the other is to cook it very quickly at a high heat. The second method is usually done in a sauté pan or a deep-fat fryer, but a very hot grill is uniquely suited for quickly seared squid. The actual cooking time is very short, and I have found that using a brick to keep the squid bodies flat ensures even, lightning-fast cooking. ◆ *Serves 4 to 6 as a light main course*

SERVING SUGGESTIONS: This dish can be served as a light main course. In fact, since it is a rather complex dish, I might serve it with an appetizer as a full dinner. For this, couple it with Grilled Sweetbreads with Wilted Southern Greens, Slab Bacon, and Balsamic Vinegar (page 206) or Grilled Chorizo Soup with Kale and Sweet Potatoes (page 31).

The Squid

✦✦✦✦✦✦✦✦✦✦✦✦✦✦✦✦✦✦✦✦✦✦✦✦✦✦✦✦✦✦✦✦✦✦✦✦✦✦

5 pounds uncleaned squid *or* 2½
  pounds cleaned squid
1 tablespoon sesame oil
Salt and freshly cracked black
  pepper to taste

1. If you have bought uncleaned
squid, clean it as follows:

  a. Remove the head with the
     tentacles from the body.
  b. Peel the thin outer mem-
     brane from the body.
  c. Pull the inner cartilage from
     the body (this is a single piece
     that looks like plastic). Dis-
     card, but save the body.
  d. Cut the tentacles off below
     the eye and remove the hard,
     pebble-like sphere that re-
     mains inside the tentacles.
     Reserve the tentacles.
  e. Wash the body thoroughly.
     It should remain in a bag
     shape after washing.

2. Rub the squid with sesame oil
and salt and pepper to taste. Set
aside while you prepare the slaw.

When buying squid, I prefer those with
a body length (not including head and
tentacles) of about 4 to 5 inches, because smaller squid are more tender.

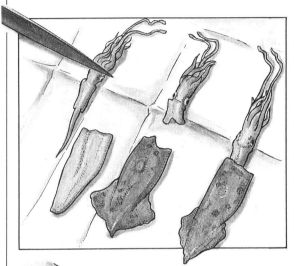

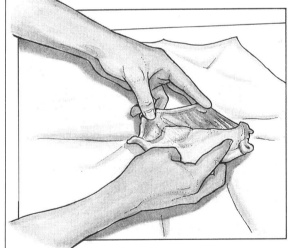

Asian Slaw

◆◆◆

1 pound green *or* red cabbage, julienned in strips about 5 inches long and ¼ inch wide

½ red bell pepper, cut into long, fine strips

2 scallions, cut thin on a sharp bias (at an angle)

½ cup rice wine vinegar

1 tablespoon sugar

1 teaspoon finely grated fresh ginger

1 tablespoon sesame seeds, toasted in a single layer in a 350°F oven for 25 minutes

1 tablespoon sesame oil

Salt and freshly cracked black pepper to taste

This rather pungent salad is a good foil for the squid and continues the dish's Eastern inspiration. It should be dressed as close to dinnertime as possible so the cabbage stays crisp in contrast to the softness of the squid. ◆ *2½ cups*

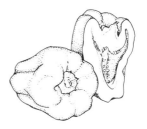

1. In a large bowl, combine the cabbage, red pepper, and scallion.

2. In a separate bowl, vigorously mix together all the remaining ingredients.

3. Just before serving time, combine the cabbage mixture with the dressing, and mix well.

Hoisin Barbecue Sauce

6 tablespoons hoisin sauce
6 tablespoons ketchup
2 tablespoons rice wine vinegar
2 tablespoons soy sauce

1. Combine all ingredients and mix well. This sauce keeps 3 weeks, covered, in the refrigerator.

Final Preparation

Okay, let's move on out to the grill, with the cabbage mixture and dressing in separate bowls ready to go, the cleaned squid in one hand and a beer in the other. Now make one more trip back to the kitchen for the Hoisin Barbecue Sauce. (Or, if you're really dexterous, you can balance the beer bottle under your chin and take everything out at once! A goal to aspire to as the summer progresses.)

You should have your squid body and tentacles oiled and salted and peppered on a plate nearby; you need to have your Hoisin Barbecue Sauce and brush; you'll need some tongs; and of course you need to have one clean, washed brick covered with foil.

Now, a brick is not generally considered a key kitchen tool, but it plays a major role here in enforcing the principle that quick, high-temperature cooking makes for tender, tasty squid. The size of your squid will de-

This is a very easy sauce to make. It's just a little twist on your basic barbecue sauce, in keeping with the Oriental theme of the dish. ◆ *1 cup*

termine how many bodies go on the grill per round. If you have squid with 4- to 5-inch bodies, you can get 3 or 4 on at once. The idea here is that the squid bodies go on the grill, and the brick goes on the bodies. Over a hot fire, cook the bodies 1½ to 2 minutes per side. Then remove the brick, slap a coat of Hoisin Barbecue Sauce on the bodies, use your tongs to roll them around on the grill for 30 seconds more, then remove them. Repeat this process with all of the bodies.

For the tentacles, you won't need the brick. Just cook them for about 2 minutes, using the tongs to roll them around on the grill so they are evenly cooked. You are looking for the tentacles to get brown and crispy. This is my personal favorite part of this dish.

When both the tentacles and bodies are cooked, brush a little more sauce on the bodies and slice them in ¼-inch slices so that they look like little rings. Serve the extra Hoisin Barbecue Sauce as a dipping sauce, and encourage your guests to try the squid and the slaw together.

If you have any leftovers, this dish is ideal for a cold salad the next day. At the end of this meal, just drop the leftover squid into the slaw. The dressing acts as a marinade that prevents the squid from toughening up, and the next day you have a chilled grilled squid salad.

Grilled Squid Pasta with Roasted Red Pepper and Basil

HIGH

◆◆

1½ pounds squid bodies and
   tentacles
Salt and freshly cracked black
   pepper to taste
1 pound dried pasta (linguine *or*
   spaghetti)
4 tablespoons unsalted butter,
   cut into 8 pieces
2 roasted red peppers, diced
   small (see Pantry, page 368)
½ cup chopped fresh basil
¼ cup chopped parsley
¼ cup toasted pine nuts
1 tablespoon minced garlic
2 dashes of Tabasco sauce
8 tablespoons lemon juice
   (about 2 lemons)

1. Clean the squid, salt and pepper it, and grill it as described on page 108. Remove it from the grill and cut the bodies into thin circles.

2. In 4 quarts of salted, boiling water, cook pasta until al dente, about 8 to 10 minutes.

3. Drain the pasta and put it into a large stainless steel mixing bowl.

4. Add the butter, squid, and all the remaining ingredients. Toss well, making sure the butter is melted, and serve hot.

I didn't see a lot of squid when I was growing up in Virginia, but living in Boston and eating it frequently in Italian restaurants with huge quantities of garlic and olive oil, I have become a big fan. Having the reputation of grilling anything, I was encouraged to adapt the classic Italian flavor combinations used with squid, then grill away.

This is a "bowl" recipe. The squid is grilled, sliced, and added to the bowl with pasta, garlic, basil, etc. Then everything is tossed and served. You really have to serve it with some hunks of Italian bread, some extra virgin olive oil, and a little freshly grated Parmesan or pecorino cheese. With a salad and a bottle or two of red wine, this is quite an enjoyable way to spend an evening. ◆ *Serves 4 as a main course*

SERVING SUGGESTIONS: Serve this with Cold Orzo Salad (page 316), Grilled Eggplant with Olive Oil, Parsley, and Capers (page 298), Grilled Hearthbread with Sopressata, Melon, and Torta Basil (page 182), and a bowl of Parmesan cheese.

Grilled Steamed Littlenecks Johnson

MED-HIGH   MED-LOW

◆ ◆

½ pound unsalted butter
½ cup white wine
36 littleneck clams
2 lemons, cut in half
2 tablespoons chopped parsley
Salt and freshly cracked pepper
   to taste (white is best if you
   have it)

1. Combine the butter and wine in a shallow baking pan that can hold all of the clams and withstand low heat on your grill.

2. Wash the clams well to remove sand and excess dirt.

3. Approach the grill: You should have your tongs, your pan containing the butter and wine, a serving platter, and another large platter containing the clams, lemons, parsley, and salt and pepper. Some particular attention should be paid to the fire for this preparation. You want to have half of your fire medium-high heat, and the other half medium-low.

4. Place the pan with the butter and wine in it on the low-heat side of the grill, and place the clams on the rack on the high-heat side.

5. The clams will open when cooked. This should take about 8 to 11 minutes, depending on your fire.

I got this recipe from my friend Steve Johnson, who owns a catering company. He found that this simple preparation made a nice display on the grill while he was cooking other dishes, and I recommend that you try it. Just set the butter-wine pan on the cool side of the grill and whip the clams in there as they open up. Eat some yourself while you cook, and when folks wander over to admire your incredible creativity at the grill . . . offer 'em a clam.

   If you want to make the presentation slightly more elegant (or if you just don't like serving clams in their shells), you can remove the shells and serve the clams as they are or over pasta.
◆ *Serves 4 as a light main course*

SERVING SUGGESTIONS: Serve this as a light main course. It pairs well with Grilled Shrimp Pasta with Sun-dried Tomatoes and Basil (page 129) or Grilled Chicken Breast with Fresh Herbs and Lemon (page 167) for a more hearty meal. For a very esoteric dinner, serve it followed by Grilled Venison Loin with Bourbon Peaches (page 208) and Basil Tabbouleh (page 313).

6. As the clams open, place them in the butter-wine mixture. When all the clams have opened, place them on a serving platter, squeeze the lemon halves over them and sprinkle them with parsley and salt and pepper to taste.

Dinner for a Whole Gang

Grilled Vegetable Antipasto
with Braised Garlic Bread
Page 41

Chili Auténtico con
Mucha Cerveza
(Real Chili with Lots of Beer)
Page 46

Grilled Steamed
Littlenecks Johnson
Page 113

Green Bean Salad
with Tomatoes and Jicama
Page 290

Roasted Eggplant
and Pepper-Garlic Purée
with Lemon and Thyme
Page 297

Quesadilla Bread
Page 326

Chocolate Bourbon
Pound Cake
Page 340

Pear-Blueberry Crisp
Page 344

Grilled Sea Scallops with Coconut–Chile Sauce

HIGH

✦ ✦

½ cup coconut milk (see Pantry, page 368)
4 tablespoons lime juice (about 2 limes)
1 teaspoon fresh minced ginger
1 teaspoon red pepper flakes
2 tablespoons chopped cilantro

1½ pounds large sea scallops
Salt and freshly cracked black pepper to taste

A little Indonesian treatment here. I like the combination of the smooth texture of the scallops and the velvety flavor of the coconut milk, with some red chile pepper flakes added so that no one falls asleep. The thin consistency of the sauce belies its intensity. This goes well with plain steamed white rice. Use chopped scallions and toasted sesame seeds for garnish if you want to break out the china for this one. ✦ *Serves 4 as a main course*

1. Make the sauce in a bowl, combine the coconut milk, lime juice, and ginger, and mix well.

2. Add the pepper flakes and cilantro, and mix well. Set aside. This will be a thin, very light, milky sauce.

3. Put the scallops in boiling water to cover for 1 minute (otherwise they stick to the grill). Drain them, thread them on skewers, and season them with salt and pepper to taste.

4. On a hot fire, cook the scallops until light brown, 2 to 3 minutes per side.

5. Remove the scallops from the skewers, pour the sauce over them, and serve with a small amount of white rice.

SERVING SUGGESTIONS: Serve this with Grilled Duck Breast with Kumquat-Sugarcane-Basil Glaze (page 198) or Chili Auténtico con Mucha Cerveza (page 46) and East Coast Grill Corn Bread (page 324).

Grilled Sausage and Scallops with Peppers, Lemon, Basil, and Garlic

MED

◆ ◆

1½ pounds fresh sea scallops

4 freshly ground sausage links
   (3 to 4 ounces each)

1 large yellow onion, cut into cubes

1 large red bell pepper, seeded and cut into about 12 large squares

1 large green bell pepper, seeded and cut into about 12 large squares

Salt and freshly cracked black pepper to taste

4 tablespoons chopped fresh basil

1 teaspoon minced garlic

2 tablespoons extra virgin olive oil

8 tablespoons lemon juice (about 2 lemons)

2 tablespoons balsamic vinegar

Scallops are one of those seafoods so delicate they stick to the grill unless you blanch them first. Sausages also have to be precooked, otherwise they burn on the grill before they are cooked through.

Adding the herbs *after* cooking allows their flavors to come through more clearly in this dish. The lemon juice provides competition for the mellow texture of the scallops and the spicy character of the sausage. Try this dish with heavily garlicked bread or over pasta. ◆ *Serves 4 as a main course*

SERVING SUGGESTIONS: Serve this with plain, buttered pasta, Celeriac and Fennel Slaw (page 81), and Grandma Wetzler's Sweet-and-Sour Wilted Chicory (page 285). Some French bread might be nice, too.

1. Blanch the scallops in boiling salted water for 1 minute. Drain and allow to cool.

2. Cook the sausage in boiling water until completely cooked, approximately 5 minutes. Drain and allow to cool.

3. Thread the scallops, sausages, and vegetables on skewers and season with salt and pepper to taste.

4. Cook the skewers over a medium fire until all the ingredients have attained some brown crusting, about 3 to 4 minutes per side.

5. Slide the scallops, sausages, and vegetables off the skewers into a large bowl. Add the basil, garlic, oil, lemon juice, and balsamic vinegar. Shake the bowl until everything is well mixed and serve.

Grilled Scallops with Rocotillo-Mango Relish

MED-HIGH

◆◆

1 cup fresh green *or* red rocotillo chile peppers (you may substitute your favorite chile peppers)
1 small red onion
1 green bell pepper, seeded
1 red bell pepper, seeded
2 ripe mangoes, cleaned
Juice of 3 oranges
½ cup pineapple juice
8 tablespoons lime juice (about 4 limes)
¼ cup chopped cilantro
2 pounds sea scallops
Salt and freshly cracked black pepper to taste

1. Dice the rocotillos, onion, bell peppers, and mangoes.

This Caribbean-inspired dish features the rocotillo pepper. The sharp spiciness (*not* heat) of the pepper combines easily with the mellow sweetness of the mango, creating a strong but not overpowering accompaniment for the creamy taste of the scallops. ◆ *Serves 8 as an appetizer or 4 as a main course*

SERVING SUGGESTIONS: Serve this with Grilled Plantain with Molasses-Citrus Glaze (page 306), or couple it with Grilled Sweetbreads with Wilted Southern Greens, Slab Bacon, and Balsamic Vinegar (page 206).

2. In a large mixing bowl, combine the diced ingredients with all the remaining ingredients except the scallops, and mix well. Season with salt and pepper to taste.

3. Blanch the scallops in boiling water for 1 minute (otherwise they stick to the grill). Drain and pat them dry and sprinkle them with salt and pepper to taste.

4. Thread the scallops on skewers and grill them over a medium-hot fire until they are golden brown outside and opaque throughout, about 2 to 3 minutes per side.

5. Make a bed of the relish on each plate and place the scallops on top.

The rocotillo has been described as the best eating chile pepper in the world. People speak of its fullness of flavor combined with a virtual absence of heat. To me the rocotillo has all the aromatic nature of my favorite, the Scotch Bonnet, and the lack of heat lets you consume large quantities without feeling that your mouth has turned to cinders.

World-Famous Fried Soft-shell Crab Sandwich with Tartar Sauce

◆◆

1 cup milk
2 eggs
Dash of Tabasco sauce
Salt and freshly cracked black
    pepper to taste
8 soft-shell crabs, cleaned (see
    the drawings on page 120)
1 cup flour
¼ pound unsalted butter
¼ cup olive oil
16 pieces Wonder *or* other
    nutritionally worthless bread

1. In a fairly large bowl, whisk together the milk, eggs, Tabasco sauce, and salt and pepper to taste.

2. Dredge the crabs in the flour, shake off the excess, and dunk them into the milk-egg mixture. Then dredge them in the flour a second time.

3. In a frying pan, heat the butter and oil over medium-high heat until hot but not smoking. Drop in the breaded crabs to fill the pan without crowding them. Cook 3 to 4 minutes per side, until the crabs are golden brown.

4. Remove the crabs from the pan and drain them on newspaper or a brown paper bag. Slap each crab on a slice of bread, whip a little

The soft-shell is not really a type of crab, but the molting stage of the blue crab. The soft-shell is more of a commercial phenomenon than the blue crabs I caught as a youth in Virginia, since the soft-shell must be held in a tank until it sheds its shell. It is in season only from late May to early June, and it's not easy to find fresh soft-shells because of their extreme perishability and because, like lobsters, they must be alive just before being eaten. However, they are available all year long frozen. While some feel this makes an inferior product, I personally think frozen stands up fine in this preparation.

Until my stint in a number of upscale restaurants showed me any number of creative and intricate preparations for the soft-shell crab, the only preparation I'd known was this sandwich. My fellow cooks just refused to believe this, and so when the first soft-shells would arrive in the late spring, I'd pick one out, bread it, deep-fry it, put it between some white bread, and enjoy the classic Eastern Shore soft-shell crab presentation. I still think it's the best. ◆ *8 sandwiches*

Tartar Sauce (recipe follows) on it, cover with another piece of low-rent bread, crack open a cold beer, and enjoy a true American classic.

SERVING SUGGESTIONS: Serve with Tidewater Coleslaw (page 274), Sweet Potato Salad (page 302), and Grilled Chicken and Black-eyed Pea Salad with Chipotle Vinaigrette (page 70).

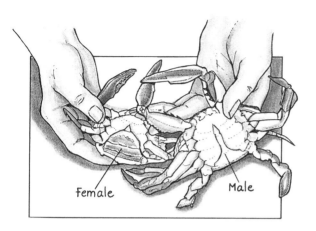

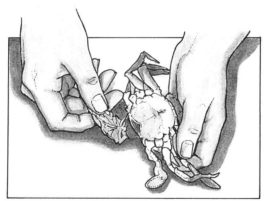

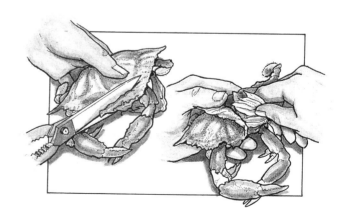

Tartar Sauce

2 tablespoons finely chopped
  parsley
1 tablespoon finely chopped,
  fresh chervil *or* 1 teaspoon
  dried
1 tablespoon prepared relish
Dash of Tabasco sauce
3 tablespoons lemon juice
  (about
  1 lemon)
Salt and freshly cracked black
  pepper to taste
¾ cup Homemade Mayonnaise
  (page 248)

Mix all the ingredients into the
mayonnaise until well blended.
Keeps up to 1 week, covered, in
the refrigerator.

Where I grew up, my seafood was fried,
and when you eat fried seafood, you eat
it with tartar sauce. ◆ *About 1 cup*

The blue crab is found mostly between Cape Cod and Florida and in the Gulf of Mexico, but it has been known to pop up in places like France, Greece, and even Egypt. Its largest concentration, however, is in the Chesapeake Bay, where the brackish freshwater/saltwater mix is ideal for these little crustaceans. Since I grew up by the mouth of the Chesapeake, the blue crab was a creature of my childhood. And now, when I watch my niece and nephew crabbing along the estuaries of southern New England, I remember the pure joy of eating something I had caught and prepared myself. Nothing else could ever make me feel quite so proud and strong and adult as this culinary rite of passage. A righteous culinary tradition continues as I see my niece and nephew jumping about, bragging and boasting of their biggest catches, the infamous "dinner plates."

Caribbean-Style Grilled Seafood Soup

◆ ◆

10 16/20 count (medium-size) shrimp, peeled and deveined

12 medium sea scallops

1 10-ounce mackerel *or* kingfish fillet

1 8- to 10-ounce spiny lobster tail, shelled (available frozen in supermarkets)

3 tablespoons vegetable oil

2 large yellow onions, diced small

3 stalks celery, diced small

2 tablespoons minced garlic

1 cup white wine

1½ quarts bottled clam juice

½ teaspoon ground cumin

¼ teaspoon allspice

2 large sweet potatoes, cut into large cubes

½ pound fresh okra, thickly sliced

2 fresh tomatoes, cut into large chunks

Salt and freshly cracked pepper to taste (white is best if you have it)

4 tablespoons lime juice (about 2 limes)

2 tablespoons minced fresh green *or* red chile peppers of your choice

3 tablespoons chopped cilantro

Even though this soup is served hot, it is an excellent choice for a hot summer day because it is also spicy. This follows a precept commonly accepted in tropical cultures, that eating hot foods will bring your body temperature down and make you feel cooler. (My travels to tropical areas bear this out, and as a matter of fact, this isn't limited to tropical cultures. A friend of mine who grew up in Iowa—decidedly untropical—tells how his grandfather always used to drink hot coffee when baling hay in the broiling Midwest sun, since it gave him more relief from the heat than the cold lemonade that others drank.)

Unlike most soups of this type, in which the fish is actually cooked in the broth, here the seafood is grilled and then added to the broth at the very end. This prevents overcooking and also keeps the individual flavors of the different seafoods strong and distinct. The broth serves as a background, but it is also flavorful and spicy in its own right.

This recipe is easily doubled and makes a fantastic meal with salad and bread. Served with a drink such as East Coast Grill Lemonade (page 358) laced with liberal amounts of rum, this is one of my personal favorites. ◆ *Serves 6 as a main course*

1. Over a hot fire, grill each kind of seafood separately. The shrimp will take approximately 3 to 4 minutes per side, the scallops 3 minutes per side, the kingfish 5 minutes per side, and the lobster 4 minutes per side. As each is done, remove it from the grill, and set aside. (Note: You are looking for the seafood to get some color on its surface: Don't worry too much about cooking it completely, since it will finish in the broth.)

2. In a large saucepan or soup pot, heat the oil until very hot but not smoking. Sauté the onion and celery in the hot oil until clear, about 5 minutes. Add the garlic, and sauté an additional minute.

3. Add the wine, clam juice, cumin, and allspice to the pot, and bring to a simmer.

4. Add the sweet potato, okra, and tomato, and continue to simmer for 30 minutes.

5. At this point, add any of the seafood that is not completely cooked, and simmer for 4 more minutes.

6. Just before serving, add the remainder of the seafood, and simmer for 1 minute, just to warm it through. Remove the pot from the heat and add salt and pepper to taste. Just before serving, toss in the lime juice, chile peppers, and cilantro, and stir briefly.

SERVING SUGGESTIONS: Serve this with Plátanos Fritos (page 145) and Salad of Green Mango, Coconut, and Hot Chile Peppers (page 295) or Corn Bread Salad with Lime Juice and Cilantro (page 312).

SMALL THINGS TO COOK IN THE COALS

There are any number of small treats you can make for yourself as long as you are grilling anyway. Just rub them with salt and freshly cracked black pepper to taste, wrap them in foil with the accompanying items, and throw them in the coals to cook. The proportions will depend upon your individual taste.

Zucchinis, cut into 1-inch slices, with garlic, thyme, and olive oil
Halved red onions with rosemary and balsamic vinegar
Small red potatoes with butter and garlic
Mushrooms with butter, sherry, and basil
Sweet potatoes, cut into 1-inch slices, with brown sugar and butter

Grilled Rum-Soaked Shrimp with Mango-Lime Relish

MED-HIGH

◆ ◆

32 16/20 count (medium-size)
   shrimp (about 2 pounds)
8 tablespoons lime juice (about
   4 limes)
1½ cups canned pineapple juice
½ cup dark rum
2 tablespoons finely chopped
   cilantro
1 teaspoon chopped garlic
Salt and freshly cracked black
   pepper to taste

1. Peel the shrimp and make a ¼-inch-deep incision on the top of each one (the side without the feet) from tail to head. Under cold running water, open the incision and wash away any brownish-black waste matter.

2. In a large stainless steel bowl, combine the lime juice, pineapple juice, rum, cilantro, garlic, and salt and pepper to taste. Add the shrimp. Cover and refrigerate and allow the shrimp to soak in the marinade for 2 to 4 hours—no longer, or they will start to cook in the lime juice. Remove the shrimp from the marinade and discard it.

3. Run a skewer through each shrimp so it is skewered in two places: Put the skewer through the tail area, then bend the shrimp over and put the skewer through

I'm not sure exactly why, but I always get a big kick out of grilling shrimp. It is commonplace these days, but not too long ago grilled shrimp were pretty radical in this country. The ingredients are abundant in both the Yucatán region of Mexico and the Caribbean, and similar dishes are served in both.

I leave the skins on the shrimp to protect the meat from burning while grilling. Because of this, you'll want to pay some attention to the size of the shrimp you use, since the bigger the shrimp the easier they are to peel (see page 59).

The slight rum flavor in the shrimp and the mango-lime relish reproduce the island/beach inspiration of this dish. On a hot day, lean back with a rum drink and these shrimp, close your eyes . . . can you hear the steel band? Probably not. Well, anyway, it's a fun dish that requires your guests to participate by peeling their own food. ◆ *Serves 4 as a main course or 8 as an appetizer*

the thick section in the upper body area. You should be able to fit 4 shrimp on a 6″ skewer, 8 on a 10″ skewer. (If you are using wooden skewers, be careful not to leave any gaps between the shrimp, or the skewer will burn through and the fire will get the shrimp.)

4. Place the skewered shrimp on the grill over medium-high heat. Grill about 3 to 4 minutes on each side, until the shells turn bright red. It's easy to check to see if they are done by probing the incision you made in Step 1. The meat should be an even opaque white.

5. Remove the shrimp from the grill and serve them on a bed of Mango-Lime Relish, either skewered or unskewered as you prefer.

SERVING SUGGESTIONS: If I used this as a first course, I would follow it with a big, hearty meat course such as Grilled Lamb Steaks with Rosemary, Garlic, and Red Wine (page 150) or Simple Grilled Whole Beef Tenderloin (page 146). If the shrimp is the main course, accompany it with West Indies Breadfruit Salad (page 312) or Grilled Sweet Potatoes with Molasses Glaze (page 304).

Mango-Lime Relish

◆◆

3 ripe mangoes
1 small red bell pepper, seeded
1 small green bell pepper, seeded
1 small red onion
1 cup canned pineapple juice
4 tablespoons lime juice (about 2 limes)
1 teaspoon chopped garlic
15 to 20 whole cilantro leaves
4 tablespoons red wine vinegar
1 tablespoon curry powder
Salt and freshly cracked black pepper to taste

About 2½ cups

1. Peel the mangoes and, using a sharp knife, slice the fruit away from the central pit (see diagrams on page 126).

2. Dice the mango fruit, red pepper, green pepper, and onion.

3. Combine all the remaining ingredients in a bowl. Mix lightly, then add the diced mango, pepper, and onion, and mix once again. This mixture will keep 3 days, covered, in the refrigerator.

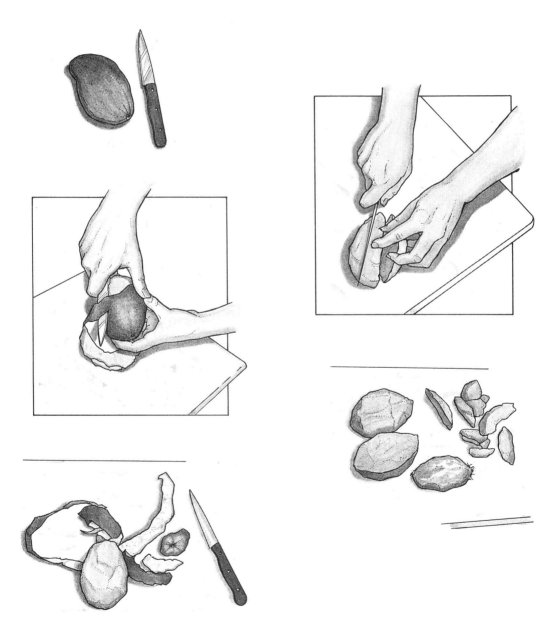

Shrimp Steamed in Beer

5 pounds 16/20 count (medium-size) shrimp, unpeeled
2 quarts beer of your choice
½ cup pickling spices
½ cup Old Bay brand seafood seasoning

Place all the ingredients in a big pot, add water to cover the shrimp completely, and bring to a simmer over medium-high heat. Simmer for 3 minutes, then remove one shrimp, peel it, and check it out to be sure it's done. Drain the shrimp and serve with cocktail sauce and saltine crackers.

SERVING SUGGESTIONS: Serve with Tidewater Coleslaw (page 274), Sweet Potato Salad (page 302), and Grilled Chicken and Black-eyed Pea Salad with Chipotle Vinaigrette (page 70).

When I was a kid, Friday night to me meant the "All You Can Eat" shrimp dinner at the local restaurant. I had become addicted to shrimp at a very young age, and the owner's face always dropped as I walked through the door. Even though you had to peel your own shrimp, I had the determination of an eight-year-old making a name for myself. Long after the rest of the family was through, I was still calling for bowl after bowl and had developed a highly efficient method for peeling shrimp which even today is the marvel of my co-workers.

Due to my semilegendary appetite, the owner eventually let me go back in the kitchen to watch the cooks prepare the weekly feast. The shrimp were steamed in a big kettle full of beer and spices, and the aroma of this combination was unmistakable. Served with cocktail sauce and saltine crackers, these little creatures were my Friday night dinner for years.

Any size shrimp are suitable for this dish. The main factor is how hard you want to work for your food: the larger the shrimp, the less peeling per bite. I call for the 16/20 count, which are a good size (see page 59). In keeping with tradition, I recommend you serve these with Tommy's Hot Cocktail Sauce (page 50) and saltine crackers—the kind that come in packs of two wrapped in shiny paper. • *Serves 8 as an appetizer or 4 as a main course*

Grilled Shrimp with Dandelion Greens and Ginger

MED

2 pounds dandelion greens (you may substitute arugula)
1 large red onion
½ red bell pepper, seeded
4 scallions
1 pound 16/20 count (medium-size) shrimp
Salt and freshly cracked black pepper to taste

For the dressing

½ cup olive oil
1 tablespoon sesame oil
¼ cup rice wine vinegar
1 tablespoon soy sauce
1 tablespoon minced ginger
1 tablespoon sugar
3 to 6 dashes of Tabasco sauce

4 tablespoons sesame seeds, toasted in a single layer in a 350°F oven for 25 minutes, for garnish

This dish features a nice combination of flavors: the mellow shrimp, the sharpness of the greens, and a little ginger to add a touch of sweetness. I suggest that you allow your guests to pour the dressing on to their personal taste. ◆ *Serves 6 as a salad or an appetizer*

SERVING SUGGESTIONS: Serve this with Rice Salad with Wasabi-Miso Dressing (page 315), Chilled Grilled Tomato Soup with Fresh Basil (page 29), and/or Grilled Basque Wings (page 66).

Eastern Shore Seafood Festival

Raw Bar Variations with Fresh Horseradish
Pages 48 and 254

Shrimp Steamed in Beer
Page 127

World-Famous Fried Soft-shell Crab Sandwich with Tartar Sauce
Page 119

Tidewater Coleslaw
Page 274

---

1. Separate, wash, and dry the dandelion greens and put them into a large bowl. Slice the onion, pepper, and scallions very thinly and add them to the greens.

2. Peel and devein the shrimp, thread them on skewers, and season them with salt and pepper to taste.

3. Grill the skewers over a medium fire until the shrimp are completely opaque, about 3 to 4 minutes per side.

4. Meanwhile, whisk the oils, vinegar, soy sauce, ginger, sugar, and Tabasco sauce together in a bowl until homogenous.

5. Add the shrimp to the greens, pour the dressing on, and toss well. Garnish with the toasted sesame seeds.

Grilled Shrimp Pasta with Sun-dried Tomatoes and Basil

MED

2 pounds 16/20 count (medium-size) shrimp
Salt and freshly cracked black pepper to taste
1 pound fettuccine
12 sun-dried tomatoes, cut into thin strips (see Pantry, page 369)
¼ cup fresh black olives, halved and pitted
1 tablespoon minced garlic
1 tablespoon capers
½ cup chopped fresh basil
¼ cup pine nuts, toasted
2 tablespoons unsalted butter, cut into eighths
4 tablespoons lemon juice (about 1 lemon)

Lemon wedges for garnish
Basil leaves for garnish

½ cup grated Romano cheese

I love grilled shrimp and will eat them any way I can get them. Here I use them with pasta and basil for a refreshing light dinner entrée for a hot summer evening. ◆ *Serves 4 as a main course*

SERVING SUGGESTIONS: Serve this with Chilled Grilled Tomato Soup with Fresh Basil (page 29), Hearthbread with Sopressata, Melon, and Torta Basil (page 182), and Romaine-Feta Salad with Lemon–Olive Oil Dressing (page 286).

1. Peel and devein the shrimp and remove their tails.

2. Thread the shrimp on skewers, season with salt and pepper to taste, and grill them 3 to 4 minutes per side over medium heat.

3. Cook the fettuccine in 4 quarts of boiling salted water until al dente, 8 to 10 minutes for dried, 3 to 4 for fresh. Drain and put it into a large bowl.

4. Add the tomatoes, olives, garlic, capers, basil, pine nuts, and butter, and toss well. Season with salt and pepper to taste, then stir in the lemon juice.

5. Add the shrimp to the bowl, garnish with the lemon wedges and basil leaves, and serve with grated Romano in a separate bowl.

Grilled Shrimp with Greens, Bacon, and Sweet Potato

◆ ◆

16 16/20 count (medium-size) shrimp (about 1 pound)
Salt and freshly cracked black pepper to taste
½ pound slab bacon, medium-diced
1 cup cooked sweet potatoes (about ½ pound), diced small
1 pound chicory, cleaned, washed, and dried
½ pound mixed greens (mustard, beet, turnip, dandelion, etc.), cleaned, washed, and dried
¼ cup balsamic vinegar
Pinch of sugar

1. Peel and devein the shrimp, but leave the tails on. Thread them on skewers, season with salt and pepper to taste, and grill them over a medium fire, 3 to 4 minutes per side. Remove and set them aside.

2. Sauté the bacon over medium heat until crisp, about 5 minutes, and remove it from pan. Do not pour off the bacon fat. Instead, add the sweet potatoes, and cook for 2 minutes. Then add the chicory and greens and turn furiously, just until the leaves are well covered with the bacon fat.

3. Remove the greens mixture from the heat, add the vinegar, sugar, and salt and pepper to taste,

I've said it once and I'll say it again—grilled shrimp make me happy. Their small size means they don't stay on the grill long enough to acquire a char that overcomes the delicate flavor, and their firm texture lets them remain juicy through the quick searing.

Here grilled shrimp is combined with traditional Southern ingredients and flavors, producing a dish that has a lot of action. ◆ *Serves 4 as an appetizer or 2 as a main course*

SERVING SUGGESTIONS: Serve this in combination with Clam Posole (page 36), or in front of Grilled Butterflied Leg o' Lamb (page 153).

and toss. Place a portion on individual plates and put a skewer
of shrimp on each.

Plain Grilled Lobster

MED-LOW

◆◆◆◆◆◆◆◆◆◆◆◆◆◆◆◆◆◆◆◆◆◆◆◆◆◆◆◆◆◆◆◆◆◆◆◆◆◆◆

4 2 to 2½-pound whole lobsters
Salt and freshly cracked black
   pepper to taste

Melted butter
Lemon halves

1. Split the lobsters in half lengthwise. To do this, place each lobster on its back and insert the point
of a large French knife into the
head just below the eyes. Bring
the knife down through the tail,
making sure to cut just through
the meat and to leave the shell
connected. Lay the lobster open,
leaving the two halves slightly attached.

2. Pull off the claws and legs from
the lobsters and crack them
slightly with the knife handle. You
just want to fracture the shell a
bit here.

3. Place the claws and legs on the
grill over medium-low heat and
cover with a pie pan. Cook them
for 5 to 7 minutes per side.

If you have a problem with killing living
things, stop here. For the beauty of this
dish is that you're eating something
superfresh, and that means that you
must be the executioner. To be merci-
ful, make your actions swift and delib-
erate. For me, there is a certain culinary
essence in taking food from "live" to
"eaten" so quickly.

   The flavor of this dish is direct, honest, and impeccable, and its simplicity is
a tribute to the inherent beauty of food.
As is true in most cases, if you use high-
quality fresh ingredients, the best thing
to do is leave them alone and let the
taste come through. Grilled corn on the
cob is a great side dish here. ◆ *Serves
4 as a main course*

SERVING SUGGESTIONS: Serve this with
Your Basic Grilled Corn (page 317),
Grilled Sweet Potatoes with Molasses
Glaze (page 304), and Chilled Spinach
with Soy and Ginger (page 287), or
combine it with Grilled Steamed Littlenecks Johnson (page 113) for a seafood
dinner.

4. Sprinkle the lobster bodies with salt and pepper to taste and place them flesh-side down on the grill over medium heat. Grill for 8 to 10 minutes. (You don't need to turn these guys at all.) Check to see if they are done by removing the tail from the shell of one of the lobsters. The exposed meat should be completely opaque.

5. Remove the lobsters from the grill and serve them with melted butter, lemon halves, and nutcrackers if you have them. If not, use a hammer for the claws. Make sure you have paper towels handy, because this is a messy one.

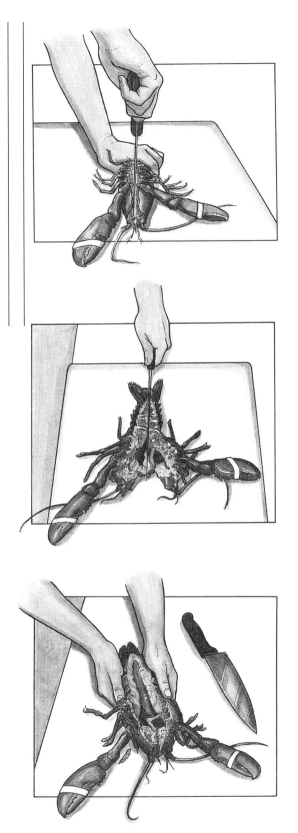

Birds and Things with Hooves

‹•◆›

The basic principle involved in grilling is that it is a quick cooking process that uses high heat to seal in juices while creating a concentration of flavor in the form of a crust on the exterior of the food. This naturally leads to certain general rules for choosing meat and poultry for grilling. Things to be grilled must be relatively small in mass in order to be properly cooked inside before they are burned beyond recognition on the outside. Also, they must be tender, free of a lot of sinews and connective tissue, since they cannot stay on the grill long enough for these tissues to be broken down during cooking. Chops, steaks, and chicken breasts fit these guidelines; roasts and whole chickens do not.

Another factor you might want to consider when deciding what meats are best for the grill is the presence or absence of bones. Except for wings and thighs, you want chicken to be free of bones, since this provides the smaller mass needed for quick cooking. Wings and thighs, on the other hand, need the bone to provide the proper amount of mass so that they will not cook completely through before they have a chance to get any sear on the outer surface.

With red meat, you want to leave the bones in whenever possible. This is not only because you can gnaw on the bone when you've eaten all the meat—a factor not to be taken lightly—but also because the meat seems to be tenderer and sweeter next to the bone. This is partially due to the fact that muscles next to the bone get used less by the animal; partially due to the ability of bones to protect meat in their immediate proximity from heat and shrinkage during cooking; and partially due to the fact that the juices are driven to the bone during cooking. Because of these phenomena, I would always choose to grill, for example, a T-bone steak as opposed to a boneless New York strip, or choose a lamb chop over a lamb fillet.

When shopping for a piece of meat or poultry to grill, just remember that what you are doing is taking a tender piece of meat and imparting additional flavor to it by means of grilling it. If you are more familiar with sautéing, it might be helpful to remember that grilling and sautéing call for similar cuts of meat.

Is It Done Yet?

The cooking times provided with the recipes in this chapter, as in the others, are approximate guides. No two fires are ever exactly the same, and part of the fun of grilling is the challenge of mastering the ever-changing dynamics of a live fire. I suggest that you learn to outsmart the vagaries of the fire by concentrating on your favorite method of checking the degree of doneness.

Red Meats

In checking the degree of doneness of beef, lamb, pork, and veal (your basic "red meats"), there are a couple of methods that I recommend.

THE "JUST POKING AROUND" METHOD: This is the way the pros do it and is based on the fact that as meat cooks it becomes firmer. By poking a piece of meat with his finger, a pro can judge the relative degree of doneness based on the meat's firmness. This is based on years of experience poking meat and then knowing by the touch how done it is.

You can shorten the learning curve for this technique by using it in conjunction with the "Hand" Method. In this method, you poke the meat and judge its degree of doneness by comparing it to the feel of a particular place on your hand. As a general rule of thumb, meat is rare when it has the same feeling as the connective tissue between the ball of your thumb and the knuckle of your index finger, progressing to very well done when it has the feel of the base of the ball of your thumb (see the diagram). Remember that a professional cook might do this 150 times a night, so don't get discouraged if it takes you a while to master this technique. Just be sure to try it for each piece of meat you cook before you check it by some other method, and trial and error will eventually lead you to mastery of the technique.

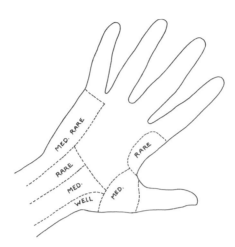

THE "SCIENTIFIC" METHOD: This method is also extremely popular with the pros, although few will admit it. It is also variously known as "peeking" or "cheating." In this method, you nick the meat with a sharp knife, or bend it, or rearrange it, or fondle it—whatever is required to get a look inside to see how done the meat actually is.

This technique has the unbeatable advantage of eliminating guesswork, but it can be deceiving to the uninitiated because the interior of any red meat will continue to cook for a few minutes after you remove it from the grill, moving up approximately one level of doneness. This is known as "carryover cooking." Also, since the juices are driven to the center of the meat during grilling, the meat has a redder appearance on the grill than it will have after resting, when the juices become evenly redistributed throughout. So if I want my steak done medium rare, for example, I nick it, and if it looks rare I pull it off. After it rests for two to three minutes, it should be a perfect medium rare.

While I am on the subject of red meat and doneness, a word about pork. The degree to which it should be cooked is still controversial, but as far as I can see it's up to the individual. The once-popular taboo against pink pork has changed, and personally I like mine medium to medium rare. But, hey, you bought it—cook it any way you like.

Chicken

The last section of a piece of chicken that cooks is the joint. This is why the classic test is to pierce the joint with a sharp object. If the juices run clear, then there is no blood left at the joint and the chicken is properly cooked. However, this technique is really meant for whole chickens, and whole chickens are not suitable for grilling. For the recipes in this book, the most accurate method is, once again, the "Scientific" Method. Cut into the thickest piece of chicken and check to be sure that the meat has a consistent white texture with no signs of translucence.

Final Tips

Before you grill red meat, you should take it out of the refrigerator and let it stand, covered, for one hour to bring it up to room temperature.

Before grilling poultry, trim off all the fat. This prevents flare-ups from the fat dripping into the fire.

Grilled Veal Chop with Artichoke Hearts, Sun-dried Tomatoes, and Pine Nuts

◆◆

4 fresh artichokes
4 tablespoons olive oil
8 tablespoons lemon juice
  (about 2 lemons)
8 sun-dried tomatoes, finely
  julienned (see Pantry, page
  369)
¼ cup Kalamata black olives,
  halved and pitted
¼ cup fresh basil, julienned
4 tablespoons pine nuts, toasted
4 veal chops (12 to 14 ounces
  each, at least 1 inch thick)

1. Prepare the artichoke hearts: Remove the outside leaves from the artichokes, and cut off the top two thirds of the artichokes. Remove the chokes and trim around the outside, leaving only the hearts. Cook the hearts in boiling salted water to cover until tender, 8 to 10 minutes. Remove from the heat, drain, and cool. When cool, slice each heart into 4 slices.

2. In a small bowl, combine the olive oil with the lemon juice. Place the artichoke hearts in the bowl and toss gently to cover with the oil-juice mixture. Add the sun-dried tomato, olives, basil, and pine nuts, and mix well. Set aside.

I usually stay away from veal when grilling for two reasons: First, the subtle flavor and tenderness that you pay for when you buy veal is covered up by the grilling process; and second, I think pork is more flavorful and makes a fine substitute in most veal recipes. The veal chop is the sole exception. This is not a dainty cut, and because of its mass it can stand up to grilling quite well. The large bone in the chop provides the necessary durability, protecting the meat and keeping it tender.

In other words, this is a delicate meat in the form of a hearty cut, and therefore suitable for a strong preparation. We get back to featuring the subtlety by serving it with a mild relish of fresh artichoke hearts and sun-dried tomatoes. ◆ *Serves 4 as a main course*

SERVING SUGGESTIONS: Serve this with Grilled Eggplant with Olive Oil, Parsley, and Capers (page 298) and Basil Tabbouleh (page 313), or preceded by Steamed Clams with Lemongrass and Chiles de Árbol (page 52) as an appetizer.

3. You want a medium-low fire for the chops, since searing is not as important with white veal meat as it is with red meat. Over this fire, cook the chops for 8 to 10 minutes per side. Check for doneness by nicking one of the chops and peeking at the interior. It should be slightly pink for medium, which is how I like to cook veal.

4. Remove the veal from the grill and allow it to repose for 5 minutes. Serve each chop topped with a couple of tablespoons of the relish.

Grilled Lime-Marinated Flank Steak with Chipotle-Honey Sauce

◆•◆

1 2½-pound flank steak

For the marinade

1 canned chipotle, chopped (see Pantry, page 369)
2 garlic cloves, minced
1 tablespoon chopped cilantro
4 tablespoons vegetable oil
10 tablespoons lime juice (about 5 limes)

For the sauce

¼ cup honey
2 tablespoons peanut oil
3 to 5 (depends on how hot you want this) canned chipotles
2 tablespoons balsamic vinegar
2 tablespoons brown mustard
8 tablespoons lime juice (about 4 limes)
2 garlic cloves
1 teaspoon ground cumin
2 tablespoons chopped cilantro
1 teaspoon salt
Freshly cracked black pepper to taste

1. Place the steak in a large dish or baking pan. Mix all the marinade ingredients together, then pour the marinade over the steak. Cover the steak and let it mari-

The flank is not the tenderest cut of beef, but it may be the most flavorful. To make it tenderer, I marinate it and slice it against the grain very thin on the bias after cooking it. So what you start with is very thin steak, and what you end up with is large thin slices of char-flavored meat that resembles roast beef. The acid in the lime marinade is very complementary to the char flavor of the meat. Marinate it anywhere from 4 to 6 hours: Any longer than that, and the lime juice will actually cook the steak, leaving you with gray meat.

Make sure your grill is really hot. Because this thin cut of meat takes very little time to cook, you need that intense heat to give it the color you want.

The sauce is a sweet/hot combination that features chipotles, which are dried smoked jalapeño chile peppers with a very distinctive flavor. Adjust the heat to the level you want, using the chipotle as your fuel. ◆ *Serves 4 as a main course*

SERVING SUGGESTIONS: Black Bean Salad (page 319), Corn Bread Salad with Lime Juice and Cilantro (page 312), and fresh tortillas combine well with this dish for a full dinner. You might want to start with Green Bean Salad with Tomatoes and Jicama (page 290).

nate in the refrigerator for 4 to 6 hours, turning occasionally.

2. Make the sauce: Combine the honey, peanut oil, chipotles, vinegar, mustard, lime juice, garlic, and cumin, and purée in a blender or food processor. Stir in the chopped cilantro and add the salt and pepper to taste.

3. Salt and pepper the steak to taste. Over very high heat, grill the steak for 5 to 7 minutes on each side (for medium rare).

4. Remove the steak from the grill and let it rest for 3 to 5 minutes so the juices that were drawn to the center by cooking redistribute for even color. Then, using a very sharp knife, slice the steak as thin as you can, against the grain and on a very sharp angle.

5. Serve the steak, which should be very juicy, either plain or on top of sliced French bread, and accompany each serving with several tablespoons of the sauce.

Come Back, Summer—A Dinner in the Dead of Winter

✦✦✦✦✦✦✦✦✦✦✦✦✦✦✦

Grilled Top Round, Cuban Style, with Plátanos Fritos

HIGH

◆ ◆

1 2½-pound top round steak,
  about 1½ inches thick
Salt and freshly cracked black
  pepper to taste
1 large red onion
1 red bell pepper, seeded
1 green bell pepper, seeded
10 radishes
¼ cup virgin olive oil
1 tablespoon Tabasco sauce
1 tablespoon minced garlic
2 tablespoons finely chopped
  parsley
2 tablespoons finely chopped
  cilantro
1 tablespoon ground cumin
1 tablespoon chili powder
6 tablespoons lime juice (about
  3 limes)

1. Season the meat with salt and pepper all over and grill it over a hot fire. You want to grill it until it is dark brown and very crusty —the crustiness is the key to the taste of this preparation. The inside should be rare/medium rare, which should take 4 to 6 minutes per side.

2. Remove the meat from the grill and let it stand about 5 minutes.

3. Cut the meat into cubes about the size of dice. (The kind you

This dish provides an interesting combination of classic Caribbean ingredients with an Asian twist in the preparation in that the vegetables and meat are both cut into small pieces and combined. Unlike traditional Asian dishes, however, the ingredients are combined after cooking, rather than before.

I use round steak here, which can often be found in your local supermarket disguised under the obsequious name of London broil. It's not considered the tenderest cut of meat, but as with most tougher cuts, it's very flavorful. The key to the taste of the meat in this dish is complete and total searing, which develops a very heavy crust with a distinctive grilled flavor that stands up to the spicy preparation.

The fried plantains are a staple of Caribbean and Central American cuisine, and this is the standard preparation, which calls for them to be fried once, smashed, and then fried again. Make sure you use green plantains, because in this state they are more like a potato than a banana, which they resemble when they are ripe. These are the French fries of the tropical world. ◆ *Serves 4 as a main course*

SERVING SUGGESTIONS: This is a fairly loud dish, and I would recommend serving it with Your Basic Black Beans

roll, not the kind you hang from your rearview mirror.)

4. Put the diced meat into a large mixing bowl. Dice the red onion and red and green bell peppers, slice the radishes very thin, and mix well with the meat.

5. Add all the remaining ingredients except the lime juice and toss well.

6. Seconds before serving, add the lime juice and toss one more time. Serve with Plátanos Fritos and rice and beans.

(page 318), Salad of Green Mango, Coconut, and Hot Chile Peppers (page 295), and plain boiled rice for a fine Cuban-style dinner.

Plátanos Fritos

2 green plantains
2 cups vegetable oil
Salt and freshly cracked black
  pepper to taste

Serves 4 as a side dish

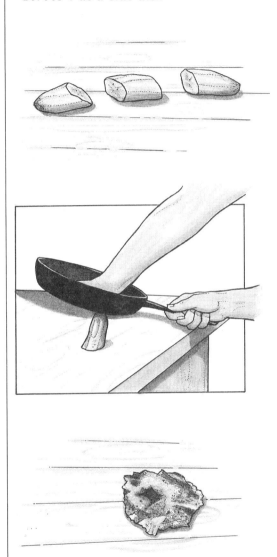

1. Peel the plantains and cut them into 2-inch rounds.

2. In a small saucepot, heat the oil until very hot but not smoking.

3. Drop the plantain rounds into the oil three at a time and cook them until well browned, about 2 to 3 minutes. Remove them from the oil and drain them on a paper towel or brown paper bag.

4. Stand each fried section upright on a table and with a heavy object smash it as flat as a pancake, using steady pressure rather than a sharp blow. (I use a small cutting board for this, but a frying pan will do fine.)

5. Put the smashed sections back into the hot oil, two or three at a time, and cook 2 minutes or so, until the entire surface is golden brown.

6. Remove, drain, and season them liberally with salt and pepper.

Simple Grilled Whole Beef Tenderloin

◆ ◆

1 whole, unpeeled tenderloin of
   beef (5 to 6 pounds)
Salt and freshly cracked black
   pepper to taste

1. Trim the excess fat off the tenderloin and cover it heavily with salt and pepper to taste.

2. Over high heat, sear the tenderloin well on both sides. This will take about 10 to 12 minutes per side. Have your tongs ready, as a large flare-up may well occur. A flare-up in this situation actually aids in the searing process. If the flames are higher than 18 inches, though, I would take the tenderloin off and allow the flames to subside. In any case, large flame-ups tend to impress your guests. Always remain calm.

3. Remove the meat from the grill, then remove the grill and push your coals over to one side.

4. Replace the grill and put the tenderloin back on the grill, over the side with no coals.

5. Place the cover on the grill, and open the stop vent slightly, 1 to 2 inches or so.

6. Continue to cook, 25 minutes for rare meat, 30 minutes for medium rare.

This cut of meat comes from the steer's back, a body part that gets very little exercise. This produces a very tender cut of meat, but one with little inherent flavor. Grilling, however, solves this problem without sacrificing the cut's melting tenderness. The heavy char that results from the grilling has its own delicious taste and crusty texture. To cook it properly on the grill takes a very moderate fire and lots of patience. I suggest having a fire in only half of the grill and placing the tenderloin where it is not directly over the heat.

This is a good dish to serve as part of a buffet, since the meat can be cut into small pieces and put on bread. I like to serve it with a couple of different condiments to complement the subtle beef flavor. The meat is also a great leftover, particularly in a salad with lemon and olive oil. ◆ *Serves 7 to 8 as a main course*

SERVING SUGGESTIONS: I would serve this with grilled fresh Pita Bread (page 327), Your Basic Grilled Corn (page 317), and West Indies Breadfruit Salad (page 312). Also, use either a single condiment or a selection of them. This is a great vehicle for just about any condiment you like. I am partial to Fresh Horseradish (page 254), but check out Spicy Oyster Sauce with Lemongrass (page 241), Very Aromatic Tomato-

7. Remove the meat from the grill and let it recline 15 minutes before serving (this lets the juices return from the center of the meat, where they have retreated during cooking).

8. Serve 2 slices per person.

Ginger Jam (page 231), Pebre: Chilean Hot Sauce (page 239), or anything that strikes your fancy.

You can buy a whole tenderloin either peeled or unpeeled. I like to get an unpeeled one and trim off some of the fat. The traditional school of thought is that the meat should get trimmed completely because there is some very tough sinew right under the surface called "silver skin," and you want to get rid of this. I say don't bother. Grilling with some of the fat on protects the delicate cut and also adds to the flavor. You can always trim the fat off after cooking if you want. This cut of meat is shaped sort of like a baseball bat: very thick at the head and tapering rather sharply down to the small tail. Some people like to tuck the tail back under and tie it up so that it won't get burned, but I just put the tail over the cooler part of the fire. Also, with the number of people that you are going to be serving when cooking a whole tenderloin, you'll want some portions more well done than others. The tapering of the meat plays into this situation nicely, since in order to get the head to a nice rare/medium rare, you will be cooking the tail to medium or even medium well.

After you pull the loin off the grill it is very important to let it stand, rest, recline (your choice) for at least 10 minutes so that the juices that have been driven to the center by the heat return back throughout the meat. This results in a perfectly consistent color right through the meat, which will totally impress your guests and make for great eating.

But, Chris, you may say, what happens if I come up short, underestimate the cooking time, and when I slice the meat it's totally rare? How will I face my guests? Now is the time when you find out what it takes to be a great chef—you improvise. It goes something like this: You cut into the meat in front of your guests and it's totally raw. First thing you say is, "Perfect. That's just perfect." Then as you slice the meat into 1-inch slices, you remark on the new trend toward roasted then grilled meats. Meanwhile you sprinkle a little salt and pepper on the slices and put them back on the grill, asking all the guests how they would like their individual portions cooked. Sometimes if the tenderloin is really large, I actually plan in advance to do this. This method has the advantage of allowing more surface area to be flavored by direct contact with the grill.

Grilled Big Black-and-Blue Steak for Two

◆ ◆

1 giant 1½-inch-thick steak
(choose one of the following):
1 2-pound boneless
Delmonico
  or
1 2½-pound bone-in
Delmonico
  or
1 2½-pound T-bone
  or
1 2½-pound porterhouse
¼ cup olive oil
Kosher salt and freshly cracked
  black pepper to taste

1. Allow the steak to come to room temperature, then rub it with oil and salt and pepper to taste.

2. Over a medium-hot fire, grill the steak until the exterior is very brown, almost black, and very crusty, about 8 to 9 minutes per side. Some flare-ups might occur. If they do, remove the steak from the grill using long tongs, allow the fire to calm down, and place the steak back on the grill. To check for doneness, nick the meat on one side and look at the color. It will appear slightly rarer than it will actually be after resting.

3. Remove the steak from fire, allow it to rest 5 minutes, and serve with a baked potato and green salad.

The ultimate red meat experience. The beauty of this dish lies in its simplicity, and the key is to buy the highest-quality meat possible and let the huge steak shine through in its own natural glory.

Now, this might sound a little religious to some of you, but in my childhood eating grilled steak on Saturday nights was very close to a spiritual experience. My father would go to the butcher shop Saturday afternoon, get a steak big enough for the whole family, and bring it home, where I helped him grill it. When it came to food my folks did not make a lot of fuss over the children—we ate it the way they cooked it, and for that reason I developed at a very young age a fine appreciation for good steak cooked hard (some might say burned) on the outside and rare (meaning raw) on the inside. So I'm very fussy about the way steaks are prepared, and usually only have them at home.

There is a reason why steaks are served with baked potatoes and salad. I'm not sure what it is, and I never bothered to ask; it's just one of those things that feels so right. I like this recipe with a big showy red wine but have also been known to accompany it with a couple of cold ones.

In restaurants a steak ordered "black and blue" means burned on the outside and raw on the inside. "Black" refers to the outer crust, and "blue" is the French term for superrare. It's also called "Pittsburgh," a reference I've never understood, but maybe it has something to do with the color of steel.

The reason I don't trust restaurants to undertake the task of satisfying my need for red meat is because, as usual in seemingly simple preparations, there is a difficulty. In this case, the problem is that it's hard to find a steak sufficiently thick to stay on the grill long enough to form the desired outer crust and still be red/raw in the center. In fact, you need a steak at least two inches thick to accomplish this, an item almost impossible to find in a single-portion size.

Now, filet mignon might meet the thickness criterion, but it is disqualified on the grounds of its inherent lack of flavor. To me the best cuts are the Delmonico, which is a cut from the prime rib in steak form, and the T-bone or porterhouse, which includes the sirloin and a small section of the tenderloin with a bone. The Delmonico, being well marbled, is the more tender, but I prefer the T-bone or porterhouse because it is a bit more flavorful and the presence of the bone somehow seems to hold the juice better—not to mention that you get to chew the bone if you can talk your companion out of it.

I recommend that you go to your butcher, explain your plan, and ask him to make a special cut for you. He'll be into it because it will be obvious to him that you hold beef in high culinary regard.

Classic Steak Dinner
◆ ◆ ◆ ◆ ◆ ◆ ◆ ◆ ◆ ◆ ◆ ◆ ◆ ◆ ◆

Arugula and Dandelion
Greens Salad with Fried Oysters,
Smithfield Ham, and Peaches
Page 185

Grilled Big Black-and-Blue
Steak for Two
Page 148

Your Basic Grilled Corn
Page 317

Sweet Potato Hash Browns
with Bacon and Onions
Page 300

Chocolate Pudding Cake
Page 337

Grilled Lamb Steaks with Rosemary, Garlic, and Red Wine

MED-HIGH

◆ ◆

2 tablespoons minced garlic

2 tablespoons fresh rosemary

6-pound leg of lamb, cut into 6 steaks (have your butcher do this for you), bone in

½ cup dry red wine

1 cup olive oil

Salt and freshly cracked black pepper to taste

1. Make a paste of the garlic and rosemary and rub it into the steaks *con mucho gusto*.

2. Put the steaks into a shallow dish, add the wine and olive oil, and let the steaks wallow around in the mixture, covered, for about 2 hours.

3. Remove the steaks, season them with salt and pepper to taste, and hit the grill. Grill them over a medium-high fire, 6 to 8 minutes per side for medium rare. Serve with lemon wedges and pita.

As a child traveling in Greece with my family, I had the best lamb I ever tasted. On the way to the Oracle at Delphi, my sister and I insisted that we stop at every roadside bar and sample the lamb skewers, which were rubbed with rosemary and garlic. Ever since then, I have associated the taste of lamb with the complementary tastes of rosemary and garlic from those skewers.

I think that cutting a leg of lamb into steaks works well because the leg has enough muscle tissue to give it a very nice flavor, but not so much that it is tough. ◆ *Serves 6 as a main course*

SERVING SUGGESTIONS: This dish is great served with grilled spring onions and pita. Romaine-Feta Salad with Lemon–Olive Oil Dressing (page 286) is also a nice complement to the rich taste of this preparation, as is Grilled Eggplant with Olive Oil, Parsley, and Capers (page 298) or Basil Tabbouleh (page 313).

Sweet Milk-Marinated Grilled Lamb with Sweet and Hot Apricot Condiment

MED-HIGH

◆ ◆

2½ pounds lamb, cut into 1-inch cubes

For the marinade

1 cup milk
1 cup vinegar
2 tablespoons curry powder
2 tablespoons brown sugar
1 tablespoon chili powder
2 tablespoons minced garlic
1 teaspoon turmeric
1 teaspoon red pepper flakes
1 teaspoon black pepper
1 teaspoon coriander seed

Salt and freshly cracked pepper to taste

1. Put the cubed lamb into a large shallow dish.

2. Combine all the marinade ingredients, mix well, and pour over the lamb.

3. Cover the dish and let the lamb sit in the marinade for approximately 24 hours, refrigerated, stirring occasionally.

4. Remove the lamb from the marinade, pat it dry, and season it with salt and pepper to taste. Thread the cubes on skewers. (Discard marinade.)

Here's a good example of the kind of grilling festivities that go on in other countries. In South Africa, there is a strong tradition of backyard grilling, which they call "braa-ing." The most popular types of dishes for braa-ing are called *sos saties*, a term derived from two Malay words meaning "spiced sauce" and "skewered meat." *Sos saties* are like barbecue in the United States in that everybody has his or her own particular recipe, which of course is the only authentic one.

This dish, in which the process of marinating meat in milk again shows the strong East Indian/Indonesian influence, is a variation of a classic *sos saties*. The sweet and hot apricot condiment is my version of a South African "sambal," a type of sweet, hot, aromatic condiment traditionally served with curries. ◆ *Serves 4 as a main course or 8 as an appetizer*

SERVING SUGGESTIONS: Serve this with Sweet Potato Salad (page 302) preceded by Raw Bar Variations (page 48) or Grilled Steamed Littlenecks Johnson (page 113).

5. Over a medium-hot fire, grill the lamb skewers approximately 5 to 7 minutes per side. The meat should be juicy and pink inside. After removing the lamb from the grill, allow it to sit 3 to 5 minutes before serving it, accompanied by Sweet and Hot Apricot Condiment.

Sweet and Hot Apricot Condiment

◆◆◆◆◆◆◆◆◆◆◆◆◆◆◆◆◆◆◆◆◆◆◆◆◆◆◆◆◆◆◆◆◆◆◆◆◆◆◆

2 large yellow onions, thickly sliced
4 tablespoons peanut oil
½ cup dried apricots
¼ cup raisins
½ cup grated fresh coconut (you may substitute ¼ cup dried unsweetened coconut)
¼ cup white vinegar
¼ cup apricot jelly
3 tablespoons chopped fresh hot chile pepper
Salt and freshly cracked black pepper to taste
4 tablespoons lemon juice (about 1 lemon)

About 2 cups

1. Sauté the onion in peanut oil over medium-high heat until golden, 5 to 7 minutes.

2. Add the apricots, raisins, and coconut to the sauté pan, and continue to cook for 2 minutes.

3. Add the vinegar and jelly and cook for 1 minute.

4. Add the hot chile pepper and salt and pepper to taste and remove from the heat.

5. Just before serving, shoot the lemon juice into the mixture. This will keep, covered and refrigerated, for about 2 weeks.

Grilled Butterflied Leg o' Lamb

MED-HIGH

◆ ◆

1 4- to 5-pound boneless, butterflied leg o' lamb
3 tablespoons minced garlic
3 tablespoons chopped fresh basil
3 tablespoons chopped fresh rosemary
3 tablespoons chopped fresh thyme
Salt and freshly cracked black pepper to taste

1. Make a paste of the garlic and seasonings by mashing them together thoroughly in a mortar and pestle—or use a heavy wooden spoon and a bowl. Rub this paste into the lamb and allow it to sit at room temperature for 1 hour.

2. Build a fire in one side of your covered grill. Over high heat, sear both sides of the lamb directly over the coals until well browned, about 4 to 5 minutes per side.

Lamb is an outstanding meat for grilling. For me, the unmistakable aroma of lamb fat hitting live fire always brings back memories of eating in places like Greece and Tunisia, where grilled lamb preparations abound.

A butterflied leg o' lamb is easy to find, but if the leg you get is boned and not butterflied, it is easy to do it yourself. Simply make one cut almost completely through the lamb to lay it open, then put it on a counter and cover it with plastic wrap. Next take a mallet or heavy frying pan and whack it a couple of times, keeping in mind that your object is to flatten the meat to make the cooking time quicker (you are looking for a thickness of about 2 to 3 inches), making sure that the thickness is as uniform as possible. That's all there is to it. ◆ *Serves 6 to 8 as a main course*

3. Move the lamb to the half of the grill with no coals, cover, and cook for 15 to 20 minutes. At the 10-minute mark, check the meat by nicking a side. Remove the lamb from the grill when it is done to your liking, and allow it to rest 5 to 10 minutes before slicing it into ½-inch slices and serving.

SERVING SUGGESTIONS: This is a fantastic combination with the unusual Preserved Lemon–Honey Relish with Hot Peppers and Curry (page 228) and Marinated Feta with Roasted Red Peppers, Black Olives, and Thyme (page 293).

Grilled Country Ham and Applesauce

MED

◆ ◆

For the applesauce (about 5 cups)

10 Baldwin *or* MacIntosh apples, peeled, cored, and quartered
¼ cup maple syrup
⅓ cup sugar
½ cup orange juice
½ teaspoon cinnamon
⅛ teaspoon nutmeg
⅛ teaspoon allspice

For the ham

3-pound semiboneless Jones *or* other cured ham
Salt and freshly cracked black pepper to taste
4 tablespoons maple syrup

A standard item in my grandma's repertoire—served at breakfast, lunch, or dinner—this combination was always welcome. I grill the ham here, which is something Grandma never did, and add a little maple syrup glaze. ◆ *Serves 8 as a main course*

SERVING SUGGESTIONS: Serve this with Doc's Cheddar Biscuits (page 309) for a classic Southern-style rural American meal.

1. Make the applesauce: Put the apple quarters, maple syrup, sugar, orange juice, and spices into a stockpot. Bring to a simmer, reduce the heat, and simmer slowly for 30 to 45 minutes, stirring occasionally. The apple quarters should be quite soft.

2. Using a food processor, blender, or potato masher, purée or mash the applesauce, then put it through a strainer. Allow it to cool to room temperature before serving. It will keep, covered and refrigerated, for 3 to 5 days.

3. Slice the ham into ¼-inch-thick slices and season on both sides with salt and pepper to taste.

4. Over a medium fire, grill the ham on one side for 4 to 5 minutes, until well seared. During the last minute of cooking, brush it with maple syrup.

Grilled Pork Loin with Indonesian Chile-Coconut Sauce

◆◆◆◆◆◆◆◆◆◆◆◆◆◆◆◆◆◆◆◆◆◆◆◆◆◆◆◆◆◆◆◆◆◆◆◆◆◆

For the sauce (about 1½ cups)

10 ancho chile peppers
1 cup white vinegar
1 cup chicken stock
2 stalks lemongrass (see Pantry, page 372), minced (you may substitute 1 tablespoon dried)
4 tablespoons peeled and coarsely chopped fresh ginger
2 garlic cloves, peeled
1 tablespoon chopped cilantro
2 tablespoons lime juice (about 1 lime)
⅓ cup coconut milk (see Pantry, page 368)
Salt and freshly cracked black pepper to taste

8 pieces of pork loin (4 ounces each)

1. Soak the ancho chile peppers in water to cover for 12 hours. Drain them, pat them dry, seed them, and set them aside.

2. In a saucepan, combine the vinegar, chicken stock, lemongrass, and ginger. Bring to a boil, then lower the heat and simmer until it is reduced by one half, approximately 20 minutes. Strain the

The chile-coconut sauce in this recipe is made from Asian staples that I saw used in many different ways when I visited Thailand. With the exception of the lemongrass, though, all of the ingredients could just as well come from Mexico. The cuisines of these two countries seem very different, but in fact they share many ingredients. When I created the recipe, I was thinking of mole sauce. I use the bitter chile taste characteristic of mole, but mellow it with coconut milk and sharpen it with aromatic lemongrass and lime juice, which gives it the flavor of traditional Thai dishes. ◆ *Serves 4 as a main course*

SERVING SUGGESTIONS: If you were out on the Pacific Rim, you would probably be eating this with the Spicy Cucumber Relish (page 232). Sweet potatoes always go well with pork, so I would suggest Sweet Potato Hash Browns with Bacon and Onions (page 300) to complete the meal.

mixture and reserve, discarding the solids. Return the liquid to the saucepan.

3. Add the garlic and seeded anchos to the reserved liquid, simmer for 15 minutes, and purée in a food processor or blender.

4. Add the cilantro, lime juice, and coconut milk, and mix well. Season the mixture with salt and pepper to taste. Will keep up to 3 days, covered, in the refrigerator.

5. When you are ready to grill, place the pork pieces between two pieces of plastic wrap, and pound them until evenly thin but not torn.

6. Season the pork pieces with salt and pepper to taste, and grill them over high heat. If the pork is thin and your fire is hot, this should take about 2 minutes per side.

7. Serve 2 pieces of pork per person, partially covered by a couple of tablespoons of the Chile-Coconut Sauce.

WHEN IS THE PORK DONE?

We all remember those pork chops from our youth—gray as a February day, dry as sawdust, and tasteless as the proverbial shoe leather. Fear of trichinosis, of course, was the culprit. Today, however, many cooks refuse to overcook pork, preferring to serve it pink to rosy-gray. Personally, I agree with them. While trichinosis has not been totally eliminated, it is certainly significantly less of a problem: There were only twenty-six cases in the United States in 1986, for example, in which pork was unequivocally the cause. The risk of eating less-than-well-done pork, in other words, seems to be no more than the danger of eating soft-boiled eggs, raw shellfish, or rare chicken. Some think it is worth the chance, others don't. Since it's your health, only you can be the judge.

Grilled Pork Skewers with Green Mango

MED

◆◆◆◆◆◆◆◆◆◆◆◆◆◆◆◆◆◆◆◆◆◆◆◆◆◆◆◆◆◆◆◆◆◆◆◆◆◆◆

2 pounds boneless pork butt

For the marinade

2 green mangoes
1 tablespoon crushed red pepper
 flakes
½ cup pineapple juice
1 tablespoon white vinegar
¼ teaspoon turmeric
¼ teaspoon ground cumin
¼ teaspoon curry powder
¼ teaspoon chili powder
1 tablespoon minced garlic

1 red bell pepper, seeded
1 large red onion
Salt and freshly cracked black
 pepper to taste

1. Cut the pork butt into 1-inch cubes and put them into a large shallow dish.

2. Make the marinade: Peel one green mango and slice the fruit away from the inner pit. Put the fruit into a blender or food processor with the pepper flakes, pineapple juice, vinegar, turmeric, cumin, curry powder, chili powder, and garlic, and purée well.

3. Pour the marinade over the pork cubes. Cover, refrigerate, and marinate for 4 to 5 hours.

It was in Burmese cuisine that I first ran across the idea of using green mango as a meat tenderizer. I like to use pork butt here so I can see how well the green mango does its job. The marinade also imparts a unique flavor. ◆ *Serves 4 as a main course*

SERVING SUGGESTIONS: I'd recommend serving this on white rice accompanied by Very Aromatic Tomato-Ginger Jam (page 231) and Grilled Baby Eggplant with Miso-Soy Vinaigrette (page 296).

4. Peel the second mango and cut the fruit away from the inner pit, making as close to 1-inch cubes as possible. Cut the red pepper into about 12 chunks, and the onion into 1-inch cubes.

5. Remove the meat from the marinade, leaving as much of the marinade clinging to it as possible. Discard the remaining marinade.

6. Thread the pork cubes and pieces of mango, red pepper, and onion on skewers in a pleasing array. Season with salt and pepper to taste.

7. Grill the skewers over medium heat until the pork is cooked, about 5 to 7 minutes per side. If the pork begins to get too brown, you may cover the skewers with a pie plate to aid in cooking.

Grilled Pork Skewers with Green Tomatoes and Your Secret Finishing Sauce

HIGH

❖❖❖❖❖❖❖❖❖❖❖❖❖❖❖❖❖❖❖❖❖❖❖❖❖❖❖❖❖❖❖❖❖

Here's a good use for those green tomatoes you have still hanging on the vines two days before the frost. "Finishing sauce" is a term used in barbecue, and it refers to a sauce that is brushed on just before meat is removed from the grill. Just a minute or two before you are ready to take the skewers off, brush this sauce on, let it caramelize a little, and the dish is ready. If you're having some fancy friends to dinner, tell them that the recipe for this sauce was given to you by an old man you met while traveling in Central America, that it has been handed down from father to son in his family, and you would never part with it. This dish is rather spicy and good served with tortillas. ◆ *Serves 4 as a main course*

For the finishing sauce

1 teaspoon ground achiote seed
　(see Pantry, page 369) (you
　may substitute paprika)
1 teaspoon ground cumin
1 teaspoon chili powder
2 tablespoons balsamic vinegar
1 tablespoon molasses
1 tablespoon chopped fresh
　oregano
Juice of 1 orange
2 tablespoons lime juice (about
　1 lime)
Salt and freshly cracked black
　pepper to taste

For the skewers

2½-pound pork butt
1 pound green tomatoes (about
　4 tomatoes)
2 large yellow onions

SERVING SUGGESTIONS: Serve this with Your Basic Black Beans (page 318), Corn Bread Salad with Lime Juice and Cilantro (page 312), Sweet Potato Salad (page 302), or Quesadilla Bread (page 326). You might try putting Tropical Gazpacho (page 34) in front of it.

1. Combine all the Finishing Sauce ingredients in a saucepan, bring to a boil, and simmer over low heat for 5 minutes.

2. Remove the sauce from the heat. What you don't use for this recipe will keep, covered in the refrigerator, for about 2 weeks.

3. Cut the pork, tomatoes, and onions into chunks ¼ inch in di-

ameter and thread them alternately on skewers.

4. Place the skewers on the grill over high heat and sear well. This should take about 3 to 4 minutes per side. Just before the meat is pulled off the grill, hit it with your secret sauce. Leave the skewers over the heat long enough to get some color, then pull them off.

MED-HIGH

Grilled Pork Birdies with Tangerine-Rosemary Glaze

For the glaze

¼ cup sugar

½ cup white vinegar

1 cup fresh tangerine juice (about 3 tangerines) (you may substitute fresh orange juice)

1 tablespoon fresh rosemary needles

1 tablespoon lime juice (about ½ lime)

Salt and freshly cracked black pepper to taste

2 tablespoons unsalted butter

The distinctly earthy flavor of fresh rosemary always reminds me of fall, and I see this dish being grilled out in the backyard among the fallen leaves and early sunsets that follow Indian summer.

This recipe calls for boneless pork loin, sometimes known as cutlets or fillets or, as my grandmother always called them, pork birdies. The meat is tender and flavorful and is complemented well by the sweet tangerine sauce with the dominant aromatic rosemary flavor. If fresh rosemary is not available, substitute fresh oregano or thyme rather than

8 4-ounce boneless pork birdies (loin fillets)
Salt and freshly cracked black pepper to taste

1. In a saucepan over medium heat, boil the sugar and vinegar together for 5 minutes. Add the tangerine juice and simmer until reduced by a third to a half. At this point the mixture should coat the back of a wooden spoon.

2. Remove the mixture from the heat, add the rosemary, lime juice, and salt and pepper to taste. Mix well, then add the butter and stir gently until it is melted and well incorporated.

3. Rub the birdies with salt and pepper to taste and place them on the grill over medium-high heat for 3 to 4 minutes per side. The surface of the meat should be slightly brown and crispy, and the interior should have a hint of pinkness, depending on your preference. (Check the interior by nicking one of the birdies slightly with a knife. If you like yours cooked completely through, leave it on an additional 2 minutes per side.) Spoon the glaze generously over the grilled birdies before serving.

dried rosemary, which has quite a different flavor from fresh. ◆ *Serves 4 as a main course*

SERVING SUGGESTIONS: Accompany this with Deep-Fried Cheddar Grits (page 311) and Your Basic Grilled Corn (page 317).

Grilled Pork Tenderloin with Roasted Corn-Bacon Relish

MED

◆◆

For the relish

3 ears of corn, shucked
4 tablespoons maple syrup
3 slices of bacon, diced small
1 large yellow onion, diced small
1 teaspoon chopped fresh sage
Salt and freshly cracked black
    pepper to taste

3 pork tenderloins (10 to 12
    ounces each)
Salt and freshly cracked black
    pepper to taste

The tenderloin is the tenderest cut of pork, suitable for grilling because its large surface area allows it to acquire a good amount of exterior char. Its subtle flavor combines well with the mellow but distinct taste of the relish. As for the corn, there are many ways to grill it on the cob, the main consideration being the degree of grilled/charred flavor you want. Here we want a lot, so we encourage it by glazing the ear of corn with maple syrup while it's on the grill. ◆ *Serves 4 as a main course*

1. Cook the corn in boiling water for 4 minutes. Remove it and allow to cool to room temperature.

2. Over a medium fire, grill the corn 2 to 3 minutes, or until lightly brown. Brush on the maple syrup and continue to grill for an additional 2 to 3 minutes, or until the syrup begins to caramelize (it will turn golden brown). Remove the corn from the grill and cool.

3. With a sharp knife, remove the kernels from the cob.

4. In a sauté pan, cook the bacon over medium heat until crisp.

SERVING SUGGESTION: This dish makes a perfect combination with Boiled Collard Greens with Salt Pork (page 292).

about 5 minutes. Add the onion and cook an additional 4 to 5 minutes, or until the onion is clear. Add the corn and cook 2 minutes more.

5. Remove the corn mixture from the heat, add the sage, and season to taste with salt and pepper. Stir well and set aside.

6. Rub the tenderloins with salt and pepper to taste and grill them over a medium fire for 12 to 15 minutes, rolling them every 3 to 4 minutes to ensure even cooking. (I prefer to eat this cut slightly pink, but if you like yours cooked completely, leave it on an additional 4 to 5 minutes.)

7. Remove the tenderloins from the grill, allow them to stand for 5 minutes, then carve each into ½-inch slices. Spoon some relish over each portion of the sliced pork and serve.

Put a Little South in Yo' Mouth

Grilled Tripe and Hominy Stew
Page 38

Grilled Pork Tenderloin with
Roasted Corn–Bacon Relish
Page 163

Corn and Watermelon
Rind Piccalilli
Page 221

Leesburg Chowchow
Page 219

Boiled Collard Greens
with Salt Pork
Page 292

East Coast Grill Lemonade
Page 358

Mint Juleps
Page 358

Mississippi Mud Cake
Page 338

Grilled West Indies Spice-Rubbed Chicken Breast with Grilled Banana

◆◆◆

For the spice rub

3 tablespoons curry powder
3 tablespoons ground cumin
2 tablespoons allspice
3 tablespoons paprika
2 tablespoons powdered ginger
1 tablespoon cayenne pepper
2 tablespoons salt
2 tablespoons freshly cracked
   black pepper

4 boneless chicken breasts,
   skin on
4 firm bananas, skin on and
   halved lengthwise
2 tablespoons vegetable oil
1 tablespoon soft butter
2 tablespoons molasses

Lime halves for garnish

1. Mix all the spices together well, rub this mixture over both sides of each chicken breast, cover, and refrigerate for 2 hours.

2. Over a medium fire, grill the chicken breasts skin-side down for 7 to 8 minutes, until well browned and heavily crusted. Turn them and grill an additional 10 minutes. Check for doneness by nicking the largest breast at the fattest point: The meat should be fully opaque

This is a variation for the grill of the dry rub commonly used in barbecue. The normal searing and crusting action of grilling is enhanced by the rub, and the result is a supercrusted, flavor-concentrated surface covering a moist breast. The grilled banana provides a little sweetness and mellowness to contrast with the crispy chicken. ◆ *Serves 4 as a main course*

SERVING SUGGESTIONS: I might put a pat of butter on each breast and serve them with Black Bean Salad (page 319) and Corn Bread Salad with Lime Juice and Cilantro (page 312) as accompaniments.

with no traces of red. Remove the chicken from the grill.

3. Rub the banana halves with vegetable oil and place them on the grill, flat-side down. Grill them for about 2 minutes, or until the flat sides are slightly golden in color. Flip them and grill for an additional 2 minutes.

4. Remove the banana halves from the grill. Mix the butter and molasses together and paint this over the bananas. Serve the chicken breasts and banana halves together, sprinkled with a little lime juice.

Grilled Chicken Breast with Fresh Herbs and Lemon

MED

◆◆◆◆◆◆◆◆◆◆◆◆◆◆◆◆◆◆◆◆◆◆◆◆◆◆◆◆◆◆◆◆◆◆◆◆

4 boneless chicken breasts,
   skin on
Salt and freshly cracked black
   pepper to taste
¼ cup chopped mixed fresh
   herbs
¼ cup virgin olive oil
8 tablespoons lemon juice
   (about 2 lemons)

1. Rub the breasts all over with salt and pepper to taste and grill them skin-side down over a medium fire for 10 to 12 minutes. The skin should be quite crisp.

2. While the breasts are grilling, combine the mixed herbs, olive oil, and lemon juice in a small bowl until well blended.

3. Turn the breasts and grill for an additional 5 to 6 minutes. During the last minute of cooking, brush the herb mixture on both sides of the chicken.

4. Remove the chicken from the grill and check for doneness by cutting into the thickest part and taking a peek: There should be no pink color and the flesh should be consistently opaque.

This dish is representative of what much of today's cooking is moving toward: a simple yet high-quality preparation where the ingredients stand on their own. Dishes that highlight the food, not the cook. I use a boneless breast because in the absence of saintlike patience I find it impossible to cook a bone-in chicken breast on an open grill. Any fresh herb or combination of herbs works fine for this dish—the key word is "fresh." I would choose from some combination of thyme, basil, oregano, parsley, and rosemary. ◆ *Serves 4 as a main course*

SERVING SUGGESTIONS: I would accompany this straightforward dish with Spicy Pickled Cabbage (page 291) and Black Bean Salad (page 319).

Grilled Jamaican Jerk Chicken with Banana-Guava Ketchup

LOW

Jamaican Jerk Rub

¼ cup Inner Beauty (see Sources, page 380) *or* other Caribbean hot sauce *or* 10 puréed Scotch Bonnet chile peppers (you may substitute 15 of your favorite fresh chile peppers)

2 tablespoons dried rosemary

2 tablespoons parsley, chopped

2 tablespoons dried basil

2 tablespoons dried thyme

2 tablespoons mustard seeds

3 scallions, finely chopped

1 teaspoon salt

1 teaspoon black pepper

Juice of 2 limes

¼ cup cheap yellow mustard

2 tablespoons orange juice

2 tablespoons white vinegar

6 chicken thighs, with legs attached

1. Combine all the rub ingredients in a food processor or blender, and blend them into a paste, making sure that all the ingredients are fully integrated. The paste should be approximately the consistency of a thick tomato sauce. If it is too thick, thin it out with a little more white vinegar.

In my surfing days, I stumbled upon a beach near Port Antonio, Jamaica, called Boston Bay. It turned out to have decent waves, but more significantly to be the best place on the island for jerk chicken and jerk pork. Originally created by escaped Maroon slaves as a method of preserving pork by rubbing it with a paste and then open-pit smoking it, this uniquely Jamaican dish has evolved into pork and chicken that is rubbed with the same mixture and then grilled slowly so that it dries out. The paste is the foundation of this dish and its key ingredient is the infamous Scotch Bonnet pepper (sometimes called the habañero pepper), the hottest chile pepper in the world. This pepper is rated at between 150,000 and 300,000 on the Scoville unit measure of heat. To give you a basis for comparison, the jalapeño chile pepper is rated at between 2,500 and 5,000 Scoville units.

Scotch Bonnet chile peppers are difficult to find fresh, although sometimes you can pick them up in Spanish markets where Caribbean and South American products are sold. It is easier to find the traditional hot Caribbean table sauce that uses the Scotch Bonnet as its main ingredient. The wildly aromatic taste is unique and unmistakable,

2. Cover the paste and let it sit in the refrigerator for at least 2 hours for the flavors to blend together. Overnight is the ideal amount of time to give them to get acquainted. (Note that if you want to avoid making a fresh batch every time you make this dish, you can multiply the amount of paste easily. Don't worry about it going bad, since it keeps almost indefinitely.)

3. Rub the chicken thighs with the paste and place them on the grill over very low heat. If you have a covered cooker, put the coals to one side, the chicken on the other, and cover.

4. Cook about 1 hour without a cover or ½ hour if covered. The key here is to use a very low heat. You need to be patient and give yourself plenty of time. The chicken is technically done when the meat is opaque and the juices run clear. However, the ideal is about 10 to 15 minutes past that point, when the meat pulls away from the bone easily. It is very hard to overcook this. In fact you can only screw it up if you burn the paste by having the heat too high. The longer the chicken stays on the grill, the more superior the smoky flavor.

5. After cooking, separate the leg from the thigh by cutting at the natural joint between them. Serve one leg or thigh per person accompanied by a few spoonfuls of Banana-Guava Ketchup.

the sauce is exceptionally hot, and while it is known by many names it is always made from a mixture of cheap yellow mustard (good mustard would ruin the authenticity of the preparation), sweeteners, and the chile pepper itself. I have personally developed a sauce for the East Coast Grill that we call Inner Beauty Hot Sauce (see Sources, page 380). It is the star player in a line of different dishes to which we affix the words "from Hell," as in Pasta from Hell (page 73).

Here are two versions of the recipe, one using fresh Scotch Bonnet chile peppers and the other using the bottled sauce which is very easy to find if you've got some pals heading south to the Caribbean, live near a Spanish market, or are in striking distance of my restaurant.

I like to use chicken thighs in this dish because they have center bones and so can withstand the long cooking time on the grill and still be juicy. If you prefer serving boneless chicken, it's very easy to remove the one bone from the thigh before serving. ◆ *Serves 4 as an entrée or 6 as a light meal*

SERVING SUGGESTIONS: For a full-on Caribbean dinner, serve this with white rice, Your Basic Black Beans (page 318), and Grilled Bananas (page 165), or with Salad of Green Mango, Coconut, and Hot Chile Peppers (page 295) and Plátanos Fritos (page 145). You might want to sip on a Last Resort (page 363) before, during, and/or after dinner.

Banana-Guava Ketchup

1 yellow onion, diced
2 tablespoons vegetable oil
5 ripe bananas (anywhere from totally yellow to spotted brown) (about 2 pounds), peeled and broken into pieces
4 ounces (½ cup) guava paste combined with 1 cup orange juice *or* 1 12-ounce can guava nectar (you may substitute 8 ounces [1 cup] of guava jelly combined with ½ cup of orange juice)
2 tablespoons brown sugar
2½ tablespoons raisins
1 tablespoon curry powder
½ cup fresh orange juice
2 tablespoons white vinegar
4 tablespoons lime juice (about 2 limes)
Salt and freshly cracked black pepper to taste

1. In a heavy-bottomed pan over medium heat, sauté the onion in vegetable oil until transparent, about 5 to 7 minutes.

2. Add the banana pieces to the pan and cook over moderate heat for about 5 minutes, stirring constantly to avoid sticking.

3. Add the guava paste mixture, brown sugar, raisins, curry powder, orange juice, and 1 tablespoon of the vinegar. Bring to a boil and simmer gently for about 15 minutes. The mixture should have the consistency of apple-

Banana-guava ketchup is certainly not a traditional accompaniment to jerk chicken, but the ingredients reproduce the authentic spirit of the dish and the sweet richness of the ketchup helps people who need a cool taste against the chicken. Sweet versus hot is always a nice contrast, and both components are loud, strong flavors, so they can stand up to each other—an essential requirement in food as well as human relationships.

I use guava paste in the dish. You can probably find it in your local Spanish or Portuguese store. If you can't, substitute guava jelly or canned guava nectar. If no guava products at all are to be found in your neck of the woods, just leave it out—the bananas can carry the ketchup by themselves. ⋄ *2 cups*

sauce when hot, but will firm up as it cools.

4. Remove from the heat and stir in the remaining tablespoon of vinegar, the lime juice, and salt and pepper to taste. You may serve this hot or at room temperature. It will keep, covered and refrigerated, up to 6 weeks.

Chicken Hobo Pack

MED

Dedicated to the Boys of the Longhorn Patrol, Troop 103

1 3-pound chicken, cut in half
1 large sweet potato, quartered
1 whole head of garlic, unpeeled and sliced in half horizontally
1 large onion, quartered
1 large ripe tomato, quartered
1 ear of corn, husked and cut into 4 pieces
1 medium carrot, cut into large chunks
2 rosemary sprigs
Salt and freshly cracked black pepper to taste
4 tablespoons butter

1. Lay one chicken half on a large sheet of extra-heavy-duty tinfoil. Arrange half of the vegetables over and around the chicken, add 1 sprig rosemary and salt and pepper to taste, dot 2 tablespoons of

The hobo pack takes its place alongside a tuna fish sandwich and Jell-O as one of my earliest recipes. As the newest member of the Longhorn Patrol of my local Boy Scout troop, I was elected to be the cook on our camping trip. Unsure of what to prepare for the guys, I was forced to rely on an old Boy Scout favorite that consists of vegetables, potatoes, hamburger, and a huge amount of ketchup wrapped up in foil and put in the burning embers of the campfire. The guys loved it.

Along with the rest of my cooking repertoire, the hobo pack has evolved over the years and is now a constant menu item on day trips to the beach. The combination convection/conduction cooking method, in which the food is surrounded by coals and slow-cooked, makes it a very easy affair. You can use this method with all kinds of ingre-

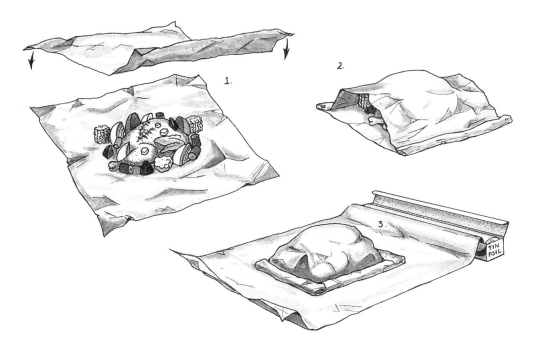

butter over all, and put another large sheet of tinfoil on top. Roll the edges of the two sheets together, closing the pack. Fold the edges up, making sure you remember which side is up (see the diagram). Now cover the entire pack with one more layer of tinfoil.

2. Repeat with the second chicken half and remaining ingredients.

3. It's best to use a campfire where you have plenty of room to work, but a large grill will do as well. Build a medium fire, place the packs on the bottom of the fire or grill, top-side up, and arrange coals all around them. Make sure to keep hot burning coals constantly around the packs, and cook for 30 to 45 minutes, depending upon the intensity of your heat.

4. Remove the packs from the coals, unroll the tinfoil, and catch

dients, but I like it with chicken and lots of garlic, which mellows when it cooks and merges with all the juice from the chicken. The packs can be made up ahead and refrigerated for 4 to 8 hours. ◆ *Serves 2*

SERVING SUGGESTIONS: Serve this with Girl Scout cookies and that nice, ice-cold beer you couldn't have when you were a Boy Scout.

the wonderful smell. For the full hobo pack experience, sit on the ground and eat it out of the tinfoil with Cokes and candy bars, then play a game of Capture the Flag and tell ghost stories. It is also okay to serve it on a plate with some crusty bread for the juices, a salad, and a bottle of white wine—but then, some people have no respect for culinary traditions.

Sand in Your Shoes— Grilling on the Beach

◆ ◆ ◆ ◆ ◆ ◆ ◆ ◆ ◆ ◆ ◆ ◆ ◆ ◆ ◆ ◆

Grilled Eggplant with Olive Oil, Parsley, and Capers
Page 298

Chicken Hobo Pack
Page 171

Marinated Feta with Roasted Red Peppers, Black Olives, and Thyme
Page 293

Pita Bread
Page 327

Watermelon

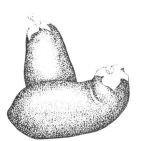

Grilled Turkey Steaks with White Grape–Cranberry Relish

◆ ◆

For the relish

½ cup fresh cranberries
½ cup blush or rosé wine
3 tablespoons sugar
½ cup orange juice
1 pound seedless white grapes, halved
2 tablespoons lime juice (about 1 lime)

4 10-ounce turkey fillets (about ½ inch thick)
Salt and freshly cracked black pepper to taste

Turkey fillets work well on the grill, since the quick cooking method retains the moistness of the interior meat while the fire gives more flavor to the exterior surface. Most supermarkets now carry boneless turkey breast cut into fillets, scallops, or steaks, which are all basically the same cut. The tang of the cranberry balances the sweetness of the grapes in the relish, making a nontraditional traditional combination. Half of the grapes are added after cooking so the relish has the added texture of the whole grapes. ◆ *Serves 4 as a main course*

1. Make the relish: In a saucepot over low heat, bring the cranberries, wine, and sugar to a boil, stirring until the sugar is dissolved. Add the orange juice and half of the grapes, reduce the heat, and simmer for 5 minutes.

2. Remove from the heat, add the rest of the grapes and the lime juice, mix well, and allow to cool. Will keep, covered and refrigerated, up to 2 weeks.

3. Rub the fillets on both sides with salt and pepper to taste and cook them over a medium-hot fire for about 4 to 5 minutes per side. Check for doneness by nicking one side; the meat should be opaque throughout. Remove them from grill and serve with the relish.

SERVING SUGGESTIONS: Serve these with Green Bean Salad with Tomatoes and Jicama (page 290) or Boiled Collard Greens with Salt Pork (page 292).

Roasted Then Grilled Half Duck

MED

◆◆

1 5- to 6-pound duck
Salt and freshly cracked black
  pepper to taste

1. Preheat the oven to 425°F.

2. Trim all the excess fat from the duck tail and remove the innards from the inside cavity of the bird. Rub the bird generously both inside and out with salt and pepper.

3. Place the duck in a roasting pan and bake for 1 hour and 15 minutes. Remove the duck from the oven and allow it to cool to the point where you can handle it comfortably.

4. Slice the duck diagonally to the bone on either side of the breastbone and backbone. Semi-bone the duck by removing the two sides from the carcass (see the diagram).

5. Over a medium fire, grill the duck skin-side up for 10 minutes, being careful of flare-ups as the remaining fat drips into the fire. Turn it and cook an additional 4 to 5 minutes, again being careful of flare-ups. If they do occur due to fat dripping into the fire, move the breasts so that they are not directly over the flames.

6. Remove the duck from the grill and serve.

This process is commonly used in restaurants because they cannot cook everything from start to finish totally *à la minute*. In this case, the duck is partially roasted at a high temperature to release its fat, then split and partially boned. With some of the fat gone to avoid constant flare-ups, the duck can then be grilled to finish the cooking process and to add the distinctive grilled flavor that is virtually impossible to achieve from a raw state. This duck derives a lot of flavor from its high fat content and its reaction to live fire, but at the same time you want to have a low fire to avoid flare-ups of flame which will blacken the bird. ◆ *Serves 2 as a main course*

SERVING SUGGESTIONS: This is especially good with Apricot Blatjang (page 225) or with Tangerine-Tamarind Sauce (page 242) brushed on after cooking. Spoon Bread with Smithfield Ham and Cheddar Cheese (page 308) is an excellent partner for this dish.

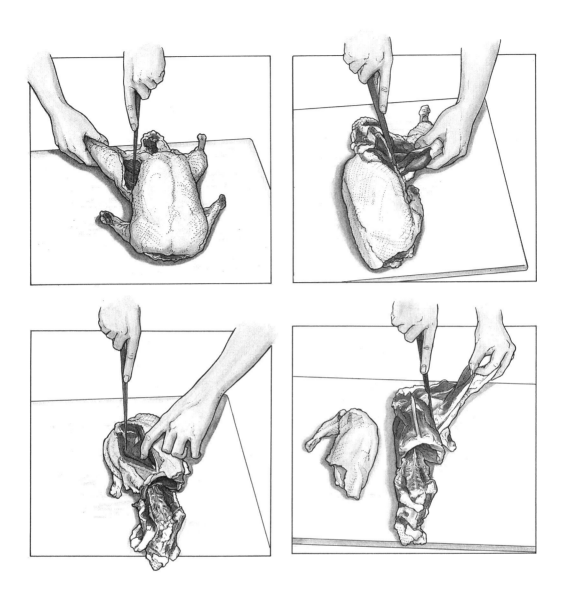

Grilling at the Ritz

◆◆

The recipes in this chapter are linked by the fact that all involve either expensive ingredients, subtle flavor combinations, or intricacy of preparation. Each dish is an example of a creative way to use the grill in a fine dining situation, taking particular care that the integrity of the delicate ingredients is not compromised by the intensity of the cooking method. This is somewhat of a departure from my usual style, in which I match the casual, everyday nature of grilling with inexpensive ingredients characteristic of "food of the people." You might say that this is the graduate course in grilling.

These are recipes for those occasions when you want to pull out all the stops. Toward the end of the summer, for example, when your technique is peaking after three months of serious grilling, it may be time to impress your friends with your range. Maybe Mr. Dithers is coming to dinner, or you are expecting your college roommate who has become a food writer for the local paper. While the dishes in this chapter are somewhat more sophisticated and ambitious than those in the rest of the book, they still retain the flavor and appeal of grilling—and there really is nothing that can beat a properly grilled shiitake or sweetbreads enhanced with just a trace of sear.

Grilled Figs with Prosciutto and Provolone

MED

◆ ◆

7 very ripe figs
3 tablespoons extra virgin olive
   oil plus more for drizzling
1 pound prosciutto, thinly sliced
½ pound hard provolone

2 limes, quartered, for garnish

1. Slice the figs in half, and rub them with the 3 tablespoons of olive oil.

2. Grill the figs skin-side up over a medium-hot fire for 2 to 3 minutes. They should attain a good amount of color.

3. Remove the figs from the fire, and arrange them skin-side down on a platter, along with the prosciutto and provolone. Drizzle olive oil over the figs, and garnish the plate with lime wedges. Serve with crusty Italian bread.

This combination could be found in most any restaurant in Italy, but I've added the slight twist of grilling the figs lightly. Make sure that you get the hard, aged provolone, as it is of much higher quality than the soft kind. Serve this with crusty Italian bread, lime wedges, and black olives, and have a bottle of extra virgin olive oil handy for drizzling.
◆ *Serves 6 to 8 as an antipasto*

SERVING SUGGESTIONS: Serve with Grill-Seared Sushi-Quality Tuna with Soy, Wasabi, and Pickled Ginger (page 192), or as a double appetizer with Grilled Sweetbreads with Wilted Southern Greens, Slab Bacon, and Balsamic Vinegar (page 206).

Grilled Expensive Mushrooms on Texas Toast

◆◆◆◆◆◆◆◆◆◆◆◆◆◆◆◆◆◆◆◆◆◆◆◆◆◆◆◆◆◆◆◆◆◆◆◆

1 pound mixed mushrooms (the bigger the better)
8 tablespoons olive oil
1 teaspoon freshly cracked black pepper
2 tablespoons unsalted butter, room temperature
2 tablespoons sherry
2 tablespoons chopped parsley
Salt and freshly cracked black pepper to taste

I have always liked the way mushrooms react to the grill, and the abundance of new varieties now commonly available makes experimentation easy. The feature of this dish is the mushrooms themselves, and the way that grilling provides the opportunity for their individual flavors and textures to be displayed. I season them with a touch of sherry and some butter and serve them on top of a lightly seasoned garlic bread to soak up the juices. ◆ *Serves 4 as an appetizer*

1. Wipe the dirt off the mushrooms with a slightly damp cloth or paper towel, and cut off the bottom third of the stems.

2. In a large stainless steel bowl, combine the mushrooms, olive oil, and teaspoon of freshly cracked black pepper. Toss until the mushrooms are well coated with oil—all of the oil should be absorbed.

3. Grill the mushrooms over medium heat, turning occasionally, until brown and crispy, about 8 to 10 minutes.

4. Remove the mushrooms from the grill, slice them into small pieces, and return them to the stainless steel bowl. Add the butter, sherry, and parsley, and toss until the butter has melted.

5. Season with salt and pepper to taste and serve on Texas Toast.

SERVING SUGGESTIONS: Serve this as an appetizer with Grilled Veal Chop with Artichoke Hearts, Sun-dried Tomatoes, and Pine Nuts (page 139), or as a main course with Arugula and Dandelion Greens Salad with Fried Oysters, Smithfield Ham, and Peaches (page 187) or Grilled Marinated Quail (page 200).

Special Dinner for Two

◆◆◆◆◆◆◆◆◆◆◆◆◆◆◆◆◆◆◆◆◆

Grilled Expensive Mushrooms
on Texas Toast
Page 179

Grill-Seared Sushi-Quality Tuna
with Soy, Wasabi, and
Pickled Ginger
Page 192

Cold Orzo Salad
Page 316

Your Basic Grilled Corn
Page 317

Chocolate Pecan Pie
Page 354

Texas Toast

4 1-inch-thick slices of Italian
bread
4 tablespoons olive oil
1 tablespoon minced garlic

Toast the bread in a low oven until hard and crispy. Combine the
oil and garlic into a paste, and coat
the bread lightly with it.

Grilled crusty bread became known as "Texas toast" because people used to think that only cowpokes on the trail would resort to grilling bread over an open fire rather than using an electric toaster. Just goes to show how much we've learned lately. ◆ *4 portions*

MUSHROOMS

Due to advances in our understanding of the growing environments of mushrooms, what was once attainable only by searching through the woods is now a common sight on produce shelves. Fungi that were once exotic, expensive, and difficult to locate are now only exotic and expensive. Grilling is an excellent way to cook these mushrooms, as it enhances their flavor without burying it. Here is a short list of some of the varieties available:

CHANTERELLES: Golden in color, delicate in nature, chanterelles grill very quickly. Use tongs to prevent them from burning.

HEN OF THE WOODS: These mushrooms are small and come in overlapping clusters that resemble a brain. Rich and tasty, they are best seared on a hot flame, then moved to a cooler part of the grill to cook until tender, about five minutes.

PORTOBELLOS: Cremini mushrooms that have been allowed to grow up, portobellos are very popular in Italy, where a single one may grow to be large enough to make a dinner. Their size and texture make them durable mushrooms, ones that stand up well to the rigors of grilling.

SHIITAKES: These mushrooms' large size, earthy taste, and firm texture make them eminently grillable, which is great because they are the easiest to find and perhaps the tastiest of the exotic mushrooms. I like them best when they are grilled until the edges are crisp, then served plain with salt and pepper.

WOOD EARS: Durable fungi that are very popular in Japan, wood ears are ear-shaped and brown in color. Their crisp texture makes them perfect for grilling. Since they have little taste by themselves, I usually add some herbs and garlic to boost the flavor.

Grilled Hearthbread with Sopressata, Melon, and Torta Basil

1 pan Hearthbread (page 183)
4 tablespoons olive oil
1 pound torta basil cheese, cut into 16 pieces (you may substitute any triple crème cheese)
1 pound sopressata, thinly sliced
1 small ripe honeydew melon, seeded, thinly sliced, and peeled
1 small ripe canteloupe, seeded, thinly sliced, and peeled

1. Make the Hearthbread.

2. When the bread has been removed from the pan, cut it into 4 sections, brush both sides of each with the olive oil, and grill them over low heat about 1 to 2 minutes per side, or until golden and crusty. Remove from the grill and cut into cracker-size pieces.

3. On a large platter, arrange the torta basil, sopressata, melon, and bread pieces in separate areas, allowing your guests to make their own combinations. (I often enjoy arranging the various parts in reproductions of famous traffic patterns. Your guests probably won't notice it, but it makes the preparation more fun.)

Hearthbread is basically a pizza dough with no topping, traditionally cooked on the floor of a wood-burning oven. In this preparation, it provides a background for the contrasting strong tastes of the sopressatta, a hard, cured Italian sausage with a semispicy, slightly gamy taste, and the intense mellow richness of the Italian layered triple crème cheese. Together with the melon, the bread helps diffuse the situation and gives your taste buds a breather. ◆ *Serves 10 as an appetizer*

SERVING SUGGESTIONS: Serve this in front of Sweet Milk-Marinated Grilled Lamb with Sweet and Hot Apricot Condiment (page 151), or in combination with Grandma Wetzler's Sweet-and-Sour Wilted Chicory (page 285).

Hearthbread

◆ ◆

3 cups lukewarm water
1 tablespoon dry yeast
1½ teaspoons sugar
1 tablespoon dried basil
1 tablespoon dried oregano
6 cups all-purpose flour
2 teaspoons salt
1½ teaspoons freshly ground
  pepper (white is best if you
  have it)
1 cup chopped scallion (about 1
  bunch: use both green and
  white parts)
6 tablespoons olive oil
3 garlic cloves, chopped
Coarse salt and freshly cracked
  black pepper to taste

Basil, oregano, and garlic provide a Mediterranean flavor for this version of hearthbread. This bread freezes well, so it can easily be made in advance, frozen, then thawed before grilling. ◆ *12 to 15 portions*

1. Preheat the oven to 450°F.

2. In a small bowl, combine the water, yeast, sugar, and dried herbs, and stir well. Set in a warm place and allow the yeast to develop. This may take 5 to 15 minutes, depending on the temperature. The yeast has developed when the mixture is foamy.

3. Meanwhile, mix together the flour, salt, pepper, and scallion in a large bowl.

4. Combine 2 tablespoons of the olive oil with the foamy yeast mixture and gradually stir into the dry ingredients. If necessary, add a bit more water to fully incorporate all the ingredients. This dough should be slightly wet and sticky.

5. Turn the dough out onto a well-floured board, and knead until the dough is smooth but not overly elastic, about 5 minutes.

6. Place the dough in a large oiled bowl, cover it with plastic wrap, and set in a warm place until doubled in volume. This may take 20 minutes to 1 hour, depending on the temperature. Check every 20 minutes or so.

7. When the dough has doubled in size, punch it down, then remove it from the bowl onto an oiled 12″ × 17″ sheet pan. Using your fingertips, spread the dough so that it covers the whole sheet pan evenly. Cover it with plastic wrap and set it in a warm place until doubled in volume. Again, check every 20 minutes or so, as the doubling in volume may take as little as 20 minutes or as long as 1 hour.

8. In a small bowl, mix together the chopped garlic and the remaining 4 tablespoons of olive oil.

9. When the dough has doubled in volume, remove the plastic wrap, and drizzle the oil and garlic mixture over the top of the dough. Sprinkle it with salt and pepper to taste, and bake about 20 minutes, or until golden brown. Remove the bread from the oven, let it cool slightly while still in the pan, then turn it onto a wire rack. May be served warm or room temperature.

Arugula and Dandelion Greens Salad with Fried Oysters, Smithfield Ham, and Peaches

◆◆◆

1 bunch arugula
1 bunch dandelion greens

For the dressing

3 tablespoons ketchup
½ tablespoon Dijon mustard
⅓ cup red wine vinegar
4 tablespoons lime juice (about 2 limes)
½ teaspoon salt
1 teaspoon freshly cracked black pepper
½ teaspoon finely chopped garlic
⅔ cup vegetable oil

For the oysters

½ cup flour
½ cup yellow cornmeal
½ teaspoon cayenne pepper
½ teaspoon salt
1 cup milk
1 large egg
12 oysters
3 to 4 cups vegetable oil for frying

¼ pound Smithfield ham, julienned (you may substitute prosciutto)
2 ripe peaches, cut into bite-size wedges (you may substitute nectarines)

This wonderfully refreshing salad is a perfect summer dish, with its combination of pungent greens, crisply breaded oysters, and rich, ripe peaches. Arugula greens are becoming easy to find due to their increasing popularity, and if dandelion greens aren't available, chicory is a good substitute. In choosing greens, look for smooth leaves with no yellowing or spotting.

As for the oysters, if shucked oysters are available, get them. If they aren't available and you aren't a proficient shucker, an easy way to open the oysters is to put them on a sheet pan and put them into a hot (350° to 375° F) oven. In 5 to 10 minutes the shells will pop open, at which point you'll be able to separate an oyster from its shell with an oyster knife (or butter knife), scraping along the shell to sever the connecting muscle. Chill the oysters immediately after shucking, and reserve them in the refrigerator until you're ready to fry them and assemble the salad. ◆ *Serves 4 as a light main course or 6 as an appetizer*

1. Trim the stems from the greens and wash the greens in cold water. Drain them well and use a lettuce spinner, if you have one, to remove any excess water. Refrigerate the greens until you're ready to use them.

2. In a food processor or large bowl, combine the ketchup, mustard, vinegar, lime juice, ½ teaspoon of salt, pepper, and garlic until well mixed.

3. Add the ⅔ cup of vegetable oil to the mixture in a slow stream, mixing constantly. (If mixing by hand, put a wet cloth under the bowl to hold it still, freeing your hands for whisking and pouring the oil.) The mixture will thicken slightly as you add the oil. Refrigerate the mixture until you're ready to serve it.

4. In a wide, shallow bowl, combine the flour, cornmeal, cayenne pepper, and ½ teaspoon of salt. In a separate bowl, combine the milk and egg, and whisk until the egg is well integrated.

5. Dip the oysters in the milk-egg mixture and then into the flour-cornmeal mixture. Then dip them in each again. This will coat the oysters well and prevent them from drying out during frying.

6. In a heavy-bottomed saucepan or flat-sided sauté pan, heat 2 inches of oil over medium-high heat for about 5 minutes or until it reaches 350°F; if the oil starts to smoke, it is too hot, and you should remove the pan from the heat immediately. Test the oil by dropping

SERVING SUGGESTIONS: For me, this would be the first course in that infamous "last meal" offered to a man about to be hanged. I would follow it with Grilled Big Black-and-Blue Steak for Two (page 148), Your Basic Grilled Corn (page 317), and a six-pack.

a pinch of the flour-cornmeal mixture into it: The oil should bubble and cook the mixture quickly.

7. In two batches, cook the twice-breaded oysters in the hot oil until just golden brown and ruffled at the edges, about 2 to 3 minutes. Wait a couple of minutes between the two batches to allow the oil to get back up to cooking temperature. (If the oil cools down too much, you will end up with greasy oysters.)

8. Drain the cooked oysters on a paper towel. You may want to hold them in a warm oven (250°F) while you assemble the salad.

9. Toss the greens with the dressing to taste. Arrange the greens on serving plates and sprinkle them with the julienned ham and peach wedges. Take the oysters from the oven and place them on top of the salads.

SMITHFIELD HAM

Made in Smithfield, Virginia, this may be the most underrated meat in the world today. Growing up in the county next to Smithfield, I enjoyed many a ham biscuit as a youth, but it was only much later that I made the connection between the classic hams of Europe and this humble Southern fare. A Smithfield ham made in the traditional manner will stand up against any prosciutto from Parma or Westphalian ham from Germany. The confusing part is that in Virginia, people insist on cooking the cured Smithfield ham and eating it in thick slices, while prosciutto and Westphalian ham are traditionally sliced paper thin and eaten in their cured state, with no additional cooking. Recently I have begun to see cooks using Smithfield ham in this way, with excellent results, so I am sure it is only a matter of time before Smithfield begins to receive the respect accorded its European cousins.

The processes used to make these classic hams are very similar, and the differences between them are the result of the particular characteristics of the regions where they are made. In the case of Smithfield ham, the hogs are fed peanuts, which darkens the meat. The meat is salt-cured, coated with pepper, hickory-smoked for up to two months, then hung up and aged for six months to a year. A true Smithfield ham has a dark red-brown color, yellowish fat, and a distinctive salty, smoky flavor.

Sake-Marinated Grilled Frogs' Legs with Japanese-Flavored Barbecue Sauce

MED

◆ ◆

For the marinade

1 cup sake
¼ cup peanut oil
1 teaspoon red pepper flakes
1 teaspoon minced garlic
Salt and freshly cracked black
   pepper to taste

16 sets of small frogs' legs, 3 to
   4 inches long (about 4
   pounds)

1. Combine all the marinade ingredients in a shallow baking pan. Add the frogs' legs, refrigerate covered, and let sit for 4 hours.

2. Remove the frogs' legs from the marinade and grill them over medium heat for about 3 minutes per side. Check for doneness by probing the meat at the juncture of the legs. It should be completely opaque.

3. Just before removing the frogs' legs from the grill, brush them with Japanese-Flavored Barbecue Sauce (recipe follows) and allow them to glaze slightly. This should take about 30 seconds— be careful, as the sauce burns easily.

Another one of those foods that falls into that huge area of flavor description, "it tastes like chicken." In this case, I would have to agree that without the proper information people would probably be saying how tasty and different these chicken wings were.

Most of the frogs' legs I've seen come from Bangladesh and India, but in the American South a lot of people have been doing very well in the frog-gigging business lately. However, I still prefer imported legs for this dish, since they are generally smaller and therefore can get well seared and crisp. Also, again like chicken wings, these small legs are a lot of fun to eat. With Spicy Pickled Cabbage (page 291) and steamed rice, they can serve as an entrée as well. ◆ *Serves 8 as an appetizer*

Japanese-Flavored Barbecue Sauce

¼ cup hoisin sauce
¼ cup ketchup
2 tablespoons rice wine vinegar
2 tablespoons sesame oil
1½ teaspoons minced ginger
Juice of 1 orange

Combine all the ingredients, and mix well. Keeps, covered and refrigerated, for up to 3 weeks.

About ¾ cup

Soy-Marinated Scallops with Grilled Shiitakes

2 pounds sea scallops
8 tablespoons soy sauce
4 tablespoons rice wine vinegar
1 tablespoon grated ginger
1 tablespoon sesame oil
1 teaspoon white pepper
1 teaspoon sugar
4 monster *or* 8 medium shiitakes
2 tablespoons vegetable oil
Salt and freshly cracked black pepper to taste
Freshly cracked pepper to taste (white is best if you have it)

2 tablespoons sesame seeds, toasted in a single layer in a 350°F oven for 25 minutes

Generally speaking, small bay scallops are prized over the larger sea scallops. For this dish, however, I prefer sea scallops, the bigger the better; their size allows them to char on the outside before they become overcooked on the inside. When buying them, try to choose scallops of uniform size; the fishmonger might not be too happy about matching sizes, but that will usually be offset by his or her joy at unloading all those giant scallops.

This dish is straightforward: The strong soy and ginger taste of the marinade goes well with the grilled scallops. I don't use a sauce here because you want the marinade to be present and

1. Rinse the scallops thoroughly and set aside.

2. In a stainless steel bowl, combine the soy sauce, vinegar, ginger, sesame oil, white pepper, and sugar, and mix well.

3. Put the scallops in the marinade mixture, cover them, and place in the refrigerator for 4 to 6 hours, turning once or twice. (No longer, or the marinade will dominate the scallop flavor.)

4. If the shiitakes are dirty, clean them by wiping them gently with a cloth or paper towel. Rub them with the vegetable oil, and season them with salt and pepper to taste.

5. Remove the scallops from the marinade and drain them. Season them with pepper to taste (no salt is needed on the scallops because of the saltiness of the marinade).

6. Place the scallops individually over a medium-high gas grill or medium-hot fire. If the scallops are too small or the spaces on the grill too large to allow you to do this, you will need to skewer them.

7. Cook the scallops, rolling them around a bit, 3 to 5 minutes, until firm. (To be sure, take one off and cut it open.)

8. At the same time you cook the scallops, if there is room on the grill, put the shiitakes on, and grill them about 3 to 5 minutes. When they have darkened slightly and have crisp exteriors, remove them from the grill and serve them with the scallops, garnished with the toasted sesame seeds.

the scallop taste to stand out. Rounding out the Japanese motif, I grill some shiitake mushrooms, which are becoming easier to find all the time. Here again, choose the monster mushrooms. When grilled, the shiitakes react almost like meat, with the outside becoming crisp and the inside remaining tender and moist. ◆ *Serves 4 as a main course*

SERVING SUGGESTIONS: Precede this with Equatorial Fruit Cocktail with Lime Juice and Jalapeños (page 85), and serve it along with José's Jicama Slaw (page 294), a simple buttered pasta, and lightly grilled red bell peppers.

HOMEMADE PICKLED GINGER

If you can't find pickled ginger—or if you just prefer to make your own—here's a simple way to do it—the key is to slice or shave the ginger as thin as possible.

⅔ cup rice wine vinegar (you may substitute white vinegar)
⅓ cup sugar
1 teaspoon salt
4 ounces peeled ginger, thinly sliced

Bring the vinegar and sugar and salt to a simmer. Drop in the sliced ginger, count to ten, remove from the heat, and cool. Then put the ginger in a glass jar and refrigerate.

Allow it to stand 2 to 3 weeks. Will keep for 3 months.

Grill-Seared Sushi-Quality Tuna with Soy, Wasabi, and Pickled Ginger

◆◆

4 8-ounce tuna steaks (3 inches thick)
4 tablespoons sesame oil
Salt and freshly ground pepper to taste (white is best if you have it)
¾ cup pickled ginger (*gari*) (see Pantry, page 370)
6 tablespoons wasabi powder (see Pantry, page 370), mixed with water to the consistency of wet sand
12 tablespoons soy sauce

1. Brush the tuna steaks lightly with the sesame oil and season with salt and pepper to taste.

2. Over high heat, place the steaks on the grill and cook 4 to 5 minutes on the top and bottom sides, or until a dark brown crispy skin has been formed.

3. Now cook the steaks for 2 to 3 minutes on each edge, trying to achieve the same dark brown crispy effect.

4. Remove the steaks from the grill, and serve with gari, wasabi, and soy sauce.

While this dish appears to be simple, it possesses an Eastern complexity within its seeming simplicity. It is one of the most popular dishes in the East Coast Grill, and is representative of some of the principles essential to my style of food.

The whole concept of this dish is to bring out the taste and texture of the tuna. This is an interpretation of one of the cardinal principles of nouvelle cuisine: Work with the highest-quality product, treat it with simplicity, honesty, and purity, and let its beauty speak for itself. Be creative in your preparation, but strive to bring out, not camouflage, the product's essential nature.

The inspiration for this particular method of preparation comes from my dad, who insisted on grilling steaks so they were burned on the outside and raw on the inside. My sister and I would always tell him that it was both too burned and too raw, but he would say that was the way meat should be cooked. He refused to cook steaks any other way, so we eventually got to like them. Tuna cooked by this method has a texture very similar to rare steak, and much like my sister and me, many of our customers find that they like this preparation despite their initial skepticism. Our serving staff always explains how we prepare the tuna, as well as the fact that it is only because of its high quality that

The "sushi-quality" tuna used here is somewhat difficult to find because what you are looking for is absolute freshness. To test for this, ask your fishmonger if you can smell the tuna. If it smells like fish, don't even consider using it here. This does not mean that the fish is not fine to eat when cooked, but when eating fish rare to raw, the taste of the fish itself comes through much more clearly. Just as an illustration, Japanese restaurants pay as much as twice the amount that other restaurants pay for fish in order to receive the quality that is necessary for serving it raw.

The tuna (for example, an 8-ounce steak) has to be cut very thick, about 3 inches, so it resembles a filet mignon. To get the proper cut, it is essential to enlist the aid of your fishmonger. The thick cut ensures that, although the fish is cooked very hard over very high heat so it is seared/charred on the outside, it will remain raw on the inside.

The inspiration for serving tuna with soy, wasabi, and pickled ginger comes from Japanese sashimi with its traditional accompaniments. These ingredients might be hard to find, but if you have a Japanese restaurant in your area, call it and ask where you can find pickled ginger (*gari*) and green Japanese horseradish (wasabi) which usually comes in powder form to be mixed with water.

we can do this, and encourages people to try it this way. If it is not to their liking, it can be very easily returned to the grill to be cooked more completely. But we are always pleased to see how many people try it, and how many tunas don't make the return trip to the grill. So even if you're not sure about this method, try it! If you don't like it, just toss it back on the grill.

When I serve this, I put the soy in a little dish along with the wasabi on an orange wedge, and serve the ginger on the side. Japanese like to mix the wasabi together with the soy, and they use the ginger to clean the taste buds. ◆ *Serves 4 as a main course*

SERVING SUGGESTIONS: Grilled Squid Pasta with Roasted Red Pepper and Basil (page 112) would get this unique seafood dinner off to a creative start. The tuna is the star of the main course, so don't serve anything to compete with it. Use simple side dishes like Chilled Spinach with Soy and Ginger (page 287), Grilled Eggplant with Olive Oil, Parsley, and Capers (page 298), and plain white rice.

RAW FISH SAFETY

There has been a lot of talk lately about the safety of eating fish, and this is certainly an important question to take into account before eating raw or partially cooked fish. The concern centers on a parasite that may exist in certain fish—including Pacific salmon, striped bass, and Atlantic cod—in their raw state, and that dies when the fish are cooked past 160°F. The disease that results from ingesting this parasite is called anisakiasis.

This parasite can be detected with the naked eye if the fish is properly inspected. Many fishmongers are not on guard for the parasite, since they assume their customers will cook the fish through. For Japanese fishmongers, however, who sell a lot of fish that is eaten raw, searching for the parasite and discarding fish that contain it is standard procedure. My advice is that you not eat fish raw or partially raw unless it has been purchased from a fishmonger accustomed to serving the raw-fish–eating public.

Tuna Sashimi with Arugula, Pickled Ginger, and Soy-Wasabi Dip

◆◆◆◆◆◆◆◆◆◆◆◆◆◆◆◆◆◆◆◆◆◆◆◆◆◆◆◆◆◆◆◆◆◆◆◆◆◆

1 pound sushi-quality tuna
(page 193)
1 pound arugula, separated,
washed, and dried
½ cup (4 ounces) pickled ginger
(see Pantry, page 370)
1 cup soy sauce
4 tablespoons wasabi, mixed
with water to consistency of
wet sand (see Pantry, page
371)

Pickled ginger for garnish

1. Cut the tuna into ½-ounce pieces. Place each piece of tuna on a leaf of arugula, and add a tiny bit of wasabi and a slice of pickled ginger.

2. Roll up the arugula leaf tightly and pin it together with a toothpick.

3. Add the remaining wasabi to the soy sauce and mix well. Serve this mixture as a dipping sauce, and use the remaining pickled ginger as garnish.

This recipe is especially good if you're having a party and want to pass hors d'oeuvres. The key to this one is the quality of the fish. Its freshness must be impeccable. If his fish is really good, ask your local sushi chef what fishmonger he uses, and go get your tuna there (see the tuna discussion on page 193).

Lay an arugula leaf out, then place a small piece of tuna on it, then ginger and a touch of wasabi. Now roll it up and "pick" it. Serve it with two soy sauces for dipping, one with wasabi and one without. I find that the sharpness of arugula, which I think is similar to a Japanese green called *shiso*, mixes well with the texture of the tuna. ◆ *Serves 8 as an appetizer*

SERVING SUGGESTIONS: Serve this as a starter before Grilled Andouille Sausage and Yam Salad (page 305) and Marinated Feta with Roasted Red Peppers, Black Olives, and Thyme (page 293).

Grilled Poussin with Grilled Leeks, Garlic, and Rosemary

❖◆❖◆❖◆❖◆❖◆❖◆❖◆❖◆❖◆❖◆❖◆❖◆❖◆❖◆❖◆❖◆❖

2 tablespoons minced garlic
2 tablespoons fresh rosemary
4 tablespoons olive oil
Salt and freshly cracked black
  pepper to taste
4 poussins, butterflied (see the
  diagram)

For the leeks

3 leeks, white part only,
  thoroughly washed and
  halved lengthwise
3 tablespoons extra virgin olive
  oil
2 tablespoons balsamic vinegar
Salt and freshly cracked black
  pepper to taste

1. In a small bowl, mix the garlic, rosemary, olive oil, and salt and pepper to taste until well combined. Rub this mixture on the poussins, inside and out.

2. Place the poussins on the grill skin-side down over medium-low heat, and cook for 15 minutes. The skin should be brown and crispy.

3. Turn the poussins over and cook an additional 10 minutes. To see if they are properly cooked, cut into a joint and check the color. It should be fully opaque with no redness.

Poussins are baby chickens, each of which serves one person nicely. They make a beautiful presentation and are easier to grill than regular-sized chickens because they take less time and are therefore less likely to burn. This is basically chicken grilled with garlic and rosemary. But eat a bit of the grilled leek with each bite of chicken, and try a touch of balsamic vinegar on the leek for a subtle combination. ◆ *Serves 4 as a main course*

SERVING SUGGESTIONS: Serve this with Grilled Sweet Potatoes with Molasses Glaze (page 304) and Celeriac and Fennel Slaw (page 81).

4. Meanwhile, place the leeks on the grill cut-side down. Grill them 3 to 4 minutes per side, remove them from the fire, and place them in a medium bowl. Add the olive oil and vinegar, and toss well. Season with salt and pepper to taste, and serve alongside the poussins.

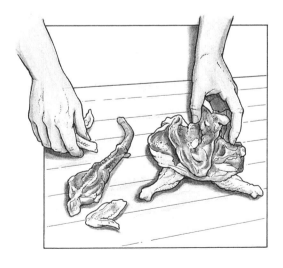

Grilled Duck Breast with Kumquat-Sugarcane-Basil Glaze

◆ ◆

10 kumquats, quartered
1 5-inch length of sugarcane, peeled and julienned
1 cup white vinegar
2 cups fresh orange juice
4 tablespoons soy sauce
4 tablespoons lemon juice (about 1 lemon)
Salt and freshly cracked pepper to taste (white is best if you have it)
¼ cup chopped fresh basil

6 duck breasts from 3- to 5-pound ducks, with the wing joints and breastbones attached (freeze the legs from these ducks to make Duck Barbecue [page 266])
Salt and freshly cracked white pepper to taste (white is best if you have it)

For the glaze

1. Place the quartered kumquats, sugarcane, and vinegar in a sauté pan over low heat. Cook this until reduced by two thirds, about 10 minutes. You should have about ⅔ cup left.

2. Add the orange juice and soy sauce, and continue to cook the mixture until reduced by a half, 10 to 15 minutes. The glaze should coat the back of a wooden spoon.

Duck à l'orange was so ingrained into my taste as a child that I find it difficult to use duck without something orange-like such as tangerines or, in this case, kumquats. The sweetness of the sugarcane offsets the tartness of the kumquats in the sauce, and the experience is further enhanced by the interesting textures of both these ingredients. This has a quasi-tropical feel, even though I don't think ducks fly that far south. Leave the breastbone on during grilling to protect the meat, prevent shrinkage, and preserve the juices. Allow the breast to repose after cooking, and then remove the bone. ◆ *Serves 4 as a main course*

SERVING SUGGESTIONS: For a quixotic, exotic dinner, start with Sake-Marinated Grilled Frogs' Legs with Japanese-Flavored Barbecue Sauce (page 188), and follow with this dish accompanied by Rice Salad with Wasabi-Miso Dressing (page 315) and Sweet Potato Hash Browns with Bacon and Onions (page 300).

3. Remove the glaze from the heat and stir in the lemon juice, salt and pepper to taste, and basil.

To grill the duck

4. Rub the breasts well with salt and pepper. Place each one, fat-side down, on the grill over a very low fire, and cook for about 6 minutes per side. Patience and a low fire are essential here. This dish has a high potential for developing the "burned duck from hell" syndrome. If flare-ups do occur because of fat dropping into the fire, move the breasts so that they are not directly over the flames. You want them to cook slowly, allowing the fat to drip off at an even pace and giving the skin time to get a bit crisp, although you will still have a thin layer of fat and the skin will not become very crispy. The fat here acts much like the fat on a steak; it both protects and flavors the meat.

5. When the duck breasts are nicely browned and as firm to the touch as the heel of your hand (this is for medium-rare), turn them bone-side down and cook them an additional 5 to 7 minutes. Since most of the fat should be gone, there is not as much danger of flare-ups at this point.

6. Remove the breasts from the grill, cool for 10 minutes, and with a small knife remove the breast-bones, leaving the first wing joints. Slice the boned breasts thinly on the bias.

    Pour the glaze over the slices of breast.

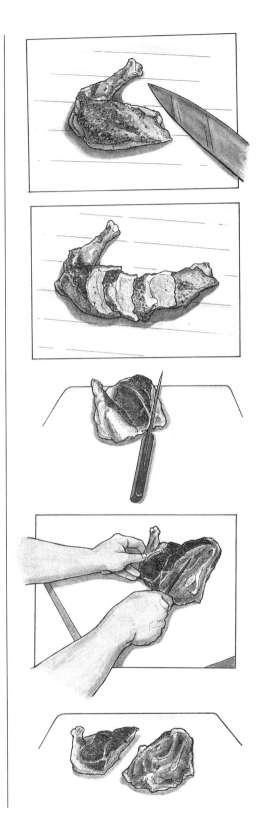

Grilled Marinated Quail

MED-HIGH

6 quail
1 tablespoon minced garlic
1 tablespoon fresh rosemary
   leaves
Salt and freshly cracked black
   pepper to taste
4 tablespoons olive oil
4 tablespoons red wine vinegar

2 lemons, cut into wedges, for
   garnish
4 tablespoons chopped parsley
3 tablespoons capers

1. Butterfly the quail (see diagram).

2. Rub the butterflied quail with the garlic, rosemary, and salt and pepper to taste, and place them skin-side down in a shallow pan.

3. Pour the oil and vinegar over the quail, and let stand for 3 to 4 hours.

4. Remove the quail from the pan, and grill them over medium-high heat for 6 to 8 minutes per side. They should be cooked through, but pinkish in appearance.

5. Serve the quail on a platter garnished with lemon wedges and sprinkled with parsley and capers.

I like food that I can eat with my hands, food that has a lot of bones in it, that requires a lot of lip smacking to eat properly. A knife and fork simply do not do justice to this dish. I'd serve it plain with some hunks of bread, lemons for squeezing, and extra virgin olive oil for drizzling. ◆ *Serves 6 as an appetizer*

SERVING SUGGESTIONS: Serve this with Grilled Expensive Mushrooms on Texas Toast (page 179) as an appetizer, and accompany it with Grilled Sweet Potatoes with Molasses Glaze (page 304) and a relish or sauce such as Tangerine-Tamarind Sauce (page 242), Black Olive and Citrus Relish (page 226), or my personal favorite, Raisin-Ginger Chutney (page 217).

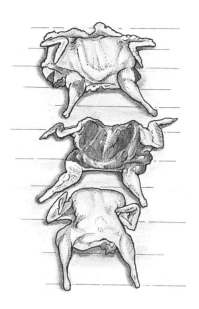

Lizzie's Totally Awesome Rosemary-Grilled Rabbit with Cumberland Sauce

◆ ◆

2 4-pound whole rabbits
Fresh rosemary from 2 6-inch
   stems
1 tablespoon minced garlic
Salt and freshly cracked black
   pepper to taste

1. Rub the rabbits with the rosemary, garlic, and salt and pepper to taste.

2. Place the rabbits on the grill over low heat and cover.

3. Cook about 15 to 20 minutes per side, until the rabbit meat is opaque throughout. It will look like done chicken.

4. Serve with Cumberland Sauce for dipping.

Rabbit is some serious good eating when grilled. Don't bother to break out the silverware for this one, because the many bones in the rabbit mean you have to use your hands to really do it justice.

I'd use Cumberland Sauce for dipping. Escoffier recommended this classic sauce for cold game, and its sweetness certainly goes well with the slightly gamy taste of the rabbit.

This dish was named after my niece's reaction when she first tasted it. ◆ *Serves 6 as a main course*

SERVING SUGGESTIONS: I suggest Sweet Potato Hash Browns with Bacon and Onions (page 300) and Boiled Collard Greens with Salt Pork (page 292) for an awesome grilled dinner.

Cumberland Sauce

✦ ✦

¼ cup currant jelly
¼ cup port wine
1 tablespoon chopped shallots
½ teaspoon grated orange rind
½ teaspoon grated lemon rind
Juice of 1 orange
2 tablespoons lime juice (about
   1 lime)
2 dashes of Tabasco sauce

About 1½ cups

1. In a saucepan, combine the jelly, port wine, shallot, and orange and lemon rind, and bring to a simmer.

2. Simmer 2 minutes, then remove from the heat.

3. Add the orange and lime juice and Tabasco and mix well. Allow the sauce to cool to room temperature before serving. Keeps up to 2 weeks, covered, in the refrigerator.

Grilled Sweetbreads with Smithfield Ham and Parsley-Caper Dipping Sauce

MED-HIGH

◆◆◆

For the dipping sauce

8 tablespoons extra virgin olive
   oil
3 tablespoons capers
1 tablespoon minced garlic
4 tablespoons chopped parsley
4 tablespoons balsamic vinegar
2 tablespoons lemon juice
   (about ½ lemon)
Salt and freshly cracked black
   pepper to taste

1 pound very fresh sweetbreads
4 tablespoons white vinegar
Salt and freshly cracked black
   pepper to taste
1 pound Smithfield ham, thinly
   sliced (you may substitute
   prosciutto)

1. Combine all the dipping sauce ingredients, mix well, and set aside in the refrigerator.

2. Rinse the sweetbreads well and place them in a large saucepan with water to cover. Add the vinegar and salt and pepper to taste, and bring to a boil. Simmer for 12 to 15 minutes until the sweetbreads are firm to the touch; they should feel like the base of your

This is a far cry from the usual subtle preparations for sweetbreads, since it calls for the sweetbreads to be grilled and coupled with salty, very distinctive Smithfield ham and flavorful parsley-caper sauce. This is a very strong preparation, but it works well and the flavor of the sweetbreads still comes through. If you have never had grilled sweetbreads, this is an interesting way of getting acquainted.

I serve these skewered with toothpicks on a platter like a new wave rumaki (chicken livers wrapped in bacon), with a bowl of the dipping sauce in the middle. ◆ *Serves 6 to 8 as an appetizer*

SERVING SUGGESTIONS: Serve this with Grilled Pompano with Lime and Olive Oil (page 95) or Red Snapper Fiesta al Carbón con Dos Salsas (page 96).

thumb when you press your finger against it.

3. Remove the sweetbreads from the water and allow them to cool.

4. When the sweetbreads are cool, clean them by gently prying the pieces from the whole and washing well. (They should separate easily into bite-size, uniform white nuggets.)

5. Skewer the sweetbreads and season them with salt and pepper to taste.

6. Over a medium-high fire, grill the sweetbreads until golden brown, about 3 to 4 minutes per side. Remove them from the grill and set aside.

7. While the sweetbreads are on the grill, cut the ham slices into strips as wide as strips of bacon but approximately half as long.

8. Remove the sweetbreads from the grill, place each sweetbread nugget at the bottom of a strip of ham, firmly roll it up in the ham, and fasten with a toothpick. Serve immediately accompanied by the dipping sauce.

SWEETBREADS

Sweetbreads are the thymus glands of calves, lambs, and kids, and in fact exist only in the young animal. Very high in protein, these glands are extremely perishable. They can be bought fresh or frozen, but either way they should be soaked in cold water for two to three hours before cooking. Fresh ones should be used the day they are bought, and frozen ones as soon as they have thawed. The mellow texture and subtle flavor of sweetbreads are enhanced by a slight smoky sear.

Grilled Sweetbreads with Wilted Southern Greens, Slab Bacon, and Balsamic Vinegar

◆ ◆

1 pound very fresh sweetbreads
1 gallon cold water
1 cup white vinegar
2 tablespoons salt
Salt and freshly cracked black
   pepper to taste
12 ounces slab bacon
2 pounds mixed greens (any
   combination of collards, kale,
   mustard greens, turnip greens,
   beet greens, dandelions),
   separated, washed, and dried
3 tablespoons balsamic vinegar
Pinch of sugar

1. Rinse the sweetbreads thoroughly and place them in a large pot with the water, vinegar, and 2 tablespoons of salt.

2. Bring the sweetbreads to a boil over high heat, and simmer for 15 minutes.

3. Turn the heat off and let the sweetbreads stand in the liquid for 5 minutes. Remove the pot from the stove, drain the sweetbreads thoroughly, and cool them in the refrigerator. When they are com-

One of the really rewarding moments in cooking is having a customer try something that previously he has always avoided, rave about it, and have it become a favorite dish—kind of like green eggs and ham. Sweetbreads provide a perfect opportunity for this kind of experience, since most people think of them in the same category as brains or Rocky Mountain oysters.

Although traditionally sweetbreads are sautéed and served in a heavy, rich cream sauce, in this dish they are grilled. The slight searing and caramelization of the sweetbreads during grilling is complemented by the balsamic vinegar which is aged in charred barrels; the greens provide a strong background for the fairly subtle sweetbreads.

Again, this is a great dish for people who have been curious about sweetbreads but reluctant to try them. And just like Sam I Am with His Green Eggs and Ham, if you can convince unbelievers to try these, they will be eternally grateful and ever after trust you enough to eat anything else you say is good.
◆ *Serves 4 as an appetizer*

pletely cool, separate them into nuggets with your fingers, and thread the nuggets on skewers. Season with salt and pepper to taste.

4. Cut the slab bacon into 12 large chunks. Cook them over low heat until crispy, then remove them and reserve, leaving the fat in the pan.

5. Grill the sweetbreads over medium-high heat until they are golden brown, about 5 to 7 minutes.

6. Turn the heat under the bacon fat to medium-high. When the fat is hot, add the greens and mix thoroughly until wilted. Add the sweetbreads and toss thoroughly.

7. Turn the heat off. Add the reserved bacon, balsamic vinegar, sugar, and salt and pepper to taste, and toss thoroughly.

8. Divide among four appetizer plates and serve at once.

SERVING SUGGESTIONS: Follow this with a light grilled fish such as Grilled Pompano with Lemon and Olive Oil (page 95), or serve it with a hot soup such as Caribbean-Style Grilled Seafood Soup (page 122) or Clam Posole (page 36).

Grilled Venison Loin with Bourbon Peaches

MED-LOW

1 2¼-pound venison loin, cut into 2 pieces
Salt and freshly cracked black pepper to taste

1. Season the venison steaks with salt and pepper to taste on both sides, and grill them over a medium-hot fire for 5 to 6 minutes per side, until well seared. Remove and allow them to rest for 5 minutes, then slice them thinly. If you find them too rare, put the slices back on the grill for a minute.

The loin is part of the deer that receives little exercise, and thus is a very tender and not overly gamy-tasting cut of meat. This dish is a good one for introducing someone to venison. When properly cooked, the loin bears a strong taste resemblance to fine aged beef. As opposed to most other cuts of venison, which require long periods of cooking to tenderize the meat, the loin is at its best when cooked quickly and served rare. Sounds like you might want to grill it, doesn't it?

I wouldn't want to serve any sauce with this; it should be enjoyed for its subtle, gamy richness. Slightly tart, sweet pickled peaches make a wonderful accompaniment. You might want to pickle the peaches during the summer, then serve them with the venison in the late fall, as it is more seasonally appropriate. ◆ *Serves 5 as a main course*

SERVING SUGGESTIONS: I recommend trying Sweet Potato Hash Browns with Bacon and Onions (page 300) and plain steamed green beans or Your Basic Grilled Corn (page 317) as side dishes with this.

When Leaves Are Falling—An Autumn Dinner

◆◆◆◆◆◆◆◆◆◆◆◆◆◆◆◆◆◆

Grilled Chorizo Soup with Kale
and Sweet Potatoes
Page 31

Grilled Venison Loin with
Bourbon Peaches
Page 208

Sweet Potato Hash Browns
with Bacon and Onions
Page 300

Grandma Wetzler's
Sweet-and-Sour Wilted Chicory
Page 285

Pumpkin Spice Cake
with Lemon-Orange Sauce
Page 332

Bourbon Peaches

◆ ◆

1 cup sugar
1½ cups water
1 cup cider vinegar
8 small peaches, quartered and
    pitted
10 cloves
½ cup bourbon
4 fresh mint sprigs

1. Combine the sugar, water, and vinegar in a saucepan, and bring to a boil, stirring until the sugar dissolves.

2. Add the peaches and cloves, simmer for 5 minutes, then remove from the heat.

3. Allow this to cool to room temperature, then pour it into a quart jar. Add the bourbon and mint, cover tightly, and refrigerate for at least 1 week. Will keep for up to 6 weeks covered airtight and refrigerated.

Sambals, Blatjangs, and Salsas

Classical cooking revolves around the "mother sauce" system. This means that a sauce is intimately connected to the item with which it is served, since the sauce is often based on a by-product of the item's cooking. Grilling does not have any by-products; it creates no natural *jus* or any equivalent. Therefore you have to look elsewhere for accompaniments.

The recipes in this chapter are not exactly condiments, and not quite side dishes. They are the "sauces" of grilled foods.

Every equatorial or hot-weather culture has some version of these accompaniments. In different countries they go by different names: Sambals, blatjangs, chutneys, salsas, ketchups, and atjars all fall into this category, as do the relishes, chowchows, and piccalillis of the American South. Some are sweet, some are sour, some are hot, and others are spicy.

What all these accompaniments have in common is that they are highly flavored, with strong, distinct tastes. This quality makes them perfect complements to the dominating character of grilled food. This combination is similar to the classic relationship between curries and the many small side dishes served with them. It is strength against strength, and neither overpowers the other.

While these preparations serve a function similar to the sauces of classical cuisine, the fact that they are not integrally connected with any particular dish means that you can mix and match them to suit your fancy. Some may be more suited to seafood and others to red meat, and if that is the case I have indicated this in the recipe. But in general, I encourage you to experiment and find out which combinations suit your taste buds.

Banana–Green Mango Chutney

1 large yellow onion, diced small
2 tablespoons peanut oil
1 green (unripe) mango, peeled
   and diced small
1 cup white vinegar
1 cup fresh orange juice
1 pound very ripe bananas,
   sliced ¼ inch thick
1 tablespoon grated fresh ginger
½ cup raisins
½ cup packed dark brown sugar
1 tablespoon finely chopped
   fresh serrano *or* jalapeño chile
   peppers (you may substitute
   ¾ tablespoon red pepper flakes)
Salt and freshly cracked black
   pepper to taste
1 teaspoon allspice

1. Sauté the onion in the oil until clear, 4 to 5 minutes.

2. Add the mango and cook 2 minutes over medium heat.

3. Add the vinegar and orange juice, bring to a simmer, and simmer for 10 minutes.

4. Add all the remaining ingredients and bring the mixture back to a simmer.

5. As soon as a simmer is reached, remove the mixture from the heat, cool to room temperature, and serve. This will keep, covered and refrigerated, for up to 2 weeks.

Your basic chutney. The sweetish taste of this condiment delivers an excellent balance to very hot dishes. ◆ *About 5 cups*

SERVING SUGGESTIONS: Serve this with Grilled Pork Skewers with Green Tomatoes and Your Secret Finishing Sauce (page 160) or Grilled West Indies Spice-Rubbed Chicken Breast with Grilled Banana (page 165).

Pear-Cranberry Chutney

◆ ◆

1 large yellow onion, diced small
2 tablespoons vegetable oil
4 firm pears of any kind, peeled,
    cored, and diced small
Juice of 2 oranges
¼ cup fresh cranberries
A pinch each of cinnamon,
    powdered ginger, and allspice

1. In a saucepot, sauté the onion in the oil over medium heat until clear, about 4 minutes.

2. Add the diced pear and orange juice. Bring to a simmer, and add the cranberries and spices. Stirring frequently, simmer until the cranberries start to burst, then remove the mixture from the heat. It should have the consistency of wet sand. Keeps, covered and refrigerated, up to 2 weeks.

This chutney has a Day-Glo translucency that is almost psychedelic, an interesting consistency, and goes well with grilled ham, turkey, or chicken. Perfect for an unusual holiday condiment.
◆ *About 2 cups*

Plum-Nectarine Chutney

4 tablespoons butter
1 small onion, sliced
3 tablespoons minced fresh
  ginger
8 tablespoons brown sugar
4 plums, pitted and cut in
  eighths
4 nectarines, pitted and cut in
  eighths
4 tablespoons golden raisins
4 tablespoons cider vinegar
½ cup orange juice
¼ teaspoon allspice
½ teaspoon nutmeg
Salt and freshly cracked black
  pepper to taste

A midsummer's chutney that when made with peak ripe fruit is a personal favorite with breakfast. And when the fruit is underripe, it creates more textural difference and the sour flavor comes in a bit clearer. ◆ *About 5 cups*

1. In a heavy saucepan, melt the butter over low heat. Add the onion slices and ginger, and cook for 10 minutes, stirring occasionally, until the onion slices are golden.

2. Add the brown sugar and stir until fully dissolved.

3. Add the plums and nectarines, raisins, vinegar, orange juice, spices, and salt and pepper to taste. Simmer over low heat, stirring constantly, for 10 minutes, until the mixture is thick. Keep a close watch on this, as it will burn easily. Will keep up to 2 weeks, covered, in the refrigerator.

Coconut and Lemongrass Chutney

◆◆◆

1 cup fresh grated coconut
4 tablespoons minced fresh
  lemongrass (see Pantry, page
  372) *or* 1 tablespoon dried
2 tablespoons minced fresh
  ginger
¼ cup roasted, unsalted peanuts
8 tablespoons lime juice (about
  4 limes)
4 tablespoons honey
2 tablespoons chopped fresh
  mint
2 tablespoons chopped cilantro
1 tablespoon fresh red *or* green
  hot chile pepper, minced

1. Grate the coconut into a me-dium-sized bowl. Add the lemon-grass and ginger, and mix.

2. Chop the peanuts coarsely and add to the mixture. Add the lime juice and honey, and mix lightly.

3. Toss in the mint, cilantro, and hot chile, and stir a couple of times to integrate them. Keeps, covered and refrigerated, 4 days.

This collection of Southeast Asian ingredients and flavors has a wonderful variety of textures. It has the unique ability to be served with subtle fish dishes and not overpower them, even though it is superspicy. ◆ *About 2 cups*

SERVING SUGGESTIONS: This is particularly good with rather heavy fish. Try it with a plain grilled kingfish or tuna.

Raisin-Ginger Chutney

1 medium yellow onion, diced
   small
2 tablespoons peanut oil
½ pound raisins
2 tablespoons minced fresh
   ginger
2 teaspoons minced garlic
1½ teaspoons red pepper flakes
1½ teaspoons curry powder
1½ teaspoons brown sugar
½ cup orange juice
2 tablespoons cider vinegar
Salt and freshly cracked black
   pepper to taste

This very potent condiment is particularly outstanding with grilled country ham. A friend of mine who loves spicy food has taken to using this as a spread on pita bread, which he claims makes a great lunch. ◆ *About 2 cups*

1. In a sauté pan, sauté the diced onion in the peanut oil over moderate heat until clear, 5 to 7 minutes.

2. Add the raisins, ginger, garlic, red pepper flakes, and curry powder, and cook over low to medium heat, stirring frequently, for 4 minutes.

3. Add the brown sugar and orange juice, and continue to cook over low heat for 10 minutes.

4. Add the vinegar and salt and pepper to taste, and bring to a boil. Lower the heat and simmer for 5 minutes.

5. Remove from the heat and cool to room temperature before serving. Keeps, in a closed container and refrigerated, up to 5 weeks.

Georgia Peach Chutney

◆ ◆

2 large yellow onions, diced small

1 to 2 tablespoons vegetable oil

4 peaches, each pitted and sliced into 16 slices

4 tablespoons packed brown sugar

4 tablespoons white sugar

1 tablespoon molasses

¼ cup raisins

1 teaspoon salt

½ teaspoon freshly cracked pepper (white is best if you have it)

¼ teaspoon allspice

½ cup white vinegar

2 tablespoons fresh lemon juice (about ½ lemon)

Here's another example of that classic tropical combination of sweet fruit and acid. The sweetness in this chutney comes from the American South in the form of peaches and molasses, and combining them with vinegar and lemon juice after cooking adds an extra jolt of tartness. ◆ *About 3 cups*

SERVING SUGGESTIONS: To finish off the Southern connection, serve this with Smithfield Ham Hush Puppies with Fresh Corn (page 43). It also goes well with Grilled Pork Tenderloin with Roasted Corn–Bacon Relish (page 163) or Outdoor Pork Baby Back Ribs (page 268).

1. In a saucepot over medium heat, sauté the onion in the oil until transparent, about 5 to 7 minutes.

2. Add the peach slices, stir, and cook for 4 minutes.

3. Add all the remaining ingredients except ¼ cup of the vinegar and the lemon juice. Simmer uncovered over low heat for 1 hour, stirring occasionally and being very careful not to burn the mixture. If necessary, add a small amount of water to prevent the mixture from burning.

4. Remove the mixture from the heat, add the lemon juice and the other ¼ cup of vinegar, and mix thoroughly. The chutney will have

the texture of thick, chunky applesauce—it will be thinner than you expect, if you are used to Major Grey's.

5. Serve the chutney at room temperature. It will keep, tightly covered and refrigerated, for about 6 weeks.

Leesburg Chowchow

◆ ◆

8 to 10 medium green tomatoes
12 cucumbers
1 medium head green cabbage
6 large yellow onions
2 cups kosher salt
6 cups water
6 cups white vinegar
8 cups cider vinegar
1 cup prepared horseradish
2 tablespoons celery seed
1 cup mustard seeds
4 tablespoons freshly ground
   black pepper
4 tablespoons turmeric
4 tablespoons cinnamon

Another great use for those green tomatoes left in your garden at the end of the summer. This recipe was inspired by an old cookbook written by a Virginia housewife. Like most pickling recipes, it makes a large quantity. This makes sense, since the pickling process takes 3 days. Fortunately it stores very well and is an excellent condiment at any time of the year. It is particularly good with barbecue. Try it with Barbecued Whole Chicken (page 263), Duck Barbecue (page 266), or The Only Real Barbecue Sandwich (page 271). ◆ *About 1½ gallons*

1. Cut the tomatoes into eighths. Peel and deseed the cucumbers, and dice the cucumbers, cabbage, and onions into 1-inch cubes.

2. In a large bowl, toss the tomato, cucumber, cabbage, and onion with the 2 cups of kosher salt. Pack the mixture into a container with a weight on top to make sure the vegetables stay submerged. Refrigerate, covered, for 24 hours.

3. After 24 hours, rinse all the ingredients in a colander, return
them to the container, and cover
them with a mixture of equal parts
water and white vinegar. Let them
soak for 24 hours, covered and
weighted. After 24 hours, rinse the
mixture again.

4. In a large stockpot, heat the cider vinegar until it just begins to
boil. Remove it from the heat and
add the horseradish, celery seed,
mustard seeds, pepper, turmeric,
and cinnamon. Mix well and pour
this over the vegetable mixture.

5. Allow everything to marinate
for another 24-hour period. You
now have an official pickle. It will
keep, covered and refrigerated, for
the rest of your life, or you can
can it and put it on the shelf.

Corn and Watermelon Rind Piccalilli

◆ ◆

1 cup sweet corn kernels, cut from the cob (about 1½ ears of corn)
1 cup cider vinegar
½ cup sugar
1 teaspoon ground cumin
1 teaspoon chili powder
Salt and freshly cracked black pepper to taste
½ red bell pepper, seeded and diced small
½ green bell pepper, seeded and diced small
½ large red onion, diced small
2 cups Watermelon Rind Pickles (recipe follows)

1. Blanch the corn in boiling water for 1 minute. Drain it and reserve.

2. Combine the vinegar, sugar, cumin, chili powder, and salt and pepper to taste in a saucepan, and bring to a boil. Add the red and green pepper and onion, and boil for 10 minutes.

3. Remove the mixture from the heat, allow it to cool to room temperature, and add the corn and cubes of watermelon pickle. Will keep up to 4 weeks covered and refrigerated.

According to my understanding, piccalilli is very similar to chowchow, which is a pickled vegetable relish with green tomatoes, cabbage, and peppers. Here I work a slight change by combining fresh corn with that old Southern standard, watermelon rind pickles, which you need to make one week before proceeding with the piccalilli. It's sweet and tart with a semicrunchy consistency. This is a dish for late summer, when watermelon and fresh corn are at their best. ◆ *About 1 quart*

SERVING SUGGESTIONS: Serve this as an accompaniment to Barbecued Whole Chicken (page 263) or Grilled Turkey Steaks with White Grape–Cranberry Relish (page 174). You might want to add Deep-Fried Cheddar Grits (page 311) as a side dish, too.

Watermelon Rind Pickles

2 cups white part of melon rind
  (no green, no red), cut into
  ½-inch cubes
2 tablespoons kosher salt
1 cup sugar
½ cup cider vinegar
5 whole cloves

About 2 cups

1. Rub the cubes of rind with salt, and allow them to sit in the refrigerator overnight.

2. Rinse the rind cubes well, and place them in a saucepan with water to cover. Bring to a boil and boil for 10 minutes. Remove them from heat, drain, and set aside.

3. In the same saucepan, combine the sugar, vinegar, and cloves, and bring to a boil. Add the reserved rind cubes, and boil again for 10 minutes.

4. Remove the mixture from the heat and allow it to cool to room temperature, then pour it into a jar and cover tightly. Allow it to stand in the refrigerator for 1 week before using. The pickles will keep, covered and refrigerated, for up to 6 weeks.

Smoked Apple-Chile Relish

4 ancho chile peppers
4 tablespoons white vinegar
12 Granny Smith apples
2 large yellow onions
4 tablespoons vegetable oil
4 tablespoons chili powder
2 tablespoons ground cumin
12 orange segments
2 tablespoons lemon juice
   (about ½ lemon)
Salt and freshly cracked black
   pepper to taste
1 tablespoon chopped fresh
   oregano

The combination of the smoky flavor and spicy chile peppers is a natural, and somehow apples seem to fit right in— maybe it's because I associate burning leaves with apple season. This relish is perfect with pork, and it is a nice accompaniment to the Corn Bread Salad with Lime Juice and Cilantro (page 312). ♦ *About 4 cups*

1. Soak the ancho chile peppers in hot water for 12 hours to reconstitute them.

2. In a food processor or blender, purée the chile peppers with the vinegar until completely puréed. Press the purée through a medium strainer. Discard the remaining skins, and reserve the purée.

3. Core and quarter the apples, leaving the skins on. Peel the onions and slice them into ½-inch slices. Lightly coat the apple and onion slices with the oil, and sprinkle them with 2 tablespoons each of the chili powder and cumin.

4. In a covered grill, build a small fire as far over to one side as possible. Wait for all of the fuel to be completely engulfed in flame.

5. Place the apple and onion slices on the grill on the side opposite the fire, cover the grill, and let it smoke for about 20 minutes. Check the tenderness of the apples: They should be slightly mushy on the outer surface, but still quite firm overall. Remove the apple slices from the heat and continue to smoke the onion slices with the cover on until cooked through, about 30 minutes in all.

6. Coarsely chop the apple and onion slices, and place them in a mixing bowl. Toss them with the remaining chili powder, orange segments, lemon juice, and the chile purée. Season with salt and pepper to taste and oregano. Will keep up to 4 days covered and refrigerated.

Apricot Blatjang

◆◆◆◆◆◆◆◆◆◆◆◆◆◆◆◆◆◆◆◆◆◆◆◆◆◆◆◆◆◆◆◆◆◆◆◆

1 pound dried apricots
1 small yellow onion, diced small
¼ pound golden raisins
½ cup plus 4 tablespoons red wine vinegar
1 tablespoon minced garlic
2 tablespoons grated fresh ginger
1 teaspoon cayenne
¼ cup blanched almonds, toasted
Salt to taste

1. In a saucepan, combine the apricots, onion, raisins, and ½ cup of the vinegar with enough water to cover.

2. Bring to a boil and simmer for 15 to 20 minutes, stirring frequently, until the mixture is the thickness of honey. Be careful not to overcook the mixture, as it will thicken as it cools. Remove the mixture from heat.

3. In a food processor or blender, combine the garlic, ginger, cayenne, almonds, and salt to taste, and purée well.

4. Add the puréed spice mixture to the apricot mixture, and mix well. Stir in the remaining 4 tablespoons of vinegar. Will keep, covered and refrigerated, up to 3 weeks.

A "blatjang" (blaht-jahng) is a South African preserve traditionally served along with pickled vegetables to balance the heat of curries. It is very similar to Indian chutney, and it shows the strong influence of the cooking of the East Indian slaves who were brought to South Africa by the Dutch. Since blatjangs are strong enough to compete with curries, they can also stand up to the strong taste of grilled foods. ◆ *About 2 cups*

SERVING SUGGESTIONS: This is good with any type of grilled satay, in particular Grilled Chicken Liver Satay with Indonesian Hot Peanut Sauce (page 78).

Black Olive and Citrus Relish

◆◆

2 oranges
2 lemons
½ cup pitted black olives,
    chopped into small pieces
1 small red onion, diced small
3 scallions, chopped
1 teaspoon ground cumin
¼ teaspoon cayenne pepper
Salt and freshly cracked black
    pepper to taste
2 tablespoons chopped parsley

1. Peel the oranges and lemons, separate them into sections, and remove the outer membranes and seeds.

2. Put the fruit into a medium-sized bowl, add all the remaining ingredients, and mix well. This will keep, covered and refrigerated, for about 4 days.

The sweet-sour taste of citrus makes a great combination with the rich, loamy taste of black olives. This relish is a variant of a North African condiment traditionally served with tagines and curries as well as with grilled meats. ◆ *About 2 cups*

SERVING SUGGESTIONS: Serve this with Grilled Chicken Breast with Fresh Herbs and Lemon (page 167), alongside Grilled Basque Wings (page 66), or as a condiment with Grilled Ham Hocks and Black-eyed Peas (page 322).

Pickled Limes with Ginger and Chiles

◆◆

10 limes, quartered
3 tablespoons kosher salt
4 tablespoons white vinegar
3 tablespoons grated fresh
   ginger
4 thinly sliced garlic cloves
5 to 6 of your favorite hot chile
   peppers, cut in half
½ cup sugar
5 to 6 fresh cilantro sprigs

1. Give the lime quarters one good squeeze, and reserve the juice for one of the many other recipes that call for it.

2. Combine the lime quarters with 2 tablespoons of the salt, mix thoroughly, and put the mixture in a tightly covered 1-quart glass (mason) jar.

3. Place the jar in a sunny window for 3 days.

4. After 3 days, mix in the remaining tablespoon of salt, replace the cover on the jar, and put the mixture in the back of your refrigerator for 4 to 6 weeks.

5. Pour the lime quarters and liquid from the jar into a saucepan, and bring to a simmer over low heat.

6. Add the vinegar, ginger, garlic, chile peppers, sugar, and cilantro. Mix well, then remove from the heat.

In the summer, when limes are plentiful and cheap, get a batch and pickle 'em. Once that's done, you can chop them up to use as part of a chutney, add them to stews and curries as a flavor enhancer, or serve them by themselves with grilled fish. ◆ *About 2 cups*

7. Cool the mixture to room temperature, then pour it back into the jar. The limes will keep, covered tightly and refrigerated, for 6 weeks.

Preserved Lemon-Honey Relish with Hot Peppers and Curry

◆◆

16 preserved lemon quarters (recipe follows)
1 red onion, diced small
1 green bell pepper, seeded and diced small
4 fresh red *or* green jalapeño chile peppers, diced small
4 tablespoons honey
½ cup red wine vinegar
8 tablespoons lemon juice (about 2 lemons)
2 tablespoons Thai-Style All-purpose Hot Mixed Curry Paste (page 255)
Salt and freshly cracked black pepper to taste

1. Dice the lemon quarters small and put them in a mixing bowl.

2. Add the onion, diced peppers, and jalapeño and mix well.

This unusual relish uses the North African preserved lemons in combination with hot peppers and the complex Thai curry paste. Plain curry can be substituted for the curry paste if necessary. ◆ *About 3 cups*

SERVING SUGGESTIONS: This relish goes well with Grilled Butterflied Leg o' Lamb (page 153) and Romaine-Feta Salad with Lemon–Olive Oil Dressing (page 286) or Basil Tabbouleh (page 313).

3. In a separate bowl, combine the honey, vinegar, lemon juice, and curry paste.

4. Combine the two mixtures and stir until well integrated. Season to taste with salt and pepper. This will keep, covered and refrigerated, for up to 1 week.

Preserved Lemons

10 lemons
4 tablespoons kosher salt
2 tablespoons freshly cracked
   black pepper

40 quarters

1. Soak the lemons in cold water to cover for 5 days, changing the water daily.

2. Drain the lemons and cut them into quarters. Sprinkle each quarter with salt and pepper, and place them in a 1-quart glass jar with screw-on or clamped-on top.

4. Place the jar in a cool place (but not the refrigerator) and leave it for 6 weeks.

5. Remove the lemon quarters from the jar and rinse them several times to remove the salt and pepper. Cut the lemon pulp from the rind and discard the pulp. Place the preserved rind in a covered container in the refrigerator. Will keep indefinitely.

Spicy Banana-Coconut Ketchup

◆◆◆

2 very ripe bananas
1 cup Indonesian Sweet Sauce
   (page 243)
⅓ cup coconut milk (see Pantry,
   page 368)
⅓ cup white vinegar
1 tablespoon minced fresh
   ginger
1 teaspoon Tabasco sauce

1. Mash or purée the bananas, then put them in a saucepan with the Indonesian Sweet Sauce. Cook over moderately high heat for 10 minutes.

2. Remove from the heat, add all the remaining ingredients, and mix until well blended. Keeps, covered and refrigerated, 1 week.

SERVING SUGGESTIONS: This sweetish, exotic ketchup goes nicely with Roasted Then Grilled Half Duck (page 175), Grilled Pork Skewers with Mango (page 158), or Simple Grilled Whole Beef Tenderloin (page 146). ◆ *About 2 cups.*

Very Aromatic Tomato-Ginger Jam

◆◆◆

1 medium yellow onion, very thinly sliced

3 tablespoons peanut oil

1 tablespoon minced garlic

2 tablespoons grated fresh ginger

2 large, ripe tomatoes, cut into small chunks

2 tablespoons sugar

2 tablespoons rice wine vinegar

1 tablespoon finely chopped scallion

1 tablespoon very finely chopped fresh lemongrass (see Pantry, page 372) *or* 1 teaspoon dried

1 tablespoon finely chopped cilantro

1 tablespoon finely chopped basil

1 tablespoon finely chopped mint

2 tablespoons lime juice (about 1 lime)

2 tablespoons lemon juice (about ½ lemon)

The main features of this jam/condiment are its strength of flavor and the potent aromatic herb combination of lemongrass, basil, cilantro, and mint, which are added at the very end of the preparation so their flavors will emerge at full strength. I have encountered these herbs together in Vietnamese as well as Thai food. I find that this jam has a unique flavor that I'd serve with just about anything grilled. ◆ *About 2 cups*

SERVING SUGGESTIONS: I might serve this as a condiment with Grilled Steamed Littlenecks Johnson (page 113), Simple Grilled Whole Beef Tenderloin (page 146), or Steamed Clams with Lemongrass and Chiles de Árbol (page 52).

1. In a large sauté pan over medium-high heat, sauté the onion slices in the peanut oil until well browned, 6 to 8 minutes. Add the garlic and ginger, and sauté 1 minute more.

2. Add the tomato and cook over low heat, stirring constantly, until the mixture is the consistency of wet sand, about 10 minutes. Be

careful that the mixture does not stick to the pan.

3. Add the sugar and vinegar, and cook, stirring constantly, for an additional 2 minutes. Again, be careful not to let the mixture stick.

4. Remove from the heat and let cool 10 to 15 minutes.

5. Add the scallion, the herbs, and the lime and lemon juice, and stir until well blended. Will keep, covered and refrigerated, 10 days to 2 weeks.

Spicy Cucumber Relish

◆ ◆

2 cucumbers
1 small red onion, diced
5 tablespoons white vinegar
4 tablespoons sugar
1 tablespoon chopped cilantro
1 teaspoon red pepper flakes
Salt and freshly cracked black
    pepper to taste

1. Wash the cucumbers well to remove the waxy deposit, cut them in half lengthwise, and slice them thin.

2. In a bowl, mix all the remaining ingredients and toss the cucumber slices with the mixture. Will keep 4 days, covered and refrigerated.

Here's another illustration of the general rule that anything used in traditional Eastern cuisine as an accompaniment to curries is also very appropriate with grilled foods. This cucumber relish appears in Thai, Indonesian, Indian, and Vietnamese cuisines, each country adding its own touch. The best one I have tasted came from a street vendor in downtown Bangkok, and here is his recipe. ◆ *About 2 cups*

SERVING SUGGESTIONS: Serve this with Spice-Rubbed Grilled Monkfish (page 90), Grilled Squid with Asian Slaw and Hoisin Barbecue Sauce (page 107), or Pasta from Hell (page 73).

Braised Garlic and Onion Jam

◆◆◆

4 tablespoons peanut oil
3 large yellow onions, very
    thinly sliced
1 large garlic bulb, braised (see
    Pantry, page 367)
2 tablespoons sugar
4 tablespoons balsamic vinegar
1 tablespoon fresh thyme
Salt and freshly cracked black
    pepper to taste

1. In a large sauté pan, heat the oil over high heat until very hot.

2. Turn the heat to medium and, being careful not to splash the oil, put in the onion and sauté, stirring constantly, until deep brown, about 8 to 10 minutes.

3. Add the garlic, sugar, and 2 tablespoons of the vinegar. Cook for 1 minute.

4. Remove from the heat, add the other 2 tablespoons of vinegar, the thyme, and salt and pepper to taste. Mix well and serve hot or cold. Keeps, covered and refrigerated, for up to 1 month.

Although this may seem an unlikely pair of ingredients for a jam, the chemical reactions accomplished during their cooking make them a fantastic duo. When the onion browns, it means the sugar in the onion has caramelized. Likewise, when the garlic is roasted or braised, it mellows and becomes slightly sweet. This is a favorite of mine for grilled steaks. It's easy, quick, and keeps for weeks. Served hot or cold, it can be used almost anyplace. ◆ *About 1 cup*

SERVING SUGGESTIONS: This is a perfect accompaniment for any grilled red meat. Try it with Simple Grilled Whole Beef Tenderloin (page 146) or Grilled Big Black-and-Blue Steak for Two (page 148).

Tomato and Peanut Salsa

1 cup roasted, unsalted peanuts
4 large, ripe, fresh tomatoes,
   diced small
1 large red onion, diced small
4 tablespoons chopped cilantro
4 tablespoons chopped parsley
1 tablespoon minced garlic
4 fresh red *or* green jalapeño
   chile peppers, diced small
4 tablespoons lime juice (about
   2 limes)
4 tablespoons olive oil
1 tablespoon sugar
Salt and freshly cracked black
   pepper to taste

This is my adaptation of a Brazilian condiment in which the peanuts show again the strong African influence on Brazilian cuisine. While it is most often used with vegetables, I actually prefer it with grilled meats, especially pork. Add a can of tomato juice and a little more hot chile pepper, and this turns into a nice salsa for chips. ◆ *About 4 cups*

1. In a blender or food processor, grind the peanuts coarsely. They should not become paste, but should have a slightly chunky, crumbly consistency.

2. Combine the peanuts with all the other ingredients in a medium bowl, and mix well. This salsa will keep, covered and refrigerated, for 3 to 4 days.

Roasted Red Pepper Coulis with Basil

•◆•

2 large yellow onions
3 tablespoons olive oil
6 roasted red bell peppers (see Pantry, page 368)
2 tablespoons braised garlic (see Pantry, page 367)
1 cup chicken stock
4 tablespoons balsamic vinegar
4 tablespoons lemon juice (about 1 lemon)
1 cup fresh basil leaves
Pinch of red pepper flakes
8 tablespoons virgin olive oil
Salt and freshly cracked black pepper to taste

This sauce is one of those accompaniments with a rich, intense flavor that can stand up to the hearty flavor that comes from grilling over wood. Excellent with any grilled seafood. ◆ *About 3 cups*

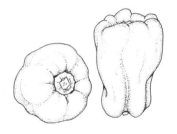

1. Peel the onions, slice them into ½-inch slices, and rub them lightly with the 3 tablespoons of olive oil.

2. Place the onion slices on a grill over a medium-hot fire. Grill them for 2 to 3 minutes per side, until golden brown. Remove them from the grill.

3. Coarsely chop the peppers, garlic, and onion.

4. Place all the ingredients except the olive oil into a food processor and purée. When everything is fully puréed, slowly add the oil, with the food processor still running. Season with salt and pepper to taste, and use the sauce hot or cold. Will keep up to 6 days, covered and refrigerated.

Chipotle-Molasses Glaze

◆◆◆

1 cup white vinegar
4 tablespoons sugar
1 cup fresh orange juice
4 tablespoons molasses
6 canned chipotles (see Pantry, page 369), puréed
4 tablespoons chopped cilantro
Salt and freshly cracked black pepper to taste
4 tablespoons lime juice (about 2 limes)

This is a combination of sweet, hot, and sour that has a distinctive flavor with a hint of smokiness. Good with game or a strong-charactered fish like bluefish or kingfish. ◆ *About 1 cup*

SERVING SUGGESTIONS: Try this with Grilled Venison Loin with Bourbon Peaches (page 208) or Lime-Marinated Grilled Kingfish with Red Onion and Mango Relish (page 91).

1. Combine the vinegar and sugar in a medium saucepan, bring to a boil, and simmer until reduced in volume by a half, about 10 minutes.

2. Add the orange juice and again simmer until reduced in volume by a half, about another 10 minutes.

3. Remove from the heat, add the molasses, chipotle, and cilantro, and stir well. Season with salt and pepper to taste, and finish by adding the lime juice and mixing well. This will keep, covered airtight and refrigerated, up to 3 weeks.

Hot Orange-Chile Glaze

2 tablespoons vegetable oil
1 medium yellow onion,
   chopped into small pieces
1 tablespoon chopped garlic
6 fresh green *or* red serrano
   chile peppers, diced small
2 tablespoons coriander seed
4 tablespoons chili powder
2 tablespoons ground cumin
Salt and freshly cracked black
   pepper to taste
1 cup orange juice
4 tablespoons molasses
1 cup vinegar
1 cup chicken stock
4 tablespoons cornstarch
4 tablespoons cold water
4 tablespoons chopped cilantro

A dandy flavor enhancer for any grilled duck or poultry dish. Try it with Grilled Chicken Breast with Fresh Herbs and Lemon (page 167), Roasted Then Grilled Half Duck (page 175), or Grilled Turkey Steaks with White Grape–Cranberry Relish (page 174). ◆ *About 3 cups*

1. In a heavy-bottomed saucepan, heat the oil until hot but not smoking. Cook the onion in the oil over medium heat until clear, 5 to 7 minutes. Add the garlic and serranos, and cook an additional 2 minutes.

2. Add the coriander seed, chili powder, cumin, salt and pepper to taste, orange juice, molasses, vinegar, and chicken stock, and bring this to a boil. Allow it to simmer for 20 minutes, stirring occasionally.

3. In a small bowl, mix the cornstarch and water together thoroughly. Slowly stir this mixture into the simmering glaze, making

sure that it is thoroughly blended in. Continue to cook, and stir for an additional 10 minutes.

4. Remove the mixture from the heat and add the cilantro. Will keep, covered and refrigerated, 1 week to 10 days.

Classic Brazilian Sauce

◆ ◆

6 fresh green *or* red serrano
   chile peppers
1 small yellow onion, diced
2 tablespoons chopped cilantro
1 tablespoon minced garlic
4 tablespoons olive oil
½ cup white vinegar
Salt and freshly cracked black
   pepper to taste

Combine all the ingredients in a food processor or blender, and purée. This sauce will keep, covered and refrigerated, for about 1 week.

In Brazil, where grilled meats are very popular, there are many versions of simple sauces served as condiments, and often 2 or 3 different sauces will be served for sampling. This is one that I like to use on steaks. The heat is supplied by the serrano but you can substitute just about any heat. ◆ *About 1 cup*

Pebre: Chilean Hot Sauce

◆ ◆

3 tablespoons extra virgin olive
   oil
1 tablespoon spicy brown
   mustard
1 tablespoon white vinegar
4 tablespoons lime juice (about
   2 limes)
1 red onion, diced small
2 scallions, diced
2 teaspoons Tabasco sauce *or*
   hot sauce of your choice
1 tablespoon minced garlic
Salt and freshly cracked black
   pepper to taste

1. Stir the oil into the mustard. Add the vinegar and lime juice, and stir well.

2. Add the red onion, scallion, Tabasco sauce, and garlic, and mix again. Season with salt and pepper to taste. This will be a rather thick sauce. Will keep, covered and refrigerated, for 4 to 6 weeks.

In Chile, the genuine term for *salsa picante*, or hot sauce, is actually *pebre*. They do a lot of grilling in Chile, and they like it hot. This is your basic all-purpose grilled condiment. ◆ *About 1 cup*

SERVING SUGGESTIONS: Serve this with Barbecued Whole Chicken (page 263), Grilled Marinated Quail (page 200), or Grilled Venison Loin with Bourbon Peaches (page 208).

Parsley Sauce

½ cup extra virgin olive oil
4 tablespoons balsamic vinegar
1 small red onion, diced
1 tablespoon minced garlic
4 tablespoons chopped parsley
2 tablespoons capers
6 tablespoons lemon juice
   (about 1½ lemons)
Salt and freshly cracked black
   pepper to taste

Put all the ingredients together in a bowl and mix well. Keeps 3 days covered and refrigerated.

This is basic sauce that, if you were living in Argentina, you might put on your fresh tomatoes from your garden or on grilled beef or pork. Of course, you can do this even if you've never been to Argentina. Just grill whatever cut of beef or pork you prefer and put this on it. Or you might try using this on pasta as you do pesto. ◆ *About 2 cups*

Spicy Oyster Sauce with Lemongrass

◆◆◆

2 cups oyster sauce (found in Asian grocery stores)
2 tablespoons minced fresh ginger
2 tablespoons minced fresh lemongrass (see Pantry, page 372) *or* 2 teaspoons dried
2 tablespoons chopped scallion
2 tablespoons sesame oil
2 tablespoons Vietnamese chili garlic paste *or* more to taste
2 cups white vinegar
Outer stalks and ends of 2 pieces of lemongrass, chopped (optional)
4 tablespoons sugar

1. In a large bowl, combine the oyster sauce, ginger, minced lemongrass, scallion, sesame oil, and chili garlic paste, and mix well. Refrigerate.

2. In a saucepan, combine the vinegar, optional chopped lemongrass, and sugar. Bring to a simmer, and simmer gently for 1 hour. You should have ½ to ⅔ cup of liquid. If there is less, add more vinegar to bring the total amount of liquid to ½ cup.

3. Strain the mixture, discard the solids, and add the liquid to the oyster sauce. Mix well. Keeps 2 weeks covered and refrigerated.

I enjoy going to ethnic markets and accumulating prepared condiments, and I always seem to have a refrigerator full of them. This is just a little Southeast Asian variation on a standard Chinese condiment. Very concentrated in flavor, it works well when brushed on grilled things a minute or so before removing them from the grill, giving a nice glaze to whatever you are grilling. If the gang that's coming tonight likes it hot, this is a good one to load up on. My heat booster of choice in this one is the prepared Vietnamese chili garlic paste described to me once by a waiter as "more exciting than Atlantic City." Or you can substitute 2 tablespoons of a mixture of: 1 tablespoon of your favorite hot chile pepper, finely chopped; 1 tablespoon minced garlic; 1 tablespoon sugar; and 1 tablespoon ketchup. ◆ *About 3 cups*

SERVING SUGGESTIONS: Serve this with red meat dishes—try Grilled Big Black-and-Blue Steak for Two (page 148), Simple Grilled Whole Beef Tenderloin (page 146), or Grilled Butterflied Leg o' Lamb (page 153).

Tangerine-Tamarind Sauce

1 cup white vinegar
½ cup sugar
Peels of 3 tangerines
1 tablespoon minced fresh
  ginger
Juice of 10 tangerines
1 tablespoon tamarind paste
  (see Pantry, page 373)

1. In a saucepan, bring the vinegar and sugar to a boil. Add the tangerine peels and ginger, and simmer until the liquid is reduced by a half, about 15 minutes. Remove from the heat, strain the liquid into a bowl, and discard the peels and ginger.

2. Return the liquid to the saucepan, add the tangerine juice and tamarind paste, bring to a simmer, and reduce by a half to a third, about 20 minutes. Remove the sauce from the heat and allow it to cool to room temperature. Keeps, covered and refrigerated, up to 2 weeks.

The tamarind is an exotic fruit indigenous to certain tropical climates. Sweet, sour, pungent, it is an excellent complement to spicy foods. I kind of fell upon this recipe, which allows the tamarind to come through in a subtle manner, when I misordered and was stuck with a full case of tangerines. I made the sauce, served it with squid and other seafood, and it has become a favorite of mine. I think you'll find that a squeeze of lime goes well with whatever you put the sauce on. ◆ *About 1½ cups*

SERVING SUGGESTIONS: Serve this on top of Grilled West Indies Spice-Rubbed Chicken Breast with Grilled Banana (page 165) or Grilled Pork Skewers with Green Mango (page 158).

Indonesian Sweet Sauce

1 cup water
½ cup rice wine vinegar
½ cup brown sugar
1 tablespoon cornstarch
1 tablespoon water
½ cup soy sauce
⅓ cup molasses
Freshly cracked black pepper to
  taste

1. Bring the water and vinegar to a boil. Stir in the brown sugar and cook, stirring constantly, until the sugar dissolves.

2. Mix the cornstarch and water together well, and add this to the vinegar-sugar mixture. Continue to cook for an additional 3 minutes, until thickened.

3. Remove from the heat, add the soy sauce, molasses, and black pepper to taste, and stir well. Keeps, covered and refrigerated, 3 weeks.

This sauce is to Indonesian food what ketchup is to American food. Just as ketchup serves as the base of many different American barbecue sauces, so does this for a whole range of Indonesian-style barbecue sauces. I have provided some suggestions for embellishments, and I encourage you to make your own special supersecret ultra-personal Indonesian barbecue sauce which you can pass on to your children. ◆ *About 2 cups*

Wild Variations

◆ ◆

For the flavors of the Pacific Rim, add one of these sets of ingredients to 1 cup of the basic sauce.

1 tablespoon minced garlic
1 tablespoon minced fresh
   lemongrass (see Pantry, page
   372) *or* 1 teaspoon dried
2 tablespoons minced hot fresh
   green *or* red chile peppers

6 tablespoons lime juice (about
   3 limes)
3 tablespoons chopped cilantro
1 tablespoon red pepper flakes

1 tablespoon shrimp paste
1 tablespoon minced garlic
2 tablespoons chopped fresh
   basil
8 tablespoons lemon juice
   (about 2 lemons)

Grilled Eggplant Condiment

3 large eggplants
4 tablespoons kosher salt
5 tablespoons olive oil
Freshly cracked black pepper to
    taste
3 tablespoons minced garlic
2 large yellow onions, thinly
    sliced
2 tablespoons grated fresh
    ginger
½ teaspoon red pepper flakes
1 tablespoon tomato paste
2 tablespoons honey
1 tablespoon brown sugar
1 teaspoon chili powder
1 teaspoon ground cumin
1 teaspoon turmeric
⅓ cup white vinegar
4 tablespoons balsamic vinegar
4 tablespoons lemon juice
    (about 1 lemon)

4 tablespoons chopped parsley
    for garnish

This Malaysian-inspired condiment is much like South African brinsal blatjang (see Apricot Blatjang, page 225), traditionally used with curries. It has very concentrated flavor, like a ketchup or bean sauce. ◆ *About 4 cups*

SERVING SUGGESTION: This goes nicely with Roasted Then Grilled Half Duck (page 175), Simple Grilled Whole Beef Tenderloin (page 146), or Grilled Pork Loin with Indonesian Chile-Coconut Sauce (page 156).

1. Cut the eggplants lengthwise into ⅓-inch-thick slices, leaving the skins on.

2. Sprinkle the eggplant slices on both sides with the kosher salt, and place them on baking sheets. Stack the sheets on top of each other, ending up with an empty sheet. Now place a fairly heavy object (a crockery mixing bowl, six-pack of beer, whatever is handy) on the top sheet. Leave the eggplant slices trapped like this

for about 45 minutes, then remove, rinse, and dry them.

3. Brush the eggplant slices with 2 tablespoons of the olive oil and cover them with black pepper to taste, and 1 tablespoon of the garlic. Grill the slices over medium-low heat until they are brown, about 10 minutes.

4. Remove the eggplant slices from the heat, let them cool to room temperature, and chop them into chunks. (The eggplant should be of a consistency that will cause it to practically fall apart by itself.)

5. In a large sauté pan, sauté the sliced onion over medium-high heat in the remaining 3 tablespoons of olive oil until golden brown, 7 to 8 minutes. Add the eggplant and all the remaining ingredients except the balsamic vinegar, lemon juice and parsley, to the pan, and cook over medium heat for 2 to 3 minutes. Remove from the heat, add the balsamic vinegar, and mix well.

6. Let the mixture cool to room temperature. Blend in the lemon juice just before serving, and sprinkle chopped parsley on top as garnish. This will keep, covered and refrigerated, for up to 3 weeks.

GASTRONOMIC ROYALTY

The nightshade family of plants is sort of the gastronomic equivalent of the royal families that dominated the early modern world. This remarkable clan has got it all—a position of prominence in cuisines throughout the world, a history filled with intrigue and triumph, even the customary nutty uncle and evil cousin. Members of the family include potatoes, tomatoes, eggplant, peppers, tobacco, the hallucinogenic jimson weed and the deadly poisonous nightshade.

Ginger-Lime Vinaigrette

2 pieces of fresh ginger, each
the size of your thumb,
freshly peeled
12 tablespoons lime juice (about
6 limes)
4 tablespoons rice wine vinegar
½ red bell pepper, seeded and
diced small
¼ red onion, diced small
4 tablespoons chopped cilantro
1 teaspoon grated lime rind
2 cups vegetable oil
Salt and freshly cracked pepper
to taste (white is best if you
have it)

1. Place the ginger in a small
saucepan and cover with cold
water. Bring to a boil, drain, and
repeat the procedure. Cool the
ginger under cold tap water. (This
will give it a milder, subtler flavor.)
When the ginger is cool, mince it
finely.

2. In a medium-sized mixing bowl,
add all the other ingredients to the
ginger except the oil and salt and
pepper, and mix well.

3. While mixing constantly, slowly
add the oil in a steady stream. Add
salt and pepper to taste. Will keep,
covered and refrigerated, for about
1 week.

This vinaigrette has a very vibrant, aromatic flavor which is great with green salads. I also highly recommend it for any fresh garden vegetable or a simple grilled fish. ◆ *About 1 pint*

Homemade Mayonnaise (with Variations)

◆◆

Yolks of 2 large eggs
1 tablespoon lemon juice (about
   ¼ lemon)
½ teaspoon salt
½ teaspoon freshly ground
   pepper (white is best if you
   have it)
1 teaspoon prepared brown
   mustard
1 cup vegetable oil

1. Blend the egg yolks and lemon juice in a food processor or blender for 30 seconds.

2. With the machine still running, add the salt, pepper, and mustard, and continue to blend for an additional 30 seconds.

3. With the machine still running, slowly add the oil in a steady stream until it is completely emulsified with the egg yolk mixture. Keeps 4 to 5 days, covered and refrigerated.

I use mayonnaises a lot with grilled fish. They are great for this because the velvety texture and plain flavor of the basic mayonnaise provides a subtle vehicle for spicy flavorings, thus giving you an accompaniment that is at once delicate and spicy. An example of this is the chipotle mayonnaise, which is an excellent partner for the strong-charactered grilled bluefish. To make the variations, just mix the ingredients into the basic mayonnaise until well blended. ◆ *About 1 cup*

Texas Pete Mayonnaise

1 cup basic mayonnaise
1 teaspoon cayenne pepper
2 tablespoons ketchup
1 tablespoon chili powder
2 dashes of Worcestershire
  sauce

Keeps 4 to 5 days, covered and refrigerated.

This is the result of my attempt to re-create a mayonnaise I had while on vacation on the Outer Banks of North Carolina, where it was served with a fried fish platter in a small seafood restaurant. The only information I could get out of the chef about this mayo was something to the effect that he put in "a bottle of Texas Pete," a local hot sauce. I made my own variation when I got back home, and it is in fact very similar to the one I had back at the fish shack on the beach. ◆ *About 1 cup*

Chipotle Pepper Mayonnaise

1 cup basic mayonnaise
1 tablespoon minced canned
  chipotles (see Pantry, page
  369)
1 teaspoon minced garlic
1 tablespoon tomato purée
2 tablespoons chopped cilantro
2 tablespoons lime juice (about
  1 lime)
Salt and freshly cracked black
  pepper to taste

Keeps 4 to 5 days covered and refrigerated.

This variation needs a major strong flavor to go up against. The chipotles, which are smoked jalapeño peppers, add a nice bit of fire to this mayo. ◆ *About 1 cup*

Sardine and Caper Mayonnaise

♦♦

1 cup basic mayonnaise
6 sardines, coarsely chopped
2 tablespoons capers
1 tablespoon lemon juice (about
   ¼ lemon)
Dash of cayenne
2 tablespoons chopped parsley

1. Chop sardines roughly. In a medium bowl, mix the sardines with all other ingredients.

2. Add to one cup mayonnaise (see recipe, page 248). Mix well. Keeps 4 to 5 days, covered and refrigerated.

♦ *About 1 cup*

Compound Butters

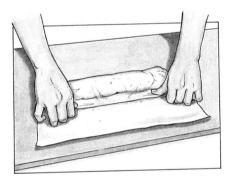

Compound butters are a quick, easy way to add a little dash to grilled fish but still let the fish be the focus. They are easy to make and you can roll them into tubes, cover them with plastic wrap, put them in the freezer, and then just cut slices the size you need. A small pat on top of your fish or chicken will melt and spread its flavor over the food. Don't forget that herb butters are a good way to use those remaining fresh herbs when the first frost is coming.

Here are some ideas to use as general guidelines for creating your own compound butters. All are added to 1 pound of very soft unsalted butter, then blended thoroughly in a food processor or by hand if necessary.

Basil-Lemon

4 tablespoons chopped basil
1 tablespoon minced garlic
4 tablespoons lemon juice
  (about 1 lemon)
Salt and freshly cracked black
  pepper to taste

Rosemary-Garlic-Black Pepper

3 tablespoons rosemary needles
1 tablespoon minced garlic
2 tablespoons freshly cracked
  black pepper
Salt to taste

Ginger-Scallion

4 tablespoons chopped scallion
2 tablespoons minced fresh
  ginger
1 tablespoon rice wine vinegar
Salt and freshly cracked black
  pepper to taste

Honey-Sage-Raisin

3 tablespoons chopped fresh
  sage
4 tablespoons honey
¼ cup raisins
Salt and freshly cracked black
  pepper to taste

Hot Chile-Cilantro

4 tablespoons chopped cilantro
2 tablespoons minced fresh red
  serrano chile peppers
2 tablespoons lime juice (about
  1 lime)
Salt and freshly cracked black
  pepper to taste

Chile

3 tablespoons chili powder
1 tablespoon ground cumin
3 dashes of Tabasco sauce
2 tablespoons tequila
Salt and freshly cracked black
  pepper to taste

Sesame

◆◆◆

4 tablespoons sesame seeds,
   roasted in a single layer in a
   350°F oven for 25 minutes
2 tablespoons sesame oil
2 tablespoons chopped scallion

Balsamic, Basil, and Black Pepper Mustard

◆◆◆

⅓ cup dark mustard seeds
4 tablespoons water
2 tablespoons balsamic vinegar
1 tablespoon dry mustard
2 tablespoons honey
1 teaspoon freshly cracked
   black pepper
2 tablespoons chopped fresh
   basil
Salt to taste

Mustards using freshly ground seeds may seem semitoxic on the first whiff, so you need to let them air out for a while. These guys are very potent and my recommendation is that they be used in conjunction with some bread and meat, as I think their power would dominate fish or even chicken. I especially like these with tenderloin sandwiches or any leftover grilled red meat. ◆ *About 1 cup*

1. Grind the mustard seeds in a spice blender or with a mortar and pestle until they have become a fine powder. Place the powder in a bowl.

2. Add the water and vinegar, stir well, and allow the mixture to stand for 1 to 2 hours.

3. Add all the remaining ingredients and blend well. This mixture will keep, covered and refrigerated, up to 4 months.

Fresh Horseradish

◆◆◆◆◆◆◆◆◆◆◆◆◆◆◆◆◆◆◆◆◆◆◆◆◆◆◆◆◆◆◆◆◆◆◆◆◆◆

1 pound fresh horseradish
4 tablespoons lemon juice
　(about 1 lemon)
Pinch of salt
Pinch of sugar

1. Peel the horseradish and either grate it very fine by hand or use the grater blade of a food processor.

2. Add the lemon juice, salt, and sugar, and mix well. This preparation will keep for weeks, covered in the refrigerator, but you should really use it within 3 days. After that, it loses a lot of its strength.

Now, let's say that somehow you came into a bushel of ultrafresh oysters or just returned from digging clams or have some gigantic shrimp steaming in beer on the stove. You're not going to want to use prepared horseradish in your cocktail sauce, for it is merely a shell and a shadow of itself in fresh form. Cocktail sauce with powerful, freshly prepared horseradish is where it's at for the modern raw bar. You can keep your wasabi tucked away, because it is tame compared to this.

You see horseradish roots every once in a while at the store, but they are very easy to grow, and the root always seems to be more potent right out of the ground. Only grate what you need because its real bite is short-lived. On the other hand, it will keep for several days refrigerated if you don't mind a lower-energy item.

By the way, if you're looking for something to serve with that rare beef you just took off the grill, this is it. ◆ *About 1½ cups*

Thai-Style All-purpose Hot Mixed Curry Paste

◆◆◆

2 fresh green chile peppers
3 tablespoons minced fresh
    lemongrass (see Pantry, page
    372) *or* 2 teaspoons dried
1 tablespoon minced garlic
2 tablespoons chopped fresh
    ginger
1 teaspoon grated lime zest
    (green part only)
1 tablespoon red pepper flakes
2 tablespoons ground coriander
    seed
2 tablespoons ground cumin
1 teaspoon ground cardamom
1 teaspoon cinnamon
1 tablespoon freshly cracked
    pepper (white is best if you
    have it)
1 teaspoon salt

Put all the ingredients together in a blender or food processor and purée into a paste. That's all, folks! Keeps, covered and refrigerated, for up to 6 weeks.

In Thailand, there is an almost infinite variety of curries served in every possible manner. Here I have made a very bold curry paste, one whose flavor will stand out when it is used with grilled foods. Keep this paste in the refrigerator and use it as a flavor enhancer. It may be substituted in any recipe that calls for powdered curry and will give you more depth of flavor. Put a couple of teaspoons in your barbecue sauce for an added whoop. Or try diluting it with a little butter and brushing it over thin pork chops before you grill them. Then serve them with Spicy Pickled Cabbage (page 291) for a complementary taste. ◆ *About 1 cup*

Slow and Low Is the Way to Go: Barbecue (Smoke Cooking)

✦ ✦

Barbecuing is *not* what Dad did in the backyard on Sunday afternoons to steaks, hamburgers, and hot dogs. As you should know by now, that is *grilling*. These two methods of cooking are sometimes confused because they are both done over live fire, but they are really quite different.

Unlike grilling, barbecuing is not listed among Escoffier's leading culinary operations. The only way to really find out about barbecue is to get into your car and drive to the South or Southwest, seeking out men like Bossi Gatson of Greensboro, North Carolina; Leo Smith of Oklahoma City, Oklahoma; or Smoky Hale of Jackson, Mississippi. Even then, you would get a different definition of barbecuing from each expert. All you can be certain of is that each explanation would be long, complicated, and colorful.

Barbecuing essentially consists of placing a large cut of meat in a closed pit and allowing it to cook indirectly by the smoke from a hardwood fire. The temperature is kept at 180° to 220°F, and the very slow cooking causes the connective tissues of the meat to tenderize and dissolve. We are talking about cooking over real wood, real slow, for a real long time. Barbecuing was created expressly to turn large, tough, inexpensive cuts of meat such as beef brisket and pork shoulder into tender, palatable eating. Since the actual cooking agent is the smoke from a hardwood fire, unlike grilling, barbecuing is a cooking method in which the fuel lends a distinct flavor to the final product. In some parts of the country pitmasters swear by hickory, in others by oak, and in still others by mesquite. (For a discussion of the flavors resulting from the use of different hardwoods in barbecuing, see Woods as Fuels, page 264.)

Barbecuing is often confused with spit roasting and smoke curing, but it differs from them in significant ways. Spit roasting is basically a grilling process for large cuts of meat in which the rotation of the spit alleviates the necessity of quick cooking; smoke curing is a preserving process in which the product is brined and smoked at very low temperatures, around 100°F, with preservation rather than tenderization as its goal.

Whatever its technical definition, barbecuing is unique to the United States, a phenomenon that transcends mere culinary methodology. As such, it should take its rightful place alongside other classic celebratory rites of world cuisine—the Hawaiian luau, in which a *kuala* pig is cooked in a pit called an *imu*, or the Tahitian pig roast in which the pig is wrapped in banana leaves and cooked in a *mhimaa*, a hole dug in the ground. Like these, barbecuing is a ritual, inseparable from the culture that gave it birth, and that it in turn reinforces and nurtures.

If this seems a bit like the raving of a barbecue lunatic, just ask any Southerner where to find the best barbecue. People who generally couldn't care less about food will argue the subtle differences of barbecue passionately and knowledgeably—and endlessly.

I am providing a few recipes for barbecue in this book so that you can enjoy the festivity and celebration that is the barbecue process. However, I think making your own barbecue is on the outer edge of what can be done in home cooking. You can do it, but it's a real effort. On the other hand, if you ever wanted to be a Southerner, this is your chance. The ability to sit out in the backyard, drinking beer and watching something cook for eight hours, is a time-honored Southern skill, handed down from father to son for generations. If you have the patience for it, then you must have a bit of Southern blood in your veins.

The Rhetoric of Barbecue

Because barbecuing is such a long process, the cooking time is always filled with a combination of beer and idle, boastful chatter, the latter being the supreme essence of barbecue. Be aware that this often calls for a whole new persona. Many people will go so far as to adopt another name, which they use only when barbecuing. This colorful custom allows normally quiet, humble people to experience a whole different part of their personality.

A prime example of this is my amigo Steve Johnson, with whom I have traveled across America searching for barbecue. Most of the time Steve is a soft-spoken, mild-mannered type of guy, but when it comes to staying up all night barbecuing a whole hog, a new person emerges. It is "Maurice" who vehemently denies the very existence of any barbecue other than shredded pork, and who has been known to threaten bodily harm to anyone who dares to suggest that a ketchup-based sauce be put on the smoky pork. This same Maurice will argue for hours the relative merits of chopped, pulled, minced, or sliced pork barbecue, and go into excruciating details on his theory about the relationship of the juicy sauce to the soaking-up power of a white bun.

So you see, giving you cooking instructions for barbecue is only providing you with half of what you need to know. Anyone familiar with the rites and rituals of barbecue knows that almost equal in importance to the actual taste of the 'cue is the amount and quality of the mumbo jumbo you put out while barbecuing. I have therefore prepared for you a primer on the subject, in which I provide the basic vocabulary essential to mastering this other, more mystical aspect—the Zen of Barbecue, as it were. Learn it well and practice it often, because only when you can go off on rants and unintelligible sermons on your preferred style of barbecue will you be a true pitmaster. Pick yourself a *nom de barbecue*, grab your cooler, and head off into the deepest recesses of your yard to practice the vocabulary below. The essence of stubborn individuality and back-woods primitivism await you.

TYPES OF BARBECUE

EASTERN NORTH CAROLINA STYLE: My personal favorite, this is no doubt the real original. It consists of either whole pig or pork shoulder cooked over hickory, then chopped or minced or pulled (depending upon which particular part of eastern North Carolina you hail from) and mixed with a light vinegar-based sauce —mention a tomato-based sauce east of Raleigh, and you had better be prepared to do some quick explaining. This style of 'cue is eaten on a cheap white bun with sweet coleslaw.

WESTERN NORTH CAROLINA STYLE: This is also pork barbecue, but the meat is dressed with a tomato-based sauce with a heavy vinegar accent. Not much different from eastern North Carolina style, right? Wrong. In the world of barbecue, even something this small becomes a serious bone of contention.

TEXAS STYLE: When you talk barbecue in Texas, you are talking beef brisket. This is one of the toughest, gnarliest cuts of meat known to humankind, but ten to twenty hours of slow cooking over mesquite or oak will turn it into one of America's original regional foods. The sauce used here is a ketchup-based blend limited only by the imagination of the cook. Chili powder and cumin are very popular additions.

KANSAS CITY STYLE: The raging debate as to whether Memphis or Kansas City is the barbecue capital of the world is as endless as it is heated. (Personally, I believe it's eastern North Carolina, but that's another story.) Barbecue is deeply embedded in the daily lives of people who live in K.C. It is a big sparerib town but also ranks high in the beef brisket department. A preparation that they think is truly unique to Kansas City, though, is "burnt ends." This is the top section of the beef brisket, which is removed from the leaner bottom and cooked even longer. The surface of the meat becomes very crispy and almost black, and the flavor is intense. Sauces in Kansas City are tomato-vinegar-based and generally pungent, strong, and assertive. The variety of sauces is immense, and some restaurants are known more for their distinctive sauce than for the actual barbecue.

MEMPHIS STYLE: If it's spareribs and brisket in Kansas City, it's ribs and shredded pork in Memphis. Home of the Memphis in May International Barbecue Championship, the city is practically synonymous with barbecue. Memphis ribs come wet or dry, but this town is best known for its amazing variety of dry rubs, served without sauce. The shredded pork is mixed with a sweet, tomato-based sauce. Not content to rest on its reputation, however, Memphis is constantly on the cutting edge of culinary development, with new menu items ranging from barbecued bologna (surprisingly awesome) to barbecue pizza and barbecue spaghetti.

OTHER TERMS YOU NEED TO KNOW

BASTING SAUCE (a/k/a mopping sauce): This is a sauce used during the long cooking process, applied with a brush or a mop, depending on the size of the piece of meat involved. The sauce can range in content from complicated concoctions of spices, herbs, and vinegar to just plain old warm beer—its purpose is to keep the meat moist. Sugar and ketchup are not generally included because they will burn during cooking. A typical recipe might be: ½ gallon white vinegar, 2 warm beers, ¼ cup cayenne pepper, and 2 secret ingredients of your choice.

FINISHING SAUCE: Now, after you've explained to your guests about your mopping sauce and the meat is ready to eat, it's time to whip out your finishing sauce. This sauce—never used during the actual cooking—varies in complexity from plain vinegar with salt and pepper to elaborate potions of over thirty ingredients. I know people who swear by a certain sauce, while others will just doctor a bottle of store-bought. In any case, it's a good condiment and should complement rather than hide the smoky flavor. Unless it is a light vinegar-based sauce, it should be served on the side, so that each individual can decide how much they want.

RIBS: Ribs can come from any animal, but here I only deal with pork ribs. Some folks will argue that beef ribs are delicious barbecued, but they are wrong, and anyway it's my book.

An old butcher I know speaks of a time when butchers gave away pork ribs due to their high fat content, toughness, and lack of meat. (Sound familiar? See page 275.) But then along came barbecuing, which gave these formerly unpopular pork parts a unique niche in culinary society. Songs, stories, and some very bad poems have been written about perfectly cooked pork ribs.

There are three types of pork ribs: 1. Country ribs, which come from the hard end of the pork loin and aren't really ribs at all but fatty pork chops. These are for grilling, not barbecuing. 2. Loin or baby back ribs, which are smaller and daintier than spareribs. This fairly tender cut does not have the fat content needed to stand up to the long cooking of proper barbecuing, although it is good for short cooking. 3. Spareribs, which come from the belly of the hog. To my mind these are the only ribs for barbecuing. They have a good amount of meat on them, but more important, this is the cut on top of which the bacon sits. We're talking serious flavor here, along with plenty of fat to keep it juicy. Spareribs come in slabs with thirteen bones. The slabs vary in size according to the weight of the pig, the most popular size being "3 and down." This means that a full thirteen-bone slab with chine bone and brisket flap still on will weigh three pounds or less. There is also a variation of the full slab called "St. Louis cut" or "Chinese cut," in which the slab is trimmed of the chine bone and brisket flap to form a slab that is of uniform size and similar in appearance to a slab of baby backs.

PORK SHOULDER: This cut is really the front leg of the pig. It is very popular for barbecue because of its low price, which in turn results from the fact that it is the most unwanted cut of pork for everything other than barbecue. Filled with fat and riddled with connective tissue, this cut is impossible to ruin unless you torch it by putting it directly over a flame. For home barbecue, I recommend the pork butt, which is a section of the shoulder which weighs four to seven pounds.

LINKS: This is a common name for sausage that is barbecued. Links are popular in Oklahoma and Texas.

MUTTON: Meat from an old sheep, this has a very distinctive flavor, and when you say "barbecue" in certain parts of Kentucky, it is mutton that you are talking about. Some folks say that its age, its strong flavor, and its general lack of popularity make it ideal for barbecue.

PITMASTER: This is a term that dates back to the time when one man would stay with the barbecue pit at all times. Today's new pit designs, however, have made the eighteen- to twenty-hour days of this tireless artisan a thing of the past.

OPEN-PIT: In this barbecue technique, used in some parts of North Carolina,

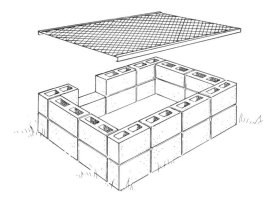

the meat to be barbecued is placed on a grill directly over a very low fire, although four or five feet above it. This technique is tricky, demanding a very watchful eye, because flare-ups are common whenever cooking is done by direct heat. Most open pits are simple affairs, consisting of cinder blocks piled six or seven high with a mesh grill laid across the top. Coals are shoveled into the bed, and sometimes corrugated tin is put on top of the meat to create an ovenlike effect.

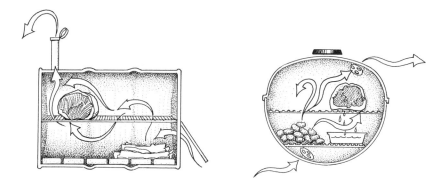

CLOSED-PIT: Despite its name, this is not a hole in the ground. This is the most common technique for cooking barbecue. The meat is cooked in an enclosed space, ranging from a 50-gallon drum to a 2-car garage, in which smoke is forced to mingle with the meat. A closed pit can use either direct or indirect fire, although indirect is far preferable because there is no danger of flare-ups.

LOG BURNER: I know it's hard to believe, but in some parts of this great land of ours people are cooking barbecue over charcoal. So when barbecuers gather, one of the standard questions is, "Are you a log burner?" If you want to be taken at all seriously, answer in the affirmative.

DRY RUB: A mixture of dry spices, this is at the very heart of barbecue. Rubbed on the meat before it is cooked, it helps form a crust on the outside that contains a tremendous amount of concentrated flavor.

PIG PICKIN': This is a gathering of people, originally for political purposes, at which a whole pig is barbecued and laid out for guests to pull apart, thus the term "pulled pork." This ritual is very popular in North Carolina and Virginia.

Barbecued Whole Chicken

◆◆

2 3½- to 4-pound whole
  chickens
1 cup All-South Barbecue Rub
  (page 273)

1. Rub the chickens well with the barbecue rub. Cover, put in the refrigerator, and let them sit for 1 hour.

2. In a covered cooker, build a small fire on one side and allow all of the fuel to become completely engulfed in flame. After it has burned down somewhat, put the chickens on the grill over the side with no fire. Cover the cooker and vent slightly.

3. Cook for 3 hours, maintaining the fire with intermittent feedings, maybe twice an hour.

4. Check the chickens by poking your fork into the thighs. If the juices run clear, dinner is ready.

The more you learn about barbecue, the more you understand that it is the *method* that makes it barbecue. In this case, I don't even use a "barbecue sauce." Instead, I rub the chicken with a dry rub, and its reaction during the cooking process results in a mellow, tender, smoky flavor and a crisp, crusty skin. The rub seems to concentrate the flavor on the surface in the same way a sauce would. I encourage you to experiment with the rub—it's a way to make your own personal barbecue statement. Some people like a lot of sugar, while others go heavy on the paprika. As is normally true with any aspect of barbecue, the quality of the barbecue is directly proportional to the quality of the patter you spin while serving it. ◆ *Serves 4*

SERVING SUGGESTIONS: Serve this with Grilled Andouille Sausage and Yam Salad (page 305) and José's Jicama Slaw (page 294).

WOODS AS FUELS

When grilling, it's important to use a hardwood, since other woods contain too much sap and will produce a lot of foul-flavored smoke. The particular type of hardwood you use, however, is not that important. While the choice of wood will have some impact on the flavor of the food, for my taste this flavor difference is much too subtle to notice.

When barbecuing, on the other hand, the long cooking time infuses the meat with the flavor of the smoke, so the choice of wood is very important. Certain regions prefer certain woods, and partisans will argue endlessly about why their particular choice is best. Pitmasters from North Carolina argue long and hard that nothing beats hickory, while Texans champion their native mesquite and oak. If you look carefully, though, you will find that each region is just using the wood most readily available in its neck of the woods, which is how it should be.

With the help of Don Hysco of People's Woods in Rhode Island, I have compiled the following list of hardwoods and their flavors. It's always fun to experiment and try to identify the wood used from the flavor of the food.

Aromatic Woods

ALDER: Very delicate, with a hint of sweetness.
APPLE: Very mild, with a subtle fruit flavor. Slightly sweet.
ASH: A fast burner, light but distinctive in flavor.
CHERRY: Similar to apple, but with a slight bitterness.

HICKORY: The favorite for barbecue. A strong, heavy, bacony flavor. Very assertive.

MAPLE: Smoky, mellow, and a bit sweet.

MESQUITE: The hottest-burning hardwood. Predominant honey and earthy flavors.

OAK: A lighter version of mesquite. (My secret barbecue fuel blend is 50 percent hickory, 50 percent oak.)

PECAN: A cool burner, nutty and sweet. Tasty, with a lot of subtle character.

Exotic and Expensive Flame Enhancers

This is where we get into what I think of as "wine snob" fuel. The superdelicate aromas of these woods are simply overpowered by the grilling process. On the other hand, I would definitely consider using seaweed as a flavor enhancer if I were grilling on the beach, or grapevines if I happened to be grilling next to a vineyard. Atmosphere, after all, is always important.

GRAPEVINES: Vines from different grape varieties give you different flavors, but generally all are rich, fruity, and very smoky.

HERBS: Smoky, herbaceous, and perfumy.

LILAC: Subtle, light, and floral.

OAKIES (shavings from the inside of a red wine barrel): Spicy and peppery, with a decided winy taste.

SEAWEED: Tangy and salty. Needs to be dried well before use.

Duck Barbecue

◆◆◆◆◆◆◆◆◆◆◆◆◆◆◆◆◆◆◆◆◆◆◆◆◆◆◆◆◆◆◆◆◆◆◆◆◆◆◆

6 duck legs from 3 5-pound
   ducks, trimmed of excess fat
Salt and freshly cracked black
   pepper to taste
4 tablespoons white vinegar
3 dashes of Tabasco sauce

1. Rub the legs with lots of salt and pepper. Build a small fire as far to one side of a covered cooker as possible. Place the legs skin-side down on the side of the grill opposite the fire.

2. Cover and cook for 1½ to 2 hours, or until a fork stuck into a leg twists easily. You will need to feed the fire slightly while they're cooking, just enough to keep it smoldering. You are barbecuing now, so grab a beer and remember the pitmaster's creed, "Slow and low is the way to go."

3. When the legs are tender, remove them from the grill, allow them to cool slightly, then remove the meat and skin from the bone and place them in a bowl. The meat should be crispy, not fatty, and you want to shred it into fairly small pieces. Add the vinegar, Tabasco sauce, and salt and pepper to taste. Mix well. This is best served immediately, but can be refrigerated, covered, for 4 to 5 days or frozen. To bring it back, place it in a pan in a 250°F oven for 20 to 30 minutes.

This is an excellent use for the extra leg meat you may have left from a grilled duck breast dish. While the exposure to smoke for long periods usually dominates its prey, the taste of duck is strong enough to stand up against the smoky tenderness of barbecuing. This freezes well and can be served in sandwiches for extra fancy barbecue or with fresh tortillas. Or reserve the breasts to make Grilled Duck Breast with Kumquat-Sugarcane-Basil Glaze (page 198) and serve the barbecue alongside. ◆ *1 pound*

SERVING SUGGESTIONS: Serve this with fresh tortillas, Black Bean Salad (page 319), and Corn Bread Salad with Lime Juice and Cilantro (page 312), or with Pita Bread (page 327) and Cold Orzo Salad (page 316).

Nouvelle cuisine reintroduced America to the practice of cooking duck breast medium-rare. This presented chefs with the problem of how to handle the legs of the duck, since it is not appropriate to undercook them and even by nouvelle standards a single duck breast does not a portion make. So we went scurrying to create interesting treatments for the legs. Some simply served the legs separately and cooked them longer. Others made duck sausage or confit. Still others made forcemeat and stuffed Chinese dumplings or ravioli. The common factor in all of these preparations is a cooking method that breaks down tough meat. One day while racking my brain for one more creative and unusual way to use the duck legs that went with a Southern-inspired duck breast preparation, I decided to fall back on the basics—why not barbecue them? Now, as you should all know, this does not mean grilling, but rather exposing the meat to wood smoke at low temperatures for a long time, allowing for the sinews to break down completely. It worked really well, proving as usual that old ways and new products are often an excellent match.

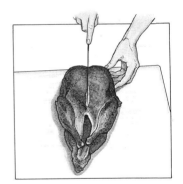

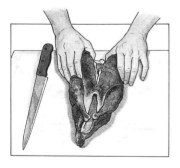

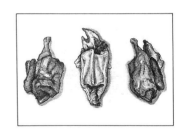

Outdoor Pork Baby Back Ribs

◆ ◆

2 slabs of baby back ribs (about 3 pounds)
1 cup basic Barbecue Rib Rub (page 269)

1. In a covered cooker, build a small fire in one half of the grill. Let the fuel become completely engulfed in flames, then wait a few minutes for the fire to burn down somewhat.

2. Rub the ribs thoroughly with the barbecue rub, put them on the half of the grill without fire under it, put the cover on the cooker, and vent slightly. Cook for 45 minutes, feeding the fire every 30 minutes or so to keep it going. Flip the ribs and cook them an additional 45 minutes, still feeding the fire regularly.

3. Remove the ribs from the fire and serve them dry (this is how the pros do it) with Basic All-American Barbecue Sauce (page 278) on the side.

Barbecuing pork spareribs outdoors on a covered grill is not an easy task, since the large surface area of the ribs makes it hard to have more than one rib on the grill without having the meat directly over the flames. For this reason I use baby back ribs in this recipe. Baby backs do not have the size or thickness of spareribs and come from the back of the pig where the meat is tenderer. While I think of that as cheating a little bit, since barbecuing is designed to break down tough meat, baby backs can carry the smoke flavor well and take less time and patience to cook. When you feel cocky with the baby backs, you can increase the level of difficulty by moving up a weight class. ◆ *Serves 6 as an appetizer*

SERVING SUGGESTIONS: I would serve this in front of Grill-Seared Sushi-Quality Tuna with Soy, Wasabi, and Pickled Ginger (page 192) or Grilled West Indies Spice-Rubbed Chicken Breast with Grilled Banana (page 165).

Barbecued Ribs, Missouri Style: Home Version

◆◆◆◆◆◆◆◆◆◆◆◆◆◆◆◆◆◆◆◆◆◆◆◆◆◆◆◆◆◆◆◆◆◆◆◆◆◆◆

2 full racks of 3/down pork
   spareribs

*For 1 cup basic Barbecue Rib
Rub*

2 tablespoons salt
4 tablespoons sugar
2 tablespoons ground cumin
2 tablespoons freshly ground
   black pepper
2 tablespoons chili powder
4 tablespoons paprika

For 2 cups basting sauce

1¾ cups white vinegar
2 tablespoons Tabasco sauce
2 tablespoons sugar
1 tablespoon salt
1 tablespoon freshly ground
   black pepper

1. Let's say dinner is at 6 P.M. Bright and early, so you can say that you've been cooking all day, preheat the oven to 180°F and rub the ribs thoroughly with the barbecue rub.

2. Place the ribs on baking sheets and put them in the oven for 3 hours. Don't bother to turn them, because all you are doing is slow cooking and infusing spices.

3. Remove the ribs from the oven. They can stand out for a while,

This method comes pretty close to true barbecuing, missing only the intense smoky flavor that can be achieved only by 3 hours of slow barbecuing. The ribs are coated with a mixture of spices, then cooked slowly in the oven and finished on the grill. The most important part of barbecuing is the slow cooking of the meat, which allows it to become tender without drying out.

The term "3/down" refers to the weight of the ribs. In this case, it is 3 pounds or under for each slab of 10 to 12 ribs.

This recipe is easily halved or doubled. Just keep the proportion of the rub to the sauce 2:1. ◆ *Serves 5 hungry folks*

SERVING SUGGESTIONS: Serve them with the traditional accompaniments: Tidewater Coleslaw (page 274), Grandma Wetzler's Baked Beans (page 321), East Coast Grill Corn Bread (page 324) or a couple of slices of cheap white bread, and watermelon, as is the prevailing tradition in sparerib country.

be refrigerated, covered, at this point for up to 2 days, or go right onto the grill.

4. You want a very low charcoal fire with the rack set as high as possible. Put the ribs on and let them stay there as long as your patience allows. A light crust on the outside and heat throughout is the goal, and depending on your fire, it can be achieved in 5 minutes per side or it can take up to ½ hour per side if you're into prolonging your guests' agony. Of course, the longer the ribs cook the better.

5. If you like your ribs "wet," coat them with sauce just before removing them from the grill. (The other option is to serve the ribs "dry" with sauce on the side.)

6. Remove the ribs from the grill and cut in between the bones.

The Only Real Barbecue Sandwich, or North Carolina Pulled Pork Barbecue Sandwich

◆ ◆

2 4- to 5-pound boneless pork butts
1 cup All-South Barbecue Rub (recipe follows)
2 cups Eastern North Carolina–style Barbecue Sauce (recipe follows)
Cheap white fluffy buns
Tidewater Coleslaw (recipe follows)

Bottle of hot sauce for garnish

The real stuff. When I think of barbecue, this is what it is. The way to eat this incomparable sandwich is sitting at a picnic table south of the Mason-Dixon Line, with a bottle of Texas Pete close at hand, a tall, frosty beer open, and George Jones on the radio. What more need be said? This amount should serve about 15 people and will keep covered in the refrigerator for 3 to 4 days.
◆ *Serves about 15*

1. Rub the pork butts on all sides with the dry rub and allow them to come to room temperature (about 2 hours).

2. Using hardwood charcoal, build a small fire in one side of a covered cooker. Allow about 40 minutes for the charcoal to become completely caught.

3. Place the butts on the grill, making sure that they are *not* above any part of the fire. Cover and vent slightly.

4. Pull a comfortable chair and a cooler full of beer out of the house and sit next to the grill, adding small amounts of charcoal when

needed to keep the fire just smoldering (about every 30 or 40 minutes or after each beer, whichever comes first).

5. Cook for 5 to 7 hours, or until the internal temperature is 165° to 170°F and the meat is super-tender.

6. Remove the pork butts from the grill and chop or shred them, whichever you prefer. Mix the pork with the sauce to taste, and pile it onto the buns, topped with coleslaw. Garnish with a bottle of hot sauce.

Good Ol' Barbecue

◆ ◆ ◆ ◆ ◆ ◆ ◆ ◆ ◆ ◆ ◆ ◆ ◆ ◆

All-South Barbecue Rub

2 tablespoons salt
2 tablespoons sugar
2 tablespoons brown sugar
2 tablespoons ground cumin
2 tablespoons chili powder
2 tablespoons freshly cracked
    black pepper
1 tablespoon cayenne pepper
4 tablespoons paprika

About 1 cup

All you do is throw them together
and mix them well.

Eastern North Carolina–Style Barbecue Sauce

1 cup white vinegar
1 cup cider vinegar
1 tablespoon sugar
1 tablespoon crushed red pepper
    flakes
1 tablespoon Tabasco sauce
Salt and freshly cracked black
    pepper to taste

About 2 cups

Once again, folks, just mix 'em
together. Keeps 2 months, covered.

Tidewater Coleslaw

◆ ◆

1½ cups commercial
  mayonnaise
½ cup white vinegar
⅓ cup sugar
1 tablespoon celery seed
Salt and freshly cracked black
  pepper to taste
1 head green cabbage, finely
  shredded
2 carrots, finely grated

About 2½ cups

1. In a small bowl, blend the mayonnaise, vinegar, sugar, celery seed, and salt and pepper to taste, and mix well.

2. In a large bowl, combine the cabbage and carrots. Pour the dressing over the mixture and blend well. Refrigerate until serving time.

Texas Barbecued Beef Brisket

◆◆

1 10- to 12-pound beef brisket
2 cups All-South Barbecue Rub (page 273)

2 cups Basic All-American Barbecue Sauce (page 278) on the side

1. Rub the brisket thoroughly on all its sides with the barbecue rub, and allow it to come to room temperature.

2. In the pit of a covered grill, build a very small fire on one side as far up against one wall as possible. Place the brisket on the grill on the side opposite from the fire so that none of the brisket is directly over the flame. Put the top on the cooker, pull up a chair, and grab the cooler.

This is where a person learns about the Zen of Barbecue. You gotta keep the fire going, but very quietly. If you've got a thermometer on your covered grill, you want to keep the temperature between 180° and 220°F. Remember, "Slow and low is the way to go." You have to figure out your own personal refueling policy. The one I like is one handful of coals or wood chunks to every beer.

This goes on for about 8 to 10 hours or however long you can

In my estimation, beef brisket just might be why the barbecue process was invented. My research, sketchy as it is, shows that there was a strong German immigrant community in Texas around the turn of the century. It has some of these Germans working in the booming Texas cattle industry, and others working in butcher shops, what with their strong background in butchering and charcuterie. It being common knowledge that butchers are constantly trying to turn tough or inexpensive cuts of meat into a usable product that brings a higher cost (witness sausages and pâtés), it has these German butchers faced with the brisket. This cut of beef is particularly unwanted because of the huge percentage of fat that runs not only on the surface, but throughout the cut. Traditional technique would braise or pickle this cut to tenderize it, but the brisket also has a lot of beef flavor. In my personal opinion, a very smart German butcher who was looking for a way to market this cut barbecued it. We're not talking here about the open-pit roasting that was already popular in this area, but rather closed-pit cooking, in which the cooking is done by convection rather than conduction. It is similar to braising in theory, with the smoke replacing the water. It is cooked at very low heat for a long period of time, and the high fat content protects the meat from drying out but also disappears through the 10- to 18-hour cooking process. What you are left

make it, the longer the better. Don't be scared by the darkening of the exterior, the outside of the brisket will be superdark—my personal favorite part.

3. Upon completion, pull the brisket out, trim off any excess fat, and slice it thin. Serve with barbecue sauce on the side—no pro would ever cover properly cooked brisket with sauce, he'd just dab on a touch.

Obviously the key here is a tremendous amount of patience and a day when you want to do nothing but sit around. But the end product is one of those great culinary events that results from spending a lot of time doing something that is relaxing and enjoyable. Make sure you have plenty of tall boys for eating this.

with is very tender meat with little or no fat and a tremendous smoky beef flavor. I think the meat and the process were literally invented for each other.

Now, I don't think that you will get any disagreement from the professional barbecue industry when I say that brisket is the hardest to master—but, hey, learning is half the fun. And, in the words of Remus Powers, famous barbecue aficionado, "The best barbecue I ever had is the one on the plate in front of me."

These are guidelines for the closed-pit barbecuing of brisket, a basic technique with many variables which is wide open for personal interpretations.

◆ *Serves 8 to 10 beer-swilling cowboys/girls*

SERVING SUGGESTIONS: I like this with Hot Pepper Corn Bread (page 325), Grandma Wetzler's Baked Beans (page 321), and Tidewater Coleslaw (page 274). Your Basic Grilled Corn (page 317) is good, too, and don't forget the watermelon.

Barbecued Bologna

◆ ◆

1 3-pound stick of bologna
1 cup All-South Barbecue Rub
  (page 273)
2 cups Basic All-American
  Barbecue Sauce (page 278)
1 loaf cheap white bread

1. Rub the bologna all over with the Barbecue Rub.

2. Build a very low fire on one side of your covered grill. Place the bologna on the side opposite the fire, cover, and allow it to smoke slowly for 1 hour.

3. Remove the bologna from the grill and slice it into ½-inch slices. Smear each slice with a little sauce, slap it between two slices of bread, and enjoy a new barbecue classic.

I don't want to ignore the cutting edge of new barbecue, so here is the latest example of a lowly piece of meat turned into a delicious, if rather unusual, delight. The weird consistency of bologna soaks up smoke like a sponge and makes it taste great. Stranger than fiction. Personally, I like my barbecued bologna sandwich with coleslaw and plenty of hot sauce. ◆ *12 sandwiches*

SERVING SUGGESTIONS: Either bottled chocolate soda or RC Cola and a Moon Pie.

Basic All-American Barbecue Sauce (with Variations)

4 large onions, chopped
3 tablespoons vegetable oil for sautéing
1 28-ounce can tomato purée
3 28-ounce cans tomatoes with juice
2½ cups white vinegar
4 tablespoons packed dark brown sugar
4 tablespoons granulated sugar
2 tablespoons salt
2 tablespoons freshly cracked black pepper
2 tablespoons paprika
2 tablespoons chili powder
4 tablespoons molasses
1 cup orange juice
2 tablespoons Liquid Smoke
8 tablespoons brown (Dijon-style) mustard

1. In a large, heavy-bottomed saucepan, sauté the onion in the oil over medium-high heat until golden brown, about 7 to 10 minutes.

2. Add all the remaining ingredients, bring to a boil, then reduce the heat and simmer uncovered at the lowest possible heat for 4 hours. (This long cooking removes as much acidity as possible from the tomatoes.)

3. Purée sauce in 2, 3, or more batches to prevent it from spilling

I define barbecue sauce as a traditional American sauce, usually made with ketchup, that is used on grilled chicken, ribs, pork, etc. There are many other sauces in this book that can be applied to grilled items, but only this one is your genuine, down-home All-American Barbecue Sauce.

Being a barbecue purist, I believe that the sauce in itself has been totally overrated as it relates to the whole of a plate of barbecue. Barbecuing is a method of cooking, not a sauce. Whether you're talking about brisket, sliced pork, spareribs, or chicken, the sauce is an accompaniment to the barbecued meat, a condiment rather than an essential ingredient. The sauce has been given prominence only as people pay less attention to the process. In North Carolina, for example, barbecued pork is served plain, either chopped or shredded, on a sandwich. The sauce—in the case of eastern North Carolina, white vinegar and red pepper flakes, in western North Carolina, a sweet-and-sour ketchup and Italian dressing mix—is served on the side to be put on the barbecue at the last minute. (For this reason, barbecue aficionados call it a "finishing sauce.") In Kansas City, where the barbecue of choice is pork spareribs which are served dry, they serve a grainy, thin, ketchup-based sauce on the side. Likewise in Texas, where the sauce for the sliced barbecued brisket is applied to one's liking just before

out of your food processor or blender.

Mexican

✦✦✦✦✦✦✦✦✦✦✦✦✦✦✦✦✦

1 teaspoon ground cumin
1 teaspoon chili powder
4 tablespoons lime juice (about 2 limes)
10 cilantro sprigs

Asian

✦✦✦✦✦✦✦✦✦✦✦✦✦✦✦✦✦

2 teaspoons minced ginger
8 tablespoons soy sauce
4 tablespoons rice wine vinegar
2 tablespoons sugar
1 tablespoon sesame oil

Caribbean

✦✦✦✦✦✦✦✦✦✦✦✦✦✦✦✦✦

2 teaspoons brown sugar
4 tablespoons pineapple juice
4 tablespoons dark rum
4 tablespoons Caribbean hot sauce
Juice of 1 orange
Pinch of allspice

eating. In fact, since barbecue sauce usually has some sugar in it, if you apply it during the grilling process, the sugar in the sauce will burn.

What I'm saying is that when you hear people talking about how they have some extra special, supersecret barbecue sauce, I would be highly doubtful that I was going to be eating any type of real honest-to-God barbecue. In fact, I've seen a lot of real barbecue pros just doctor up some ketchup with sugar, vinegar, and spices, or even take store-bought sauce and change it a little.

Having discounted barbecue sauce, I will now attempt to restore a little dignity to it. This recipe is the one we presently use at the East Coast Grill and is the result of four years' of practice and evolution. It is a "finishing" sauce to be applied either right before the meat is eaten or when it is just ready to be removed from the grill. What we're doing here basically is making our own thin ketchup heavily flavored with vinegar and sugar. I am providing you with my particular recipe and method, but I really encourage you to use this sauce as a vehicle to develop the taste you personally like best: Try a little less vinegar, maybe a little more sugar. You, too, can come up with the superspecial, ultrasecret, barbecue-snob recipe.

This recipe makes around 1 gallon of sauce. A pint or so is usually plenty to cover a grilling session for six people, and the sauce keeps up to 2 weeks covered in the refrigerator, so one batch will last a while. I have also given you some ideas for making variations from the "mother" barbecue sauce. Again, I encourage you to personalize these to your own liking. ✦ *About 1 gallon*

Honey Mustard

◆ ◆ ◆ ◆ ◆ ◆ ◆ ◆ ◆ ◆ ◆ ◆ ◆ ◆ ◆ ◆ ◆

1 cup brown (Dijon-style)
   mustard
8 tablespoons honey

Mediterranean

◆ ◆ ◆ ◆ ◆ ◆ ◆ ◆ ◆ ◆ ◆ ◆ ◆ ◆ ◆ ◆ ◆

4 tablespoons balsamic vinegar
4 tablespoons red wine vinegar
2 tablespoons minced garlic
2 tablespoons olive oil
1 large chunk of fresh tomato
   chopped
4 tablespoons lemon juice
   (about 1 lemon)
1 cup combined fresh herbs
   such as basil, thyme, sage,
   parsley, oregano, or rosemary

Variations

To 1 pint of your Basic All-American Barbecue Sauce, add these other ingredients for different variations of it. These additions should be made after the sauce has cooled to room temperature or has been refrigerated. These sauces all keep 2 weeks, covered, in the refrigerator.

UNIQUE RITUALISTIC COOKING STYLES

CARNE CON CUERO: This Argentinean cooking style was reputedly borrowed from an African technique in which a whole elephant—trunk, feet, and all—was buried in a preheated, stone-lined pit and left overnight. In the Argentinean version, the loin section of a steer is cooked in a preheated hole in the ground. It has a rather high degree of difficulty, since the *gauchos* of Argentina like their beef rare.

ASADO DE CARNERO: Argentineans are big ranchers and they have devised many ways to cook their meat. In this method, a sheep is split open and placed upright on heavy metal rods, which are then cantilevered over a fire to cook the meat.

SUCKLING PIG IN CLAY: This is a technique used in the West Indies, in which a whole pig is seasoned with herbs, wrapped in clay, and placed in a bed of hot ashes. After long, slow cooking, the clay is cracked and pulled off the tender, seasoned pork. Eating the crisp skin that has stuck to the clay is reported to be the high point of this feast.

BARBACOA SERRANA: A Mexican variation on the West Indian technique of wrapping seasoned meat in clay, in which the meat is wrapped in cornmeal dough and cooked slowly in ashes. Although part of the cornmeal bread is burned, the edible portion, soaked with meat juices, is fantastic.

SOUTH SEA ISLAND STYLE: This is yet another variation on the "wrap something up and stick it in the ashes" technique. In this one, mounds of fruit and vegetables are wrapped in large leaves and stacked closely around the meat so they will cook in its juices. All this is covered with more leaves, and then coals are tossed on top.

And All the Fixin's

◆◆◆

This is a mixed-bag collection of salads, vegetables, and side dishes that I think go well with grilled foods. Some have tropical overtones, some echo picnic foods, still others are simply ethnic favorites like Your Basic Black Beans or Spicy Pickled Cabbage, but all share a casual straightforwardness.

In these recipes I have used a wide range of ingredients, techniques, and flavor combinations. You will find tropical staples, such as jicama and breadfruit, combined with standard American preparations to create new dishes like José's

Jicama Slaw or West Indies Breadfruit Salad. In some recipes, I follow the tropical technique of using fruits such as papayas and mangoes in their green state as vegetables. Many of these dishes are cold, since cold side dishes go very well with grilled or spicy food, and most of them will keep in your refrigerator for a long time, which means you can prepare them well in advance if you wish.

The range of recipes in this chapter will allow you to take advantage of what is in season, and I think you will find some interesting and unusual combinations of ingredients. All of the dishes have strong personalities and at the same time are versatile enough to be served with just about anything.

Grandma Wetzler's Sweet-and-Sour Wilted Chicory

◆◆

1 medium-large head chicory
4 slices bacon, diced small
½ yellow onion, diced
1 tablespoon sugar
1 tablespoon white vinegar
Salt and freshly cracked black
    pepper to taste

1. Cut off the root end of the chicory. Since chicory tends to be gritty, soak it in water a couple of minutes, then dry it thoroughly in a lettuce spinner or in paper towels. After the chicory is dry, break the leaves in half.

2. In a deep saucepot, sauté the bacon pieces over medium heat until crisp, about 6 to 8 minutes. Remove the bacon and reserve, leaving the fat in the pan.

3. Add the diced onion to the fat, and cook until clear, about 3 to 4 minutes.

4. Add the chicory and stir well to coat it with the fat. Cook only until the chicory is wilted, 1 to 2 minutes. Make sure the chicory does not go completely limp.

5. Remove the pot from the heat, add the sugar and vinegar, and toss well. Add the reserved bacon pieces and salt and pepper to taste. Serve immediately.

When I visited Grandma Wetzler's house in rural Pennsylvania as a child, the table was always jammed with an incredible variety of dishes—homemade applesauce, pickled eggs, corn pudding, ham salad, homemade baked beans. It always made me think of a picnic. We'd eat hot baked beans with a massive ham at supper, then cold beans the next day at lunch with ham salad. Her common sense, unflagging practicality, and enormous repertoire of German-American dishes resulted from having cooked for her family since the age of sixteen. Today, at ninety-three, Grandma still grows all of her own vegetables and makes the best pickles and homemade tomato juice in the world.

This dish is a variation on hot German potato salad, with its traditional sweet-sour combination. The strong-flavored, slightly bitter chicory is a little too bitter to serve raw, and it needs to be cooked or, as in this dish, wilted. ◆ *Serves 4 as a side dish*

SERVING SUGGESTIONS: This dish is not great cold, but it can be reheated. It will spice up a simple grilled chicken, and the acid and sweetness of this dish balance particularly well against oily fish. Try it with Grilled Bluefish with Chipotle Vinaigrette (page 94) or Lime-Marinated Grilled Kingfish with Red Onion and Mango Relish (page 91).

Romaine-Feta Salad with Lemon–Olive Oil Dressing

◆ ◆

2 heads romaine
2 ripe tomatoes
2 cucumbers
½ cup fresh parsley
1 green bell pepper, seeded
1 red bell pepper, seeded
1 large red onion
1 cup feta cheese broken into
   smallish pieces
1 cup Kalamata olives

For the dressing

½ cup extra virgin olive oil
1 teaspoon minced garlic
Salt and freshly cracked black
   pepper to taste
12 tablespoons lemon juice
   (about 3 lemons)

This Greek-inspired salad goes well with Pita Bread (page 327), and it's also a nice accompaniment for any lamb entrée, such as Grilled Butterflied Leg o' Lamb (page 153) or Grilled Lamb Steaks with Rosemary, Garlic, and Red Wine (page 150). It's also good with Grilled Pork Birdies with Tangerine-Rosemary Glaze (page 161). I like the simplicity of the dressing. ◆ *Serves 8 as a side dish*

1. Separate the romaine leaves, wash, and dry them well. Break them in half.

2. Chop the tomatoes, cucumbers, and parsley coarsely, julienne the peppers, and peel the onion and slice it extremely thin. In a large bowl, combine all these with the romaine, feta, and olives.

3. In a small bowl, mix together the olive oil, garlic, and salt and pepper to taste. Pour these over the romaine mixture, followed by the lemon juice, then toss and serve.

Chilled Spinach with Soy and Ginger

◆ ◆

2 pounds fresh spinach,
   separated, washed and dried
3 tablespoons sesame oil
3 tablespoons rice wine vinegar
4 tablespoons soy sauce
1 tablespoon fresh ginger,
   minced
2 teaspoons sugar
3 dashes of Tabasco sauce
Freshly cracked pepper to taste
   (white is best if you have it)
3 tablespoons sesame seeds,
   toasted in a single layer in a
   350°F oven for 25 minutes

1. Plug up your sink and fill it with about 5 quarts of water and a couple of trays of ice cubes.

2. In 3 quarts of boiling water, blanch the spinach very briefly, about 15 to 20 seconds. Remove it, drain, and plunge immediately into the ice-water bath. (This is important to stop the cooking and retain the vibrant green color of the spinach.) After 30 seconds or so, drain the spinach again, chop it coarsely, and place it in a large mixing bowl.

3. Add all the remaining ingredients except the sesame seeds, and mash the liquid into the spinach with a wooden spoon for 30 to 45 seconds. This bruising technique accomplishes a thorough mixing of the spinach and the dressing.

This is a version of Japanese *sunomono*, "vinegared salads," which are actually a cross between salads and condiments. The portion is small, but the flavor is intense. When served alongside a simple grilled fish, it is clean and refreshing. ◆ *Serves 6 as a side dish*

SERVING SUGGESTIONS: I would serve this as a side dish with a simple grilled fish such as Grilled Pompano with Lime and Olive Oil (page 95), Grilled Halibut Steaks with Fresh Tomato Sauce (page 93), or Grilled Yellowtail with Water Chestnut–Scallion Relish (page 101).

4. Sprinkle the spinach with the sesame seeds, and serve at once, or refrigerate it until ready to serve, then sprinkle it with sesame seeds. This dish is definitely best when served fresh, but it will keep covered and refrigerated for 2 days.

Spicy Green Bean Salad with Grilled Pork and Peanuts

✦✦✦✦✦✦✦✦✦✦✦✦✦✦✦✦✦✦✦✦✦✦✦✦✦✦✦✦✦✦✦✦

2 pounds green beans, cleaned
½ to ¾ pound grilled pork loin, diced small
2 tablespoons sesame oil
½ tablespoon sugar
2 tablespoons soy sauce
1 tablespoon chopped chiles de árbol
4 tablespoons lime juice (about 2 limes)
4 tablespoons rice wine vinegar
2 tablespoons chopped fresh basil
2 tablespoons cilantro
2 tablespoons chopped fresh mint
1 red bell pepper, seeded and diced small
Salt and freshly cracked black pepper to taste

½ cup coarsely chopped unsalted, roasted peanuts, for garnish

This Thai-inspired dish works as either a main lunch course or the first course of a large dinner. It's nice for very hot days and is an exciting way to use up last night's grilled pork. Be careful not to overcook the beans, as their crisp texture is an important aspect of this dish. ◆ *Serves 4 as a light meal*

SERVING SUGGESTIONS: Serve this as a first course in front of Grilled Salmon, Lomi Lomi Style (page 62) or Avocado Stuffed with Seared Tuna Estilio Seviche (page 54).

1. Bring approximately 4 quarts of water to a rolling boil. In the meantime, fill a large shallow pan half full of ice water. Put the green beans in the boiling water and leave them for 3 to 4 minutes. Drain the beans and immediately dump them into the ice water. When they are completely cool, drain thoroughly, transfer to a large mixing bowl, and refrigerate.

2. In a separate bowl, combine the pork, sesame oil, sugar, soy sauce, chiles de árbol, and lime juice. Mix well and let stand for 1 hour.

3. Pour the pork mixture onto the beans, and toss well.

4. Add the vinegar, basil, cilantro, mint, bell pepper, and salt and pepper to taste. Toss well again, transfer the salad to a serving platter, and sprinkle chopped peanuts over the top.

Green Bean Salad with Tomatoes and Jicama

◆ ◆

1 pound green beans, cleaned
2 large tomatoes
1 pound jicama, peeled and
  julienned

For the dressing

⅔ cup olive oil
4 tablespoons red wine vinegar
2 teaspoons minced garlic
1 teaspoon ground cumin
4 tablespoons chopped cilantro
6 tablespoons lime juice (about
  3 limes)
Salt and freshly cracked pepper
  to taste (white is best)

This makes a light, refreshing lunch or an excellent starter for dinner. The crisp texture of the jicama and green beans is complemented by the juicy mellowness of your prize August tomatoes. Cilantro and citrus zip it up. A good salad to serve with fish. ◆ *Serves 4 to 6 as a side dish*

SERVING SUGGESTIONS: Serve with Red Snapper Fiesta al Carbón con Dos Salsas (page 96) or Grilled Yellowtail with Water Chestnut–Scallion Relish (page 101).

1. In a large pot of boiling salted water, blanch the green beans for 1 to 2 minutes. Drain and immediately place them in a bath of ice water. When the beans are fully cooled, drain and reserve them.

2. Slice the tomatoes ¼ inch thick and arrange on a platter. Arrange the green beans and jicama on top of the bed of tomatoes.

3. Blend the oil, vinegar, and garlic with the cumin, and pour it over the vegetables. Sprinkle the chopped cilantro on top. Just before serving, squeeze the lime juice over everything and add salt and pepper to taste. Will keep, covered and refrigerated, up to 4 days.

Asian Inspiration

◆ ◆ ◆ ◆ ◆ ◆ ◆ ◆ ◆ ◆ ◆ ◆ ◆

Grilled Rum-Soaked Shrimp with
Mango-Lime Relish
Page 124

Grilled Pork Skewers with
Green Mango
Page 158

Green Bean Salad with
Tomatoes and Jicama
Above

Scallion Pancakes with Spicy
Oyster Sauce with Lemongrass
Pages 329 and 241

Grilled Baby Eggplant with
Miso-Soy Vinaigrette
Page 296

Spicy Pickled Cabbage

1 medium head Chinese *or*
Napa cabbage, thinly sliced
2 large carrots, finely shredded
3 tablespoons salt
4 tablespoons white vinegar
1 tablespoon minced garlic
1 tablespoon minced fresh red *or*
green chile pepper
3 tablespoons minced fresh
lemongrass (see Pantry, page
372), *or* 3 teaspoons dried
4 tablespoons sugar
4 tablespoons ketchup
1 teaspoon freshly cracked
pepper (white is best if you
have it)
2 tablespoons minced fresh
ginger

1. Combine the cabbage and shredded carrot in a large mixing bowl, add the salt, and mix well. Allow to stand at room temperature for 4 hours.

2. Mix in all the remaining ingredients.

3. Put the mixture in a mason jar, cover tightly, and allow it to sit in the refrigerator for 3 to 4 days. Will keep refrigerated for approximately 2 to 3 weeks.

This is a Southeast Asian–style pickle, both sweet and hot, in which the liquid is created by the reaction of the cabbage with the salt. I would use it to accompany a hot dish, perhaps one using Thai-Style All-purpose Hot Mixed Curry Paste (page 255). ◆ *Serves 8 as a side dish*

SERVING SUGGESTIONS: Serve this with Grilled Pork Birdies with Tangerine-Rosemary Glaze (page 161).

Boiled Collard Greens with Salt Pork

◆◆◆

2 pounds collards, destemmed
  and washed
1 4-ounce piece of salt pork
1 large yellow onion, diced
½ cup cider vinegar
1 tablespoon salt
1 tablespoon freshly cracked
  black pepper
½ teaspoon red pepper flakes

1. Bring 1 gallon of water to a boil, then add the collards, salt pork, and onion.

2. Turn the heat down to a simmer, add the vinegar, salt and pepper, and pepper flakes. Cover and cook for 1 hour. Drain, reserving the liquid, and serve the greens hot.

3. The resulting broth is called "pot likker" and is served separately and savored as a clear soup. This flavorful liquid is appreciated even by those who don't enjoy the collards.

As a child, I always thought the "greens" served at school lunch were a cruel form of punishment. But now with the wisdom of my years (and my interest in low-cost ingredients), I have become a demi-gourmet of greens. Turnip, beet, collard, kale, poke sallet, dandelion—I've come to appreciate each of their individual characteristics. The sharpness of the dandelion green is great for salads; turnip and mustard are mellow and good for sautéing. But when it comes to what is, in my opinion, the best method for preparing greens—boiling—there is only one that can stand up to the requisite hour or more of cooking, and that's the legendary collard. This is an excellent dinner side dish and makes a hearty light lunch in combination with any soup. Hot Pepper Corn Bread (page 325) is a must accompaniment for soaking up the juices here. ◆ *Serves 4 as a side dish*

SERVING SUGGESTIONS: Serve this as a side dish with any grilled pork preparation. Try it, for example, with Grilled Pork Tenderloin with Roasted Corn–Bacon Relish (page 163).

Marinated Feta with Roasted Red Peppers, Black Olives, and Thyme

◆◆

1 pound feta cheese, diced large
   (about 16 pieces)
1 cup fresh black Greek olives,
   pitted
2 roasted red bell peppers (see
   Pantry, page 368)
½ cup extra virgin olive oil
1 small red onion, diced small
1 teaspoon minced garlic
1 tablespoon red wine vinegar
2 tablespoons fresh thyme
Salt and freshly cracked black
   pepper to taste
8 tablespoons lemon juice
   (about 2 lemons)

This southern Mediterranean combination is a fantastic addition to a large summer buffet. Its richness goes well with grilled meat and can be enjoyed by itself or with salads like Basil Tabbouleh (page 313) or Grilled Eggplant with Olive Oil, Parsley, and Capers (page 298). I would definitely be having some grilled Pita Bread (page 327) here.

◆ *Serves 6 as an antipasto*

1. In a large bowl, combine the feta, olives, and red peppers. Add the olive oil and toss lightly.

2. Add the onion, garlic, vinegar, thyme, salt and pepper, and toss again.

3. Squeeze the lemon juice over the mixture, and allow it to stand 2 to 3 hours in the refrigerator before serving. Will keep, covered and refrigerated, about 4 days.

José's Jicama Slaw

5 cups grated green cabbage
2 cups grated carrot
2 cups peeled and julienned
jicama

For the dressing

1 cup chopped cilantro
½ cup cheap yellow mustard
½ cup ketchup
4 tablespoons white vinegar
2 teaspoons sugar
1 garlic clove, minced
Salt and freshly cracked black
pepper to taste

1. Place the cabbage, grated carrot, and jicama in a large bowl.

2. In a food processor or blender, mix all the dressing ingredients until well integrated. Pour this over the vegetables, and mix well.

To me, "slaw" means an assortment of inexpensive fresh vegetables thinly sliced or grated and combined with a dressing. Cabbage is obviously the classic, but slaw can feature many other vegetables. In this case, the jicama and West Indies–slanted seasonings combine to create a new wave, island version with a slightly exotic flavor and crunchy texture—another dish created by my day chef, José Velasquz, who has the uncanny ability to make anything taste good. This is an easy dish to prepare for large groups—it's no more difficult than your basic coleslaw, but something new and unusual for your guests. ◆ *Serves 8 to 10 as a side dish*

SERVING SUGGESTIONS: Serve this with traditional barbecued meats or any grilled red meat, such as Grilled Lime-Marinated Flank Steak with Chipotle-Honey Sauce (page 141).

Salad of Green Mango, Coconut, and Hot Chile Peppers

◆◆

2 green mangoes, peeled, pitted, and thinly sliced
8 tablespoons lime juice (about 4 limes)
Juice of 2 oranges
2 fresh red *or* green jalapeño chile peppers, finely chopped
1 tablespoon chopped cilantro
½ teaspoon sugar
4 tablespoons shredded fresh coconut
1 small shredded green cabbage

Lime wedges for garnish

In this tart salad dish, the thinly sliced mangoes are allowed to marinate in lime and orange juice, which intensifies and brings out their flavor. Mangoes, used extensively in tropical areas, are considered a vegetable when green, a fruit when ripe. So . . . here is a nice, cooling summer fruit and vegetable salad to be eaten with grilled fish or chicken.
◆ *Serves 6 as a salad or side dish*

SERVING SUGGESTIONS: Try this with Grilled Swordfish Steaks with Yucatán Orange-Herb Paste (page 100).

1. Place the sliced mangoes in a shallow pan. Combine the lime juice, orange juice, jalapeño, cilantro, and sugar, and pour over the mangoes. Let them marinate for 4 to 10 hours.

2. Just before serving, toss in the coconut. Serve on top of a bed of shredded white cabbage, and garnish with lime wedges.

Grilled Baby Eggplant with Miso-Soy Vinaigrette

◆◆

4 tablespoons peanut oil
3 tablespoons sesame oil
3 tablespoons rice wine vinegar
2 teaspoons light miso
½ teaspoon sugar
1 teaspoon minced fresh ginger
12 baby eggplants
Salt and freshly cracked pepper to taste (white is best if you have it)
½ head green cabbage, very finely sliced

1. In a mixing bowl, whisk together the peanut oil, 1 tablespoon of the sesame oil, and the vinegar. Stir in the miso, sugar, and ginger. Set the mixture aside.

2. Cut the eggplants in half lengthwise, brush them with the remaining 2 tablespoons of sesame oil, and sprinkle them with salt and pepper to taste.

3. Grill the eggplants skin-side up over medium heat until golden brown, about 3 to 4 minutes. Flip them and grill an additional 2 minutes.

4. Remove the eggplants from the grill and arrange them on a serving platter that has been covered with the sliced cabbage. Dress them with the vinaigrette mixture.

Why do I specify baby eggplant here? Because it's subtler in flavor? Maybe. Because it's so cute? Maybe. And if you couldn't find baby eggplant, could you use regular eggplant without changing the taste? Probably.

Seriously, I do think that in this dish with its Eastern preparation, the baby variety adds a certain elegance that is more in keeping with the aesthetics of Japan. A traditional Japanese small salad, this is a spare little appetizer you might serve before a heavy fish course like salmon or swordfish.

♦ *Serves 4 as a salad*

SERVING SUGGESTIONS: Follow this up with Grilled Pompano with Lime and Olive Oil (page 95) or Grilled Scallops with Rocotillo-Mango Relish (page 117). Or try the Chilled Spinach with Soy and Ginger (page 287).

Roasted Eggplant and Pepper-Garlic Purée with Lemon and Thyme

◆◆◆◆◆◆◆◆◆◆◆◆◆◆◆◆◆◆◆◆◆◆◆◆◆◆◆◆◆◆◆◆◆◆◆◆◆◆◆

2 medium eggplants, skin on
1 large yellow onion, skin left
  on
2 red bell peppers
1 whole head of braised garlic
  (see Pantry, page 367)
4 tablespoons extra virgin olive
  oil
8 tablespoons lemon juice
  (about 2 lemons)
1 tablespoon fresh thyme
Salt and freshly cracked black
  pepper to taste

2 tablespoons chopped parsley
  for garnish
Lemon wedges for garnish

1. Prick each eggplant in 5 to 7 places with a fork, then place them on the grill over a medium-hot fire. Cover them, and cook until the skins are charred black and the eggplants are soft, about 8 to 12 minutes.

2. Remove the eggplants from the grill, cut them in half, and scoop out the insides. If they are properly cooked, the insides should be very mushy and easy to scoop.

3. Cut the onion in half, leaving the skin on, and place the halves

Recipes for roasting and grilling eggplants appear in most Mediterranean cuisines. This one is a glorified dip of sorts, its origin resting somewhere between the Greek/Arabic moussaka and the Italian caponata. You can slice some French bread very thin, brush it with butter, garlic, and parsley, and put it in a slow oven (250°F) for 15 to 20 minutes until the bread is like a cracker, then use it to scoop up the dip. ◆ *Dip for 6*

SERVING SUGGESTIONS: Serve this with Basil Tabbouleh (page 313), grilled Pita Bread (page 327), and Grilled Butterflied Leg o' Lamb (page 153). Or try it with Grilled Figs with Prosciutto and Provolone (page 178).

on the grill. At the same time, place the red peppers on the grill and cook, turning occasionally, as described in Pantry (page 368). The onion is done when the outer surface is dark brown, and the peppers are done when the skin is charred black. When the onion halves are done, remove them from the grill, peel off the skin, and chop fine. When done, remove the peppers from the grill, peel off the charred skin, seed, and chop into small dice.

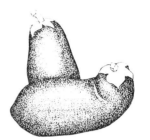

4. Add the pepper, onion, and garlic to the eggplant, and mix well. Stir in the olive oil, lemon juice, thyme, salt and pepper to taste, and mix again.

5. Garnish with chopped parsley and lemon wedges to brighten up the color.

Grilled Eggplant with Olive Oil, Parsley, and Capers

◆◆◆◆◆◆◆◆◆◆◆◆◆◆◆◆◆◆◆◆◆◆◆◆◆◆◆◆◆◆◆◆◆◆◆◆◆

2 large eggplants
¾ cup extra virgin olive oil
Salt and freshly cracked black
    pepper to taste
½ cup chopped parsley
4 tablespoons capers
8 tablespoons lemon juice
    (about 2 lemons)

Eggplant on the grill is a natural. It's straightforward, easy, and goes well as a vegetable with grilled chicken or fish. A lot of people would advise you to salt the eggplant before grilling to remove the bitterness, but I find that if the eggplant is grilled immediately after cutting, that is not necessary.

1. Just before grilling, slice the eggplants into ½-inch-thick slices. Brush with a bit of the olive oil and season with salt and pepper to taste.

2. Over medium heat, grill the eggplant slices on one side until golden to dark brown, about 3 to 4 minutes. Turn them and grill the other side in the same manner.

3. Remove the eggplant slices to a platter large enough to lay them out in a single layer. Pour the remaining olive oil over the slices, sprinkle them with the parsley and capers, and squeeze the lemon juice over them. Serve at once.

This dish adapts itself well to advance preparation. If you want to, you can grill the eggplant and refrigerate it, covered, up to 3 days, then at the last minute julienne it, mix all the ingredients together, and add a touch of red wine. ◆ *Serves 6 as a side dish*

SERVING SUGGESTIONS: Try this as a side dish with Grilled Halibut Steaks with Fresh Tomato Sauce (page 93) or Grilled Squid Pasta with Roasted Red Pepper and Basil (page 112). Or serve it in combination with Grilled Chicken Thighs with Peach, Black Olive, and Red Onion Relish (page 68).

Brunch with Three Cheeses

◆ ◆ ◆ ◆ ◆ ◆ ◆ ◆ ◆ ◆ ◆ ◆ ◆

Spoon Bread with Smithfield Ham
and Cheddar Cheese
Page 308

Romaine-Feta Salad with
Lemon–Olive Oil Dressing
Page 286

Wilted Greens with Grilled Lamb
and Blue Cheese
Page 72

Grilled Eggplant with Olive Oil,
Parsley, and Capers
Page 298

Sweet Potato Hash Browns with Bacon and Onions

◆◆◆◆◆◆◆◆◆◆◆◆◆◆◆◆◆◆◆◆◆◆◆◆◆◆◆◆◆◆◆◆◆◆◆

4 medium sweet potatoes (about
  2 pounds), peeled
6 slices bacon, diced
1 large yellow onion, sliced
½ cup peanut oil
Salt and freshly cracked black
  pepper to taste
4 tablespoons chopped parsley

Using sweet potatoes makes this a richer dish than traditional white potato hash browns. I like this with applesauce and some sort of pork, or just steak and a salad, for a right nice dinner. ◆ *Serves 6 as a side dish*

1. Place the potatoes in a saucepan with cold water to cover. Bring them to a boil and cook until a skewer can start to go through them easily, 15 to 20 minutes. If you are unsure, it is better to undercook a bit rather than overcook in this situation.

2. Remove the potatoes from the heat, drain, and cover with cold water. Allow the potatoes to cool to room temperature, then cut them into chunks the size of large dice.

3. In a large sauté pan over medium heat, cook the bacon pieces until nearly done (just starting to crisp up). Add the onion and cook both until the onion is colored gold to brown, about 7 minutes. Remove both from the sauté pan and reserve.

4. Wipe out the sauté pan and return it to the stove over medium-high heat. Add the peanut oil, and

SERVING SUGGESTIONS: Try this with Grilled Peppered Wolffish (page 89) or Grilled Big Black-and-Blue Steak for Two (page 148). Grilled Country Ham and Applesauce (page 154) also likes this as an accompaniment.

heat it until very hot but not smoking. Test the heat of the oil by tossing a chunk of potato in—you should see some action, Jackson.

5. Put the potato chunks in the oil and panfry them until golden brown, about 7 to 8 minutes, turning occasionally. Watch out for the splattering oil.

6. Remove the pan from the heat, add the bacon and onion, season with salt and pepper to taste, and sprinkle the parsley on top.

THE OTHER POTATO

The sweet potato, the root of a member of the morning glory family, is actually not related to the white potato. Nevertheless, these two tubers have been playing hopscotch on the international culinary hit parade for quite a while.

Although both roots originated in the New World, sweet potatoes were already rather popular in Europe by the sixteenth century, when white potatoes were still considered deadly poison. Of course, the white tuber soon far outdistanced its orange counterpart, becoming one of the four major food plants in the world.

Meanwhile, however, the sweet potato had become an important food plant in Africa and was brought by slaves to the American South, where it soon became a staple. With its high sugar content and rich flavor, the sweet potato is rapidly gaining popularity throughout the United States today, as Americans look for more taste in their everyday food.

Sweet Potato Salad

4 medium sweet potatoes (about
   2 pounds), peeled and cut into
   uniform large pieces
½ red bell pepper, seeded and
   diced small
½ green bell pepper, seeded and
   diced small
½ large red onion, diced small
4 tablespoons finely chopped
   parsley

For the dressing

3 tablespoons Dijon mustard
3 tablespoons ketchup
1 teaspoon minced garlic
¾ cup olive oil
4 tablespoons cider vinegar
1 tablespoon Worcestershire
   sauce
2 tablespoons lime juice (about
   1 lime)
Salt and freshly cracked black
   pepper to taste

A new variation on an old theme. I use sweet potatoes instead of the blander white potatoes and dress them with a light vinaigrette. I like it better than mayonnaise, and the resulting salad is a little more versatile. ◆ *Serves 6 as a side dish*

SERVING SUGGESTIONS: This salad goes with just about anything. Try it with Grilled Pork Birdies with Tangerine-Rosemary Glaze (page 161), Shrimp Steamed in Beer (page 127), Soy-Marinated Scallops with Grilled Shiitakes (page 189), or Sake-Marinated Grilled Frogs' Legs with Japanese-Flavored Barbecue Sauce (page 188).

1. Plug up your sink and fill it with about 5 quarts of cold water and a couple of trays of ice cubes.

2. In 3 quarts of boiling salted water, cook the pieces of sweet potato until just done, 10 to 12 minutes. Be careful not to overcook. You should be able to pierce them with a fork, but you should still feel some resistance, and the pieces should not fall apart.

3. Remove the pieces of sweet potato from the heat, drain, and im-

mediately plunge them into the ice-water bath. After about 30 seconds, drain them again, and put them into a large stainless steel bowl. Add the diced pepper, onion, and parsley.

4. Make the dressing: Place the mustard, ketchup, and garlic in a medium-sized bowl. Whisking constantly, add the olive oil in a slow, steady stream. Add the vinegar, Worcestershire sauce, and lime juice, and mix well. Season with salt and pepper to taste.

5. Pour the dressing over the sweet potato mixture, and toss gently. Serve immediately, or it will keep, covered and refrigerated, for up to 5 days.

Dinner with Friends

Grilled Basque Wings
Page 66

Grilled Halibut Steaks
with Fresh Tomato Sauce
Page 93

Sweet Potato Salad
Page 302

Chilled Spinach
with Soy and Ginger
Page 287

Chocolate
Peanut Butter Pie
Page 352

Grilled Sweet Potatoes with Molasses Glaze

◆•◆

4 medium sweet potatoes (about 2 pounds)
4 tablespoons molasses
Juice of ½ orange
1 tablespoon unsalted butter, room temperature
Pinch of allspice
Salt and freshly cracked black pepper to taste

My Grandma Wetzler's holiday spreads always include candied sweet potatoes. As a child, I thought I was getting one over on the adults by having dessert with my meal and afterwards, too. This is another one of my grandma's inspired ideas that I have adapted to the grill. ◆ *Serves 8 as a side dish*

1. Peel the sweet potatoes and slice them lengthwise into ½-inch-thick slices. Cook them in boiling salted water to cover until just done, about 8 to 10 minutes. You should be able to stick a fork through them, but you should still feel some resistance, and the slices should not break apart easily. Be careful not to overcook them, as they need to be sturdy to stand up to the rigors of the grill. Remove them from the heat, drain, and cool to room temperature.

2. While the sweet potato slices are cooling, mix together all the remaining ingredients in a small bowl. Mash the mixture with the back of a spoon until the butter is well incorporated.

3. Over a moderately hot fire, place the sweet potato slices on the grill and cook them until slightly brown on each side, about 2 to 3 minutes per side. Then brush them with

SERVING SUGGESTIONS: This dish goes very well with Grilled Turkey Steaks with White Grape–Cranberry Relish (page 174) or Grilled Country Ham and Applesauce (page 154).

the molasses mixture and cook very briefly, about 30 seconds per side, just to give the potatoes a nice glaze.

Grilled Andouille Sausage and Yam Salad

◆◆

6 medium yams
1 pound andouille sausage
3 tablespoons grainy Dijon
   mustard
⅓ cup cider vinegar
⅓ cup balsamic vinegar
1 cup virgin olive oil
1 tablespoon sugar
1 large red onion, chopped
Salt and freshly cracked black
   pepper to taste
½ cup chopped parsley

This is a relative of those Germanic sausage and potato dishes that my grandma used to make, but with a Southern touch. Andouille is a Cajun smoked pork sausage, similar to Polish kielbasa or the Portuguese linguica in that it's precooked. Any of these are good for grilling, and if you don't like your dishes spicy, you might want to substitute the milder kielbasa or linguica for the andouille, which has a good bite to it. ◆ *Serves 6 as a side dish or 4 as a light main course*

1. Bring about 4 quarts of water to a boil, add the yams, and boil until just tender, about 15 to 20 minutes. Drain and set them aside to cool.

2. Grill the sausage over a medium-hot fire until nice and crusty, about 5 to 7 minutes. (This is precooked sausage, so don't worry about cooking it through, but make sure it's well browned.) Remove it from the heat, slice it into ¼-inch slices, and set aside.

SERVING SUGGESTIONS: Serve this with Marinated Feta with Roasted Red Peppers, Black Olives, and Thyme (page 293).

3. In a medium bowl, whisk together the mustard and vinegars, then add the oil in a thin stream, whisking constantly. Add the sugar, and whisk until well blended.

4. Cut the cooled yams into ½-inch cubes and put them into a large mixing bowl. Pour the dressing over them, add the onion, sausage slices, salt and pepper to taste, and mix well. (Be careful not to mash the yams by mixing too vigorously.) Sprinkle all over with the parsley. Best eaten warm, but keeps up to 3 days covered and refrigerated, and is also great cold.

Grilled Plantain with Molasses-Citrus Glaze

◆◆◆◆◆◆◆◆◆◆◆◆◆◆◆◆◆◆◆◆◆◆◆◆◆◆◆◆◆◆◆◆◆◆◆◆◆◆

4 tablespoons molasses
Juice of 3 oranges
4 tablespoons lime juice (about 2 limes)
2 tablespoons dark rum
6 very ripe plantains (about 2 pounds)

1. Make the glaze: Combine the molasses, orange and lime juice, and rum. Mix well.

2. Do *not* peel the plantains. Slice them in half lengthwise. (The skin

The plantain is another one of those tropical staples that is used as a vegetable when green, a fruit when mature. In this preparation, care must be taken to choose only the ripest of plantains; unlike a banana, a mature plantain is dark brown to black, almost rotten-looking. At this stage its sweetness is at its peak, and it tastes rather like a banana. The lime in the glaze really perks up this side dish, which can be served as an accompaniment to any equatorial dish or by itself as a dessert. ◆ *Serves 6 as a side dish*

will serve as protection and allow the interior to cook through before the exterior scorches.) Over a medium fire, place the plantains facedown on the grill and cook for 2 minutes, or until the surface is well browned. Turn and cook them faceup for another minute.

3. Remove the plantains from the grill and either paint or spoon the glaze over them. Serve immediately.

SERVING SUGGESTIONS: Serve these with Grilled Pork Skewers with Green Mango (page 158), Roasted Then Grilled Half Duck (page 175), or Grilled Lime-Marinated Flank Steak with Chipotle-Honey Sauce (page 141).

West Indian Grill

✦✦✦✦✦✦✦✦✦✦✦

Grilled Jamaican Jerk Chicken
with Banana-Guava Ketchup
Page 168

Grilled Scallops with
Rocotillo-Mango Relish
Page 117

Grilled Plantain with
Molasses-Citrus Glaze
Page 306

West Indies Breadfruit Salad
Page 314

Daiquiris
Page 361

Jamaican Guy Flan
Page 331

Spoon Bread with Smithfield Ham and Cheddar Cheese

◆◆◆

3 cups water
4 cups milk
3 cups yellow cornmeal
2½ teaspoons salt
3 tablespoons sugar
4 tablespoons unsalted butter,
  melted
2 cups Smithfield ham, diced
  small
1 cup grated cheddar cheese
4 tablespoons very finely
  chopped fresh sage
10 eggs
2 tablespoons baking powder

1. Preheat the oven to 350°F.

2. Grease a 5-quart casserole dish or a 10-inch iron skillet.

3. In a large (6-quart) pot, combine the water and milk, and bring them to a simmer. Add the cornmeal, salt, 3 tablespoons sugar, and butter, and stir over medium-low heat until the mixture becomes thick, 5 to 7 minutes.

4. Remove the mixture from the heat, and blend in the ham, cheese, and sage.

5. Whip the eggs with the baking powder until very frothy. Fold the whipped eggs into the corn mixture, mixing lightly but thoroughly.

This is a variation on a dish from my childhood, traditional Southern spoon bread as found on the Colonial era menus of Williamsburg taverns, and it is a favorite of my sister. I have added Smithfield ham to the recipe, since it is also a traditional Virginia product and I think they make a very nice combination. With a simple salad, this dish makes a great bruch for a large group of people. ◆ *Serves 12 as a side dish*

SERVING SUGGESTIONS: This goes perfectly with Arugula and Dandelion Greens Salad with Fried Oysters, Smithfield Ham, and Peaches (page 187)—if you leave the ham out of the salad.

6. Pour into the greased casserole or skillet, and bake for 50 to 55 minutes or until the top is nicely browned. Serve hot.

Doc's Cheddar Biscuits

◆ ◆

5 cups all-purpose flour
2 tablespoons baking powder
4 tablespoons sugar
½ teaspoon salt
1 cup heavy cream
1 cup buttermilk
½ pound (16 tablespoons) butter, melted
1 cup grated cheddar cheese

1. Preheat the oven to 350°F.

2. Sift together the flour, baking powder, sugar, and salt.

3. If you have a paddle attachment on your mixer, use it at low speed to mix the heavy cream, buttermilk, and three fourths (12 tablespoons) of the melted butter in with the sifted ingredients. Otherwise, use a wooden spoon for mixing. In either case, mix only until the dough just pulls together, but is still somewhat crumbly.

4. Turn the dough out onto a floured surface and finish incorporating the dry ingredients by hand with a gentle kneading motion. Do not overwork the dough.

Another Southern tradition that has been imported to the North for my annual Christmas party, where I serve these with Grilled Country Ham with Applesauce (page 154), along with a heavily spiked eggnog. These little guys are also known in the South as "ham biscuits" and are so popular that they have almost become a generic term for hors d'oeuvres, as in "Don't y'all fill up on them ham biscuits, darlin'." ◆ *1 dozen*

5. Form the dough into a rectangular shape, and using a rolling pin on a floured surface, roll the dough out to ½-inch thickness, keeping the edges as square as possible. Brush half of the rectangle with the remaining melted butter (4 tablespoons), and sprinkle the cheese over this half. Using the edge of your hand, make an indentation at the middle of the dough (just give it a good karate chop), then fold the unbuttered half over the cheese-covered half. Press down evenly with your hands.

6. Using a rolling pin, roll the dough (which should now be about 1 inch thick) down to ¾-inch thickness. Wrap the dough in waxed paper, and chill for about ½ hour to firm it up.

7. When the dough is chilled, with a biscuit or round cookie cutter, cut rounds from the dough, place them on an ungreased baking sheet, and bake for 40 minutes, or until the tops are golden brown. The biscuits should split at the center during baking, exposing the cheese and making a handy configuration for a nice ham sandwich.

GRITS

Consumption of grits has been on the decline for the past twenty years, which gets no argument from me. Grits consist of course-ground, dried hominy which is boiled and then force-fed to children throughout the South. The outstanding characteristic of grits is profound blandness. They are served hot as a porridge and often appear alongside ham on Southern breakfast tables.

Deep-Fried Cheddar Grits

1 cup hominy grits
4 cups water
6 tablespoons butter
1 cup grated sharp cheddar
    cheese
Salt and freshly cracked black
    pepper to taste
1 cup flour
1 cup corn oil

1. In a heavy-bottomed 4-quart saucepan, heat the grits, water, and 4 tablespoons of the butter over high heat, stirring slowly with a wooden spoon, until the mixture comes to a boil.

2. Reduce the heat and simmer for 20 minutes, stirring constantly, being sure to scrape the bottom of the pan to prevent burning.

3. Add the grated cheese and stir until it is melted. Pour the mixture into a buttered 8″ × 12″ cookie sheet. Smooth evenly and allow it to cool to room temperature.

4. Cut the cooled grits mixture into 2″ × 2″ squares, and season with salt and pepper to taste. Put the flour into a pie pan and toss the squares in the flour.

5. In a large sauté pan, heat the oil until it crackles when a drop of water hits it. Place the squares in the oil and cook on one side until golden brown, about 1 minute. Turn them and cook until the second side is also golden, again about 1 minute.

This dish was developed by my friend and former sous-chef, Paul O'Connell, as a way of satisfying his desire for Italian food and mine for Southern American dishes. Somewhere between cornmeal mush and Italian polenta, it is an example of using new techniques to dress up something that was once very plain and simple. It's still not complicated, but it's got a little more pizzazz. ◆ *2 dozen squares*

SERVING SUGGESTIONS: These are good with Grilled Country Ham and Applesauce (page 154) or with Grilled Pork Birdies with Tangerine-Rosemary Glaze (page 161).

Corn Bread Salad with Lime Juice and Cilantro

◆ ◆

3 cups stale corn bread
½ red bell pepper, seeded and diced
½ green bell pepper, seeded and diced
½ small red onion, chopped
4 tablespoons chopped parsley
2 tablespoons chopped cilantro
2 scallions, chopped
2 garlic cloves, minced
1 fresh red *or* green jalapeño chile pepper, chopped (you may substitute 4 dashes of Tabasco sauce)
Salt and freshly cracked black pepper to taste
3 tablespoons good-quality olive oil
1 tablespoon white vinegar
6 tablespoons lime juice (about 3 limes)

1. Crumble the corn bread coarsely. You want to have some crumbs and some chunks, but no chunks should be larger than ½ inch in diameter. Spread the corn bread in a shallow pan and dry it in a low oven (250°F) for about 1½ hours, or until very crispy.

2. Add all the ingredients except the oil, vinegar, and lime juice, and toss well.

3. Add the oil, vinegar, and lime juice, and toss well again.

A tasty, slightly offbeat salad using the corn bread from the barbecue platter you ate last night. This salad is a good companion for grilled sausage or pork chops, or for any dish where you want a flavorful starch to soak up sauce. It is best served at room temperature or slightly heated.

Using stale crumbs from corn bread, I add oil and herbs, giving the mixture tabbouleh-like consistency. To introduce the taste of the Southwest, I add lime to the traditional Southern combination of heat and corn bread.
◆ *Serves 4 as a side dish*

SERVING SUGGESTIONS: Serve this with Grilled Pork Skewers with Green Tomatoes and Your Secret Finishing Sauce (page 160), Grilled Pork Skewers with Green Mango (page 158), or Grilled Top Round, Cuban Style, with Plátanos Fritos (page 143).

Basil Tabbouleh

⬥ ◆ ⬥ ◆ ⬥ ◆ ⬥ ◆ ⬥ ◆ ⬥ ◆ ⬥ ◆ ⬥ ◆ ⬥ ◆ ⬥ ◆ ⬥ ◆ ⬥ ◆ ⬥ ◆ ⬥ ◆ ⬥ ◆ ⬥ ◆ ⬥

⅔ cup bulgur wheat
3 large tomatoes, chopped small
1 large red onion, diced small
1 cup finely chopped fresh basil
½ cup finely chopped parsley
½ cup extra virgin olive oil
2 tablespoons finely chopped
   fresh mint
Salt to taste
8 tablespoons lemon juice
   (about 2 lemons)

The classic Middle Eastern salad with basil added for a slight change—no reason to buck tradition here. However, this version is a bit looser than you might be used to. ⬧ *Serves 6 as a side dish*

SERVING SUGGESTIONS: Serve this with Pita Bread (page 327), Grilled Butterflied Leg o' Lamb (page 153), and Roasted Eggplant and Pepper-Garlic Purée with Lemon and Thyme (page 297).

1. Place the bulgur wheat in a large bowl and pour in enough boiling water to cover. Let it stand 5 minutes, then remove it to a strainer and drain well. Press the bulgur lightly with the back of a wooden spoon to remove as much water as possible without mashing the bulgur.

2. Add all the ingredients except the lemon juice and mix very well. Refrigerate until ready to serve. Will keep covered and refrigerated for up to 4 days.

3. Just before serving, add the lemon juice and mix well.

West Indies Breadfruit Salad

◆ ◆

1 3- to 4-pound breadfruit (see Pantry, page 371)
1 cup chopped celery
1 large red onion, diced small
4 fresh red *or* green jalapeño chile peppers, finely chopped

For the dressing

1 ripe mango, peeled, pitted, and puréed
4 tablespoons cider vinegar
2 tablespoons dark rum
8 tablespoons lime juice (about 4 limes)
1½ cups mayonnaise
4 tablespoons chopped cilantro
2 tablespoons minced fresh ginger
Salt and freshly cracked black pepper to taste

1. Prepare the breadfruit: Peel and slice it in half, then remove the center core and cut the fruit into bite-size cubes. Cook them in boiling water to cover for 10 to 15 minutes, until easily pierced with a fork. Remove them from the heat, drain, and cool to room temperature.

2. Place the room-temperature breadfruit in a mixing bowl. Add the celery, onion, and jalapeño, and mix lightly.

3. Make the dressing: Whisk the mango purée, cider vinegar, rum, and lime juice into the mayon-

Breadfruit comes from the West Indies. Large and green with bumpy skin, it can get as big as 8 pounds, but it is normally smaller, with an average diameter of about 9 inches. It is a starchy vegetable and is used like a potato. It can be fried, baked, or boiled.

This is a dish to make when you are tired of getting that same ole potato salad, and it goes well with any type of Caribbean-theme dinner. ◆ *Serves 6 as a side dish*

SERVING SUGGESTIONS: Serve with Grilled Jamaican Jerk Chicken with Banana-Guava Ketchup (page 168) and Plátanos Fritos (page 145).

naise. Blend in the cilantro and ginger. Season with salt and pepper to taste.

4. Fold the dressing into the breadfruit and serve. Will keep, covered and refrigerated, 4 days.

Rice Salad with Wasabi-Miso Dressing

◆◆◆

2 tablespoons light miso (see Pantry, page 370)
1 tablespoon wasabi powder (see Pantry, page 371)
½ cup rice wine vinegar
1 teaspoon sugar
2 tablespoons sesame oil
1 teaspoon freshly cracked pepper (white is best if you have it)
3 scallions, thinly sliced
2 cups cooked white rice

1. In a stainless steel bowl, whisk the miso and wasabi powder into the rice wine vinegar.

2. Add the sugar and sesame oil and whisk until well blended. Add the pepper and scallion and mix well.

3. Pour the dressing over the rice and mix well. This will keep, covered and refrigerated, for up to 4 days.

This is a variation on a category of Japanese side dishes called *aemono*—literally "dressed things"—used to highlight the main courses with which they are served. *Aemono* are generally less strong than a condiment and more flavor-concentrated than a salad. I find that the concept fits in well with the relish-chutney-sambal theory of small, potent side dishes that highlight a grilled main course.

Here I take a small liberty with the *aemono* and make a very flavorful cold rice salad with a wasabi and miso dressing. Light yet strong, it's an excellent accompaniment for grilled fish or chicken. ◆ *Serves 4 as a side dish*

SERVING SUGGESTIONS: Serve alongside Grilled Yellowtail with Water Chestnut–Scallion Relish (page 101) or Grilled Chicken Breast with Fresh Herbs and Lemon (page 167).

Cold Orzo Salad

◆ ◆

1½ cups dried orzo
3 hard-boiled eggs, coarsely
   chopped
1 large red onion, diced small
2 tomatoes, diced medium
½ cup black olives, halved and
   pitted
1 tablespoon minced garlic
3 tablespoons capers
½ cup chopped fresh parsley
½ cup extra virgin olive oil
3 tablespoons balsamic vinegar
12 tablespoons lemon juice
   (about 3 lemons)
½ pound grated pecorino cheese

1. Cook the orzo in boiling salted water for 10 minutes. Remove it from the heat, rinse, drain, and allow it to cool to room temperature.

2. Place the cooked orzo in a large mixing bowl, add all the remaining ingredients except the lemon juice and cheese, and mix well. Cover and refrigerate for at least 4 hours. Twenty-four hours is best.

3. Just before serving, pour the lemon juice over the salad, mix well, and sprinkle with the pecorino. This dish will keep, covered and refrigerated, for up to 5 days.

Orzo is about the only pasta that I like served cold. Here it acts as a vehicle for a wide combination of Italian-style flavors. Cold salads are particularly good for summer months, as they are lighter and easily prepared in advance—in fact, the flavors in this dish peak on day two. ◆ *Serves 8 as a side dish*

SERVING SUGGESTIONS: I would serve this with Grilled Lamb Steaks with Rosemary, Garlic, and Red Wine (page 150) or Grilled Chicken Breast with Fresh Herbs and Lemon (page 167).

Your Basic Grilled Corn Strategy

◆ ◆

There are any number of methods for dealing with corn on the grill, each with its own merits. After many years of experimentation, I have settled on the following method, which is a combination of several techniques.

The traditional method has you peel away the outer husk without actually removing it, remove the inner silky threads, then wrap the outer husk back around the ear. You then soak the ear in water and finally place it on the grill, where it cooks by steaming. This method produces tasty corn, but to me it is missing the taste of the fire. So I follow this method until the corn is just cooked, which takes about 15 to 20 minutes over a low fire. I then remove the husks, brush on a little butter, season with salt and pepper, and roll the ears around on the grill ever so slightly, just to add a little char.

Another method calls for the interior silk to be removed and for the corn to then be wrapped in foil along with butter and seasonings and roasted in the coals for 12 to 15 minutes. This is also an excellent method, although again it misses the taste of the fire.

Whichever technique you use, summer corn cooked on the grill is a welcome addition to any meal, its natural simplicity making for some outstanding eating.

Your Basic Black Beans

◆ ◆

2 cups dried black beans
2 large yellow onions, diced
   small
4 tablespoons peanut oil
2 tablespoons minced garlic
1 teaspoon chili powder
1 teaspoon ground cumin
1 teaspoon Tabasco sauce
1 teaspoon sugar
4 tablespoons white vinegar
2 cups water
1 bottle of your favorite beer
Salt and freshly cracked pepper
   to taste

3 scallions, chopped, for garnish

1. Soak the beans in cold water to cover for 5 hours, then drain and rinse them well.

2. In a saucepan, sauté the onion in the peanut oil over medium-high heat until clear, 4 to 5 minutes.

3. Add the garlic, and cook another minute.

4. Add the chili powder, cumin, Tabasco sauce, sugar, vinegar, water, and beer, and bring to a simmer.

5. Add the beans, bring everything to a simmer again, then cover well and cook over low heat for 3 hours or until the beans are soft to the bite. If you think additional liquid is needed, add more beer.

A staple in much of the world. Cook a big batch and keep it in the refrigerator to heat up anytime you need 'em. These are good by themselves or with rice, providing a smooth, comforting complement to spicy grilled foods. The beer gives a touch of malty flavor. I prefer a dark or amber beer, but use what you like. ◆ *Serves 6 to 8 as a side dish*

SERVING SUGGESTIONS: Serve this with Chili Auténtico con Mucha Cerveza (page 46), Grilled West Indies Spice-Rubbed Chicken Breast with Grilled Banana (page 165), Lime-Marinated Grilled Kingfish with Red Onion and Mango Relish (page 91), or any other spicy dish.

6. Finish the dish by seasoning with salt and pepper to taste, and garnish with chopped scallion. Keeps up to 1 week, covered and refrigerated.

Black Bean Salad

◆◆

For the beans

1 pound dried black turtle beans
½ teaspoon dried thyme
½ teaspoon salt
¼ teaspoon fennel seed
2 fat garlic cloves, peeled
1 bay leaf

For the dressing

⅔ cup chopped red onion
½ cup chopped red bell pepper
2 tablespoons chopped parsley
2 tablespoons chopped cilantro
2 tablespoons chopped scallion
1 tablespoon ground cumin
⅛ teaspoon cayenne pepper
4 tablespoons olive oil
10 tablespoons lime juice (about 5 limes)
Salt and freshly cracked black pepper to taste

1. Sort the beans carefully, discarding any small pebbles that may be mixed in. Soak the beans in cold water to cover for 5 hours, then drain and rinse them well.

2. Put the beans in a saucepan and add enough water to come about 1½ inches above them.

This dish is Mexican/Southwestern in concept. It's a bit like a salad of greens, where black beans substitute for the lettuce and the rather large dose of lime juice makes it surprisingly refreshing. It travels well and is better the day after it's made: a good accompaniment to hot or cold grilled meat. You can also add cold grilled meat directly to the salad and turn it into an entrée. ◆ *Serves 6 to 8*

3. Add the thyme, salt, fennel seed, garlic, and bay leaf. Bring to a boil, then reduce the heat and simmer, uncovered, for 1 to 1½ hours, or until the beans are tender but not mushy.

4. Drain the beans and rinse them under cold water for 1 minute to stop the cooking process. Drain them again.

5. In a large bowl, combine the dressing ingredients and mix well. Add the beans, toss, and serve. This salad keeps for 4 to 5 days, covered and refrigerated.

PICKLED CHILE PEPPERS

If you find chile peppers you really like, or if you simply have an abundance from your garden, you might want to consider pickling them. There will be a slight change in their flavor, but the heat and their general characteristics will remain the same.

Make enough pickling solution to cover the amount of chile peppers that you have, mixing the ingredients in the following proportions: 1 cup vinegar to ½ cup sugar to 2 cloves of garlic. Bring this mixture to a boil over high heat, remove it from the heat, pour it over the chile peppers to cover, and cool to room temperature. Put in a jar with a tight cover, making sure that the liquid completely covers the peppers. They will keep this way for up to 3 months at room temperature.

Grandma Wetzler's Baked Beans

◆◆

½ pound bacon, diced
1 yellow onion, diced small
1 gallon water
½ cup molasses
½ cup brown sugar
2 cups ketchup
2 tablespoons cheap yellow
    mustard
1¼ pounds navy beans (soaked
    in water to cover overnight)
Salt and freshly cracked black
    pepper to taste

Made from my grandma's Pennsylvania Dutch recipe, these beans just can't be beat. Filling, satisfying, and slightly sweet, no picnic or barbecue feast is complete without them. ◆ *Serves 10 as a side dish*

SERVING SUGGESTIONS: Serve these with any picnic food or barbecue. They are a virtually indispensable accompaniment to The Only Real Barbecue Sandwich (page 271), Texas Barbecued Beef Brisket (page 275), and Barbecued Ribs, Missouri Style (page 269).

1. In a large pot, sauté the bacon over medium heat until browned, about 5 minutes.

2. Add the diced onions and cook until browned, about 5 minutes.

3. Add the water, molasses, brown sugar, ketchup, and mustard, and bring to a boil.

4. Add the beans, bring back up to a boil, then reduce to a slow simmer and cook 4 to 5 hours until the beans are soft, adding water from time to time if necessary and stirring often to prevent burning. Season with salt and pepper to taste. These beans will keep, covered and refrigerated, about 1 week.

Grilled Ham Hocks and Black-eyed Peas

◆◆

2 1-pound ham hocks
2 yellow onions, diced medium
2 celery stalks, diced medium
2 carrots, diced medium
4 tablespoons peanut oil
½ cup white vinegar
1 pound dried black-eyed peas
½ teaspoon red pepper flakes
Salt and freshly cracked black
   pepper to taste

1. Grill the ham hocks on all sides over a low fire until well browned, about 10 to 12 minutes. Remove them from the grill and set aside.

2. In a small saucepan over medium heat, sauté the onion, celery, and carrot in the peanut oil until clear, about 7 minutes.

3. Add the ham hocks, vinegar, and enough water to cover. Bring to a simmer, cover, and simmer very slowly for 2 hours.

4. Add the black-eyed peas, pepper flakes, and salt and pepper to taste. Bring this back to a simmer, and cook until the peas are soft but not mushy, about 1½ hours. Check every 20 minutes or so to see if more water is needed. When finished, all the water should be absorbed. Keeps up to 4 days covered and refrigerated.

Just a slight deviation on the Southern staple. In this preparation although the hocks are already smoked, they are also seared on the grill, which gives the dish an extra smoky, charred dimension.
◆ *Serves 6 as a side dish*

SERVING SUGGESTIONS: Serve this with Doc's Cheddar Biscuits (page 309) and Grilled Country Ham and Applesauce (page 154).

Breads and Desserts

In this chapter mainly on desserts I've also included a couple of breads. Some are good for cooling down hot foods, others are ideal for scooping up the different dips and chutneys that accompany grilled food. Still others are good for grilling themselves, and appear in a number of guises throughout the book.

The desserts are simple, down-home desserts—easy to make, satisfying, hearty, and rich. I find that I can eat them night after night, and that they are a perfect touch after grilled foods.

East Coast Grill Corn Bread

◆ ◆

4 cups all-purpose flour
2 cups yellow cornmeal
1½ cups sugar
1 teaspoon salt
2 tablespoons baking powder
4 eggs
3 cups milk
2½ tablespoons vegetable oil
½ cup melted butter

1. Preheat the oven to 350°F.

2. Lightly oil a 2″ × 12″ × 8″ pan.

3. Sift together the flour, cornmeal, sugar, salt, and baking powder.

4. In a separate bowl, mix together the eggs, milk, and vegetable oil.

5. Pour the wet ingredients over the dry ingredients, then add the melted butter. Stir until just mixed.

6. Bake for approximately 1 hour, or until a cake tester comes out clean. The corn bread should be brown on top when done.

The ubiquitous companion to Southwestern and Southern dishes, from Chili Auténtico con Mucha Cerveza (page 46) to Barbecued Ribs, Missouri Style (page 269) to Boiled Collard Greens with Salt Pork (page 292). This slightly sweet version is perfect for mopping up pot likker or cooling off your palate after hot dishes. If you have any left over, use it in the Corn Bread Salad with Lime Juice and Cilantro (page 312), or cut it into small cubes and bake them in a 350°F oven for 30 to 45 minutes, until brown and toasty, and you have marvelous croutons for your green salads.

◆ *12 thick pieces*

Hot Pepper Corn Bread

1¼ cups yellow cornmeal
1¼ cups all-purpose flour
3 tablespoons sugar
2 teaspoons baking powder
1 teaspoon salt
1 cup canned cream-style corn
¾ cup buttermilk
6 small, fresh red *or* green chile
  peppers of your choice, finely
  chopped
1 whole small yellow onion,
  grated
1 egg, lightly beaten
1 cup grated sharp cheddar
  cheese
4 tablespoons vegetable oil

1. Preheat oven to 350°F. Grease a 2″ × 12″ × 8″ pan.

2. In a large mixing bowl, sift together the cornmeal, flour, sugar, baking powder, and salt. Set aside.

3. In a saucepan, heat the corn and buttermilk until warm, but do not boil. Remove from heat, add the chile peppers and onion, and mix well.

4. Add the egg and cheese to the buttermilk mixture and mix well.

5. Add the egg-buttermilk mixture to the dry ingredients, pour in the oil, and mix just until well combined.

6. Pour the batter into the greased pan and bake for 30 minutes, or until the top is nicely brown.

This is a slightly more ambitious and complex version of traditional down-home corn bread, sort of a nouvelle Tex-Mex variety. ◆ *12 thin pieces*

SERVING SUGGESTIONS: Serve this with Grilled Marinated Quail (page 200) or Grilled Venison Loin with Bourbon Peaches (page 208) for a fancy feast, or try it with Clam Posole (page 36) for a simpler meal.

Quesadilla Bread

1 cup pastry flour
2 cups all-purpose flour
1 tablespoon baking powder
1 tablespoon salt
1 tablespoon freshly cracked
  pepper (white is best if you
  have it)
12 eggs, separated
½ cup sugar
1 pound unsalted butter, melted
3 cups grated sharp cheddar
  cheese (approximately ¾
  pound)
1½ cups sour cream

1. Preheat the oven to 375°F.

2. Grease a 12″ × 17″ baking pan.

3. Sift together the flours, baking powder, salt, and pepper, and set aside.

4. Beat the egg yolks and sugar together until light. Beat the egg whites until they form stiff peaks, then fold in the yolk mixture.

5. Working steadily, fold in the dry ingredients, the melted butter, the grated cheese, and finally the sour cream.

6. Pour the batter into the greased pan and bake for 20 to 30 minutes, or until the entire top of the bread is golden brown and a cake tester comes out clean.

7. Let the bread cool slightly in the pan, then turn it out onto a wire rack and cool completely.

We developed this bread at the East Coast Grill to serve as a polentalike foil for spicy Latin recipes. The cheese and sour cream tend to cool the palate after these fiery dishes. ♦ *One 12″ × 17″ pan*

SERVING SUGGESTIONS: This bread goes very well with Grilled Tripe and Hominy Stew (page 38), Clam Posole (page 36), or Chili Auténtico con Mucha Cerveza (page 46).

Pita Bread

1 tablespoon dry yeast
½ tablespoon sugar
1½ cups lukewarm water
1½ tablespoons dried rosemary
    (optional)
½ cup whole wheat flour
3 cups all-purpose flour
2 teaspoons salt
½ teaspoon freshly cracked
    pepper (white is best if you
    have it)
1 tablespoon olive oil
Approximately 2 tablespoons
    yellow cornmeal

1. Preheat the oven to 500°F.

2. Mix the yeast, sugar, water, and rosemary in a small covered bowl, and set it in a warm place to allow the yeast to develop. This can take from 5 to 30 minutes, depending on the temperature. Just check every few minutes, and when the surface of the mixture is foamy, the yeast is ready.

3. Meanwhile, sift the flours, salt, and pepper together into a large bowl.

4. Add the olive oil to the ready yeast mixture, then stir the yeast mixture into the dry ingredients gradually, using a wooden spoon, until the wet ingredients are fully incorporated. Turn the dough out onto a well-floured board and knead until the dough is firm and has some elasticity, about 5 to 10 minutes.

I call for grilled pita often in this book because it is so versatile and goes so well with grilled food. Most store-bought pita is fresh and tasty, but if you feel like making your own, here's a recipe that really works. The pitas actually puff up and separate into two layers, and the optional rosemary adds an aromatic earthiness that you can't get in commercial pita. Brush these babies with a little olive oil and grill them about 30 seconds or so, just until they are brown. They are perfect for scooping things up, stuffing things into, or dipping into things. This recipe was developed by Laura Bezel. ◆ *12 small pitas*

5. Place the dough in an oiled bowl, cover with plastic wrap, and set in a warm spot. Allow the dough to rise until doubled in volume, which will take 15 minutes to 1 hour, again depending upon the temperature. Be careful not to let the dough more than double in volume, or it will not rise fully when you bake it.

6. When the dough has doubled in volume, turn it out onto a floured cutting board. Cut the dough into 12 pieces and roll them around until they are round, even spheres. The spheres should be slightly larger than Ping-Pong balls. Cover them with a damp kitchen towel and allow them to rest for 5 minutes.

7. Remove the towel and gently roll the dough spheres into circles, using plenty of flour on the cutting board to keep the dough from sticking. The circles should be 5 to 6 inches in diameter, and a little less than ¼ inch thick. Cover the circles with the damp towel and allow them to rest for 20 minutes.

8. About 10 minutes before baking, sprinkle 2 baking sheets with the cornmeal and put them into the oven to get hot. (What makes these breads rise is not just the yeast, but the moisture in the dough turning to steam when it hits the hot surface: This causes the big air bubble in the center that separates the pitas into two parts.)

9. Pull out 1 hot pan, place 6 circles on it, and pop the pan back into the oven as quickly as you

---

Good Things to Eat in or on Grilled Pita

◆◆◆◆◆◆◆◆◆◆◆◆◆◆

Banana–Green Mango Chutney
Page 213

Raisin-Ginger Chutney
Page 217

Black Olive and Citrus Relish
Page 226

Grilled Eggplant Condiment
Page 245

Roasted Red Pepper Coulis with Basil
Page 235

Very Aromatic Tomato-Ginger Jam
Page 231

Braised Garlic and Onion Jam
Page 233

Spicy Banana-Coconut Ketchup
Page 230

can. Let the pitas bake for 4 to 5 minutes, being sure not to open the oven door. The pitas should be puffy and just slightly brown when done.

10. As soon as the first pan is done, remove it from the oven and set it aside to cool. Now repeat the baking procedure with the second pan and the second set of pitas. The pitas will flatten as they cool.

Scallion Pancakes

◆◆

1 cup all-purpose flour
1 cup pastry flour
1 tablespoon baking powder
1½ teaspoons salt
½ teaspoon freshly cracked pepper (white is best if you have it)
3 scallions, finely chopped
1 cup cold water
½ cup olive oil
2 tablespoons sesame oil

These Chinese pancakes are easy to make and have a wonderful, unique flavor. Serve them with a small bowl of hoisin sauce for spreading on them. ◆ *6 pancakes*

SERVING SUGGESTIONS: Serve these with Grilled Duck Breast with Kumquat-Sugarcane-Basil Glaze (page 198), Grilled Squid with Asian Slaw and Hoisin Barbecue Sauce (page 107), or Spicy Green Bean Salad with Grilled Pork and Peanuts (page 288).

1. In a large bowl, sift together the flours, baking powder, salt, and pepper. Add the scallion, pour in the cold water, and mix with a wooden spoon until the water is well incorporated. The dough should be fairly wet and sticky. If it is dry add additional water.

2. Turn the dough out onto a floured cutting board and knead until it has some elasticity and is smooth, about 1 to 2 minutes.

3. Divide the dough into 6 pieces and form each piece into a ball, using the palm of your hand. Cover with plastic wrap, and let them rest in a cool spot (but not refrigerated) for 15 minutes.

4. On a floured cutting board, roll out each piece of dough to form a disc approximately 6 inches in diameter and ¼ inch thick. (If the dough is pliable enough, you can use your hands instead of a rolling pin.) Cover the discs with plastic wrap and leave them in a cool place, but not the refrigerator, for at least 30 minutes, or up to several hours.

5. Heat the olive and sesame oils in a frying pan until they just begin to smoke slightly. This is very important, since the oil must be very hot or the dough will absorb it instead of floating on top.

6. Gently slide the dough discs, one at a time, into the oil and cook them for 1 to 2 minutes, until brown and puffy. Then flip them over and cook for another minute. Drain them on paper towels.

Jamaican Guy Flan

✦✦✦✦✦✦✦✦✦✦✦✦✦✦✦✦✦✦✦✦✦✦✦✦✦✦✦✦✦✦✦✦✦✦✦✦✦✦

1 12-ounce can evaporated milk
4 tablespoons sugar
3 large eggs
3 tablespoons Tia Maria (you may substitute Kahlúa)
About 4 tablespoons brown sugar

1. Preheat the oven to 350°F.

2. In a medium-sized bowl, mix all the ingredients except the brown sugar well with a mixer or beater until the sugar is thoroughly combined.

3. Ladle the mixture into 8 4-ounce ramekins, and put them into a small roasting pan. (If you don't have ramekins, use any small oven-proof containers. In a pinch I've used ceramic coffee cups.) Fill the pan with hot water halfway up the sides of the ramekins, and cover the pan with tinfoil.

4. Bake covered for 50 minutes. Use a wooden skewer or cake tester to check whether the flans are done. They should come out wet but clean. Don't despair if after 50 minutes the flans aren't set. Depending on the efficiency of your oven, they may take a bit longer. After 5 minutes, uncover them and check again.

5. Remove the flans from the water bath and refrigerate them for at least 1 hour, or up to 24 hours.

Go to any tropical climate, and you'll find that one of the most popular desserts is some version of this classic custard. It's light, easy to prepare, and a soothing touch after eating spicy dishes. This Caribbean-inspired version follows custom and uses evaporated rather than fresh milk, which is not readily available in many island locations, and sports a bubbly brown sugar crust.

Why Jamaican guy? Because the guy who makes it in our restaurant kitchen is Jamaican, and his version uses Tia Maria. Depending on your mood (or the contents of your liquor cabinet), add brandy or Grand Marnier for French Guy Flan, Kahlúa for Mexican, Amaretto or Frangelico for Italian.
✦ *Serves 8*

6. Just before serving, sift the brown sugar through a wire colander or flour sifter onto the top of the flans. You want a thin layer of sugar, but you also want the top of the custard well covered.

7. Light your broiler, put the flans on a baking sheet, and slide the sheet under the broiler. Broil about 1 to 2 minutes, just until the brown sugar is melted. Watch carefully so it doesn't burn.

Pumpkin Spice Cake with Lemon-Orange Sauce

◆·◆

1⅔ cups all-purpose white flour
¾ teaspoon salt
¼ teaspoon baking soda
1½ teaspoons baking powder
2 teaspoons powdered ginger
½ teaspoon cinnamon
¼ teaspoon nutmeg
¼ teaspoon ground cloves
1 cup canned pumpkin
⅓ cup water
8 tablespoons unsalted butter, softened
1½ cups sugar
2 large eggs
½ cup walnuts, coarsely chopped

This moist cake keeps well for days on end. I like its combination of the earthy spice taste with the sophisticated citrus sauce. ◆ *Serves 8*

1. Preheat the oven to 350°F.

2. Butter and flour a 9-inch cake pan.

3. In a large bowl, sift together the flour, salt, baking soda, baking powder, and spices, and set aside.

4. In a small bowl, combine the pumpkin and water.

5. Using an electric mixer, cream the butter until it turns white, 2 to 3 minutes. Add the sugar and continue to cream until very well mixed and fluffy in texture.

6. Add the eggs to the butter-sugar mixture, and continue to beat until ribbons form when the beaters are lifted, at least 2 to 3 minutes.

7. Alternately fold in thirds of the dry ingredients and the pumpkin mixture. Gently fold in the nuts.

8. Pour the batter into the buttered and floured pan and bake for 1 hour, or until a cake tester comes out clean when inserted in the middle of the cake. Allow it to cool before removing it from the pan, and serve each slice drizzled with Lemon-Orange Sauce.

Lemon-Orange Sauce

3 large eggs
¾ cup granulated sugar
8 tablespoons lemon juice
   (about 2 lemons)
2 tablespoons grated orange zest
5 tablespoons unsalted butter,
   room temperature
2 tablespoons Grand Marnier *or*
   other orange liqueur

About 1½ cups

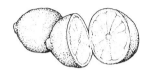

1. Using an electric mixer on high speed, whip the eggs and sugar together in a stainless steel bowl until doubled in volume, about 7 minutes.

2. Beat in the lemon juice and orange zest.

3. Place the mixture in the top of a double boiler and, over medium heat, cook until it is very thick. Stir the mixture frequently with a rubber spatula so that it cooks evenly.

4. Remove it from the heat. Add the butter and liqueur, and stir until the butter is completely melted.

5. Strain the sauce through a fine sieve and serve warm or chilled.

East Coast Grill Maple-Pecan Bread Pudding

◆◆

8 large eggs
¼ cup all-purpose flour
4 cups half-and-half
1½ cups maple syrup plus extra
   for topping
1 teaspoon vanilla
Dash of salt
Dash each of cinnamon and
   nutmeg
1 large loaf stale bread (Italian
   or French is best, but use
   Wonder if you prefer), sliced
½ cup toasted chopped pecans

From a time when people did not have year-round access to exotic ingredients for desserts—this sweet, custardy pudding uses staples that everybody has on hand. It may not be intricate or delicate, but it's filling and delicious. Besides, what else can you do with the extra loaf of bread that didn't get eaten at last night's dinner? ◆ *Serves 8*

1. Preheat the oven to 350°F.

2. Butter and flour an 8″ × 12″ baking dish.

3. In a large mixing bowl, beat the eggs lightly. Add the flour and continue to beat until smooth. Add the half-and-half, 1½ cups maple syrup, vanilla, salt, and spices, and beat the custard until well mixed.

4. Using a serrated knife, remove the crusts from the bread and cut it into 4″ × 2″ rectangles. If the bread is not stale, place the slices in a 200°F oven for about 15 minutes, until dried but not toasted.

5. Layer the bread lengthwise in the baking dish, overlapping slightly, in 3 or 4 rows (this is known as shingled bread). The bread should be at about a 45-

degree angle from the bottom of the pan and should fit snugly.

6. Ladle the custard over the bread evenly until the pan is full. Let the bread soak in the custard for about 5 minutes, pressing the bread down if necessary to be sure it is fully submerged.

7. Sprinkle the pecans over the top of the pudding and cover the pan with tinfoil. Place a baking dish full of water on the bottom shelf of the oven, place the pudding on the middle shelf, and bake for 1 hour, turning the pudding after ½ hour to ensure even baking.

8. After 1 hour, remove the tinfoil and continue baking for 15 minutes or until the top is golden brown and the custard firmly set. Serve with a bit of maple syrup trickled over the top.

MAYBE IT'S IN THE GENES

Bread pudding is one of those desserts that is very simple to make, but that some people just make better than anybody else. Rosemary Mack, the original baker at the East Coast Grill, could make a bread pudding that was like manna from heaven. Our customers clamored for it, and no one else could even come close to achieving the same result.

One day, just as an experiment, I stood beside her and made a batch right along with her, mimicking her every move. Sure enough . . . when they came out of the oven, mine was mighty good, but hers was simply out of this world. I never will understand why some people are born bakers, but I sure can appreciate the results.

Chocolate Pudding Cake

2 cups all-purpose flour
1½ cups plus ⅔ cup granulated
   sugar
4 tablespoons baking powder
½ teaspoon salt
1¼ cups unsweetened cocoa
1 cup milk
1 tablespoon vanilla
¼ cup melted butter
½ cup brown sugar
2 cups freshly brewed coffee
1 cup water

Whipped cream for garnish
   (optional)

1. Preheat the oven to 350°F.

2. Butter a 9″ × 12″ pan.

3. In a large mixing bowl, sift together the flour, 1½ cups sugar, baking powder, salt, and ½ cup cocoa. Set the mixture aside.

4. In another bowl, combine the milk, vanilla, and melted butter, and mix well. (Don't worry if the butter starts to solidify, just mix it in well.)

5. Add the dry mixture to the liquid mixture, and mix only until combined well. You will end up with a gooey, thick batter.

6. Spoon the batter into the buttered pan, spreading it evenly over the bottom.

This gooey chocolate brownie cake which bakes in its own chocolate sauce is a sold-out favorite. A childhood fantasy come true. Don't let the many steps intimidate you here, this is actually a simple, no-fail recipe. And no, that's not a misprint: The four tablespoons of baking powder are what lift the batter up through the sauce! Since it's equally delicious hot from the oven or cold the next day, this is an ideal do-ahead dessert. ◆ *Serves 12*

7. In a bowl combine the brown sugar, ⅔ cup white sugar, and remaining ¾ cup cocoa. Mix well with a fork and sprinkle the mixture evenly over the top of the batter.

8. Mix together the coffee and water, and pour over the sugar mixture on top of the batter.

9. Bake 30 to 40 minutes. Check every 5 minutes after the first 30 minutes. You will know the cake is done when it pulls away from the sides of the pan and some sauce comes bubbling through the top surface. Serve it with whipped cream if you wish.

Mississippi Mud Cake

◆◆

6 ounces unsweetened chocolate
½ cup strong-brewed coffee
½ cup bourbon
½ pound (2 sticks) butter
1½ cups sugar
2 cups flour
2 teaspoons baking powder
1 teaspoon salt
4 large eggs
2 teaspoons vanilla

This dense chocolate cake is a Southern tradition, as rich and thick as the river mud that gives it its name.
◆ *Serves 10*

1. Preheat the oven to 350°F.

2. Butter and flour a 9-inch springform pan. If you don't have a springform, you may use a standard 9-inch round cake pan.

3. Put the chocolate, coffee, bourbon, and butter into the top of a double boiler. Cook over medium heat, stirring occasionally, until the chocolate is melted.

4. Remove from the heat, add the sugar, and stir until it is completely dissolved. Set aside.

5. Sift together the flour, baking powder, and salt.

6. Whisk together the eggs and vanilla. Slowly whisk ¼ of the chocolate mixture into the egg mixture, then whisk the egg mixture back into the chocolate mixture.

7. Add the dry mixture to the liquid mixture in small batches, stirring after each addition just until flour is fully incorporated.

8. Pour the batter into the greased and floured pan and bake for 1 hour, or until the cake pulls away from the sides of the pan. If you aren't sure if the cake is done, give it a shake—if the whole top moves as one piece, it's done. If a section in the middle moves separately, bake it a few more minutes.

SOUTHERN HOSPITALITY, DESSERT DIVISION

Southerners are justifiably renowned for their sweet tooth, and a rich, hearty dessert is the favored ending to a meal south of the Mason-Dixon Line. Somehow a delicate pastry just doesn't seem to fit with the type of food that Southerners do best.

On a recent trip through Mississippi, I ate in a family-style restaurant where the owner brought to the table not only his version of Mississippi Mud Cake, but also banana pudding, sweet potato pie, and pound cake with a heavily sugared glaze. This was not so folks could have a choice, he explained—most of his regular customers would have all four. I did my best, but was probably branded as a Yankee, since I could only work my way through two.

Chocolate Bourbon Pound Cake

◆ ◆

3 cups brewed coffee (preferably espresso)
1 cup cheap bourbon
3 cups sugar
1 pound unsalted butter
12 ounces unsweetened baking chocolate, in small pieces
4 eggs
2 tablespoons vanilla
4 cups all-purpose flour
2 tablespoons baking soda
1 teaspoon salt

Spongy, rich, heavily flavored with the favorite liquor of the Old South, this is an easy, satisfying recipe. ◆ *Serves 10*

1. Preheat the oven to 350°F.

2. Butter and flour a 10-inch Bundt pan.

3. In a large bowl, mix the coffee, bourbon, and sugar together. Set aside.

4. Place the butter and chocolate in the top section of a double boiler over medium heat to melt. Stir occasionally until the mixture is smooth.

5. Add the coffee mixture to the chocolate mixture, remove from the heat, and stir well.

6. Beat the eggs and vanilla together lightly. Add ¼ of the chocolate-butter mixture to the beaten eggs, and mix well. Stirring constantly, pour the egg mixture back into the chocolate-butter mixture and mix very well.

7. In a large bowl, sift together the flour, baking soda, and salt. Pour the wet mixture into the dry mixture and mix well.

8. Pour the batter into the greased and floured pan and bake for 1 hour. The cake is done when a cake tester inserted into the center comes out clean.

9. Remove the cake from the oven and allow it to cool for 30 minutes in the pan, then turn it out onto a wire rack and cool completely.

Cary's Chocolate Cloud with Raspberry Sauce

◆◆

1 pound semisweet chocolate, coarsely chopped
6 large eggs
1 tablespoon dark rum
1 tablespoon brandy
1 cup heavy cream

Dense and intensely chocolate, this smooth terrine, which is the specialty of my partner, Cary Wheaton, will satisfy the strongest dessert cravings.
◆ *Serves 8*

1. Preheat the oven to 350°F.

2. Butter and flour a 6″ × 3″ loaf pan.

3. Melt the chocolate in the top of a double boiler and set aside.

4. Put the eggs, rum, and brandy into a stainless steel mixing bowl set over the bottom of the double

boiler. Over low heat, whisk this mixture vigorously, being careful that the egg does not coddle or cook on the sides of the bowl. If this should happen, remove the bowl from the heat and continue to whisk. Whisk for about 10 minutes. The eggs should become thick.

5. Remove the bowl from the heat and whisk in the melted chocolate.

6. Whip the cream until it holds soft peaks, then fold it into the chocolate mixture. Turn the mixture into the loaf pan.

7. Place the loaf pan inside a large baking pan and fill the baking pan with hot water to come halfway up the sides of the loaf pan. Place it on the center rack of the oven and bake for 1 hour and 20 minutes. When the Cloud is done, a toothpick inserted into the center should come out clean.

8. Let the Chocolate Cloud cool in the refrigerator for at least 2 hours before removing it from the pan to serve. Spoon several tablespoons of Raspberry Sauce onto a plate and top with a thin slice of Cloud.

Raspberry Sauce

◆ ◆

½ cup water
½ cup sugar
1 tablespoon grated orange rind
1 cup fresh *or* frozen
   raspberries
1 tablespoon Grand Marnier *or*
   Cointreau

About 2 cups

1. Boil the water, sugar, and orange rind together for 1 minute.

2. Add the raspberries and continue to boil for 2 more minutes.

3. Purée the mixture in a blender or food processor and strain through a fine sieve.

4. Cool to room temperature and add Grand Marnier or Cointreau. Keeps 10 days covered and refrigerated.

Pear-Blueberry Crisp

◆◆◆

For the topping

1 cup all-purpose flour
½ teaspoon cinnamon
¼ teaspoon nutmeg
⅓ cup dark brown sugar
2 tablespoons granulated sugar
1 cup chopped walnuts
6 tablespoons (3 ounces) cold
   butter, cut into 24 pieces

For the filling

3 large Anjou pears, cored and
   unpeeled
3 large McIntosh apples, cored
   and unpeeled
4 stalks rhubarb
1 pint blueberries
1 cup sugar
½ teaspoon cinnamon
¼ teaspoon ground ginger
⅓ teaspoon nutmeg
Dash of ground cloves

1. Preheat the oven to 350°F.

2. Butter a 10″ × 12″ × 2″ baking pan.

3. Make the topping: In a medium-sized mixing bowl, mix together all the dry ingredients. Add the butter and mix with a fork or your fingers until well incorporated. The mixture should be coarse and lumpy.

4. Cover the topping mixture and refrigerate.

Another of those simple desserts you can eat day after day. Blueberries and pears are a particularly pleasing combination, and the rhubarb adds just the right touch of tartness. The apples, for those of you who were wondering, act as a natural thickener without diluting the flavor of the berries and pears.
◆ *About 8 servings*

5. Make the filling: Cut the pears, apples, and rhubarb into bite-size chunks, and mix together with the blueberries in a large mixing bowl.

6. In a separate bowl, mix the sugar and spices for the filling together well.

7. Add the spices to the fruit mixture, mix well, and pour into the buttered pan. Cover with the topping and bake for 1 hour. The topping should be golden brown and the fruit quite soft when done. Remove and serve hot or at room temperature.

Apple Crisp

◆◆◆

Adapted from Jake and Earl's Dixie Barbecue

12 tart apples (about 4½ pounds)
1 cup granulated sugar
2 tablespoons lemon juice (about ½ lemon)
¼ teaspoon plus ⅛ teaspoon nutmeg
8 tablespoons brown sugar
2½ cups flour
½ teaspoon cinnamon
½ pound (2 sticks) cold butter
1½ cups coarsely chopped toasted walnuts

Whipped cream for garnish

Some call it Apple Pan Dowdy, but whatever you call it, it is the true original of down-home desserts. ◆ *Serves 8 to 12*

1. Preheat the oven to 375°F.

2. Wash the apples, then quarter and core them. Cut each quarter into thirds, and toss with ¾ cup sugar, the lemon juice, and ¼ teaspoon nutmeg. Allow this to sit for 20 minutes.

3. Combine the remaining ¼ cup sugar, the brown sugar, flour, the remaining ⅛ teaspoon nutmeg, and the cinnamon in the mixing bowl of an electric mixer.

4. Cut each stick of butter in half lengthwise and then into 6 pieces.

5. Using a paddle attachment, turn the mixer on to low speed and add the butter, mixing only until the mixture resembles coarse cornmeal. Do not overmix or the topping will not crumble properly.

6. Arrange the apple pieces in one layer in an 11″ × 15″ baking dish. Sprinkle the topping over them evenly and then sprinkle on the walnuts.

7. Bake for about 40 minutes, until the apples soften and the top browns.

8. Serve warm from the oven or at room temperature with whipped cream.

Peach Cobbler

◆◆◆

For the topping

2 cups all-purpose flour
1 tablespoon baking powder
¼ teaspoon salt
2 tablespoons sugar
1 tablespoon finely grated
    orange zest
4 tablespoons cold butter, cut
    into 16 pieces
½ cup milk
2 large eggs

For the filling

14 peaches, pitted and unpeeled
1½ cups sugar
1 teaspoon cinnamon
¼ teaspoon nutmeg

1. Preheat the oven to 350°F.

2. Butter a 10″ × 12″ × 2″ baking pan.

3. Make the topping: Mix all the dry ingredients, including the orange zest, in a medium-sized bowl. Using a fork, cut the butter into this mixture until it has the consistency of coarse meal. Add the milk and eggs, and mix until smooth. Cover and refrigerate.

4. Make the filling: Cut the peaches into bite-sized chunks. In a large mixing bowl, combine the sugar and spices. Add the peach chunks and toss until they are well coated.

A classic country dessert which I always eat topped with heavy cream. The technique of cooking the peach mixture before adding the topping avoids the twin perils of cobblers: undercooked fruit or overcooked topping. You can substitute apples or pears or most any other fruit for the peaches in this recipe, but vary the sugar and spices accordingly.
◆ *About 8 servings*

5. Place the fruit mixture in the pan and bake for 20 minutes. Remove from the oven and spoon the topping over the fruit until the fruit is covered.

6. Put it back into the oven for another 20 to 25 minutes, or until the top is light brown.

Sweet Potato–Peanut Pie

◆ ◆

For the topping

- 4 tablespoons cold butter, cut into 8 pieces
- 4 tablespoons brown sugar
- 4 tablespoons all-purpose flour
- 4 tablespoons roasted, unsalted peanuts, finely chopped

For the filling

- 1 medium sweet potato
- 8 tablespoons unsalted butter, room temperature
- ¾ cup brown sugar
- 3 large eggs, separated
- ¾ cup milk
- ⅛ teaspoon salt
- ¼ teaspoon each of allspice, ground cloves, and nutmeg
- ¼ cup rum
- 4 tablespoons chopped roasted, unsalted peanuts

This is a combination of two holiday pies from my Southern childhood. Sweet potatoes and peanuts were abundant staples of eighteenth-century Southern cooking, so pies made from these two ingredients were a fixture in the taverns of colonial Williamsburg. Combining them results in a mixture of smooth and crunchy textures, and folding the beaten egg whites into the filling before baking gives you a lighter version of the traditional pie. The topping is really a peanut streusel, which seemed to me to be a natural Southern variant on Scandinavian walnut streusel. ◆ *One 9″ pie*

1. Preheat the oven to 375°F.

2. Prepare the partially baked shell (recipe follows) and set aside.

3. Make the topping: Place all four ingredients in a bowl and mix them with your fingers until just combined. Do not overmix—the topping should look crumbly.

4. Make the filling: Peel the sweet potato, cut it in half, and boil until tender, testing with a fork.

5. Cool the potato and mash it until smooth. A ricer makes the smoothest potatoes, but a potato masher or electric mixer also works fine.

6. In an electric mixer, cream the butter and brown sugar together until light and fluffy.

7. Add the sweet potato to the butter mixture and mix well, then beat in the egg yolks and milk until thoroughly combined.

8. Add the salt, allspice, cloves, nutmeg, and rum, and mix again.

9. In a clean bowl, beat the egg whites until stiff (not dry) peaks form.

10. Stir a third of the egg whites into the potato mixture. Gently fold in the remaining egg whites. Gently fold in the peanuts.

11. Pour this mixture into a partially baked pie shell.

12. Sprinkle the topping evenly over the pie and bake in the center of the oven until the pie is set, about 40 minutes.

Short Pie Dough

2¼ cups all-purpose flour plus extra for rolling the dough
1 tablespoon sugar
¼ teaspoon kosher salt
½ pound (2 sticks) cold butter
½ cup cold water

♦ *Enough for two 9″ pies*

1. Preheat the oven to 350°F.

2. In a mixing bowl, sift together the flour, sugar, and salt.

3. Cut the cold butter into 8 to 10 small pieces and, using 2 forks or a pastry cutter, cut into the flour mixture until it resembles coarse meal.

4. Add the water and mix briefly, just until the dough comes together.

5. Divide the dough into 2 equal parts, wrap each half in plastic wrap, and refrigerate for at least 15 minutes. (The dough has to be chilled thoroughly so that the butter doesn't melt while the dough is being rolled out.)

6. Rolling the dough: Remove 1 piece of the dough from the refrigerator and place it on a lightly floured surface. Dust the rolling pin and the dough itself with flour as well. Using your hands, shape the dough into a thick circle, about 5 inches in diameter. Then use the rolling pin and roll the dough from the center out, rotating it with your hands from time to time. Each time you rotate, dust the dough with

flour so it doesn't stick to the table. Always apply pressure on the rolling pin very evenly and gently so the dough is a uniform thickness. For a 9-inch pie, roll the dough out to a circle about 13 inches in diameter.

7. Brush the excess flour off the dough. To get the dough from the table into the pie pan, fold it in half, pulling the top half toward yourself, then gently slide your fingers under the dough and lift it into the pan. Now unfold the dough so it fills the pan. There should be about 1 to 1½ inches of dough overlapping the edge of the pan. Gently tuck the dough so it fits snugly into the pan, then trim the overhanging dough with a paring knife so there is an even 1-inch overhang. Gently press the dough into the sides of the pan.

8. Refrigerate the dough for about 15 minutes or until it is firm again. When it is firm, pinch the edges together to form a pretty border around the shell.

9. Prebake the shell. Fit a piece of tinfoil into the chilled shell and place an empty pie pan over it so it fits snugly. Bake for about 15 minutes or until the edge of the crust is fully cooked but the shell is semiraw in the center.

Pie dough freezes well. Save the other half for another pie.

Chocolate Peanut Butter Pie

◆ ◆

For the graham cracker crust

¾ cup graham cracker crumbs
4 tablespoons granulated sugar
2 tablespoons brown sugar
4 tablespoons butter, melted

For the filling

1½ cups heavy cream
8 ounces cream cheese, room
    temperature
¾ cup sugar
1 cup creamy peanut butter
1 tablespoon vanilla

For the chocolate sauce

¾ cup heavy cream
8 ounces semisweet chocolate,
    grated

This easy-to-make pie is like a giant, creamy peanut butter cup. Need I say more? ◆ *One 9" pie*

1. Make the crust: In a food processor or blender, blend the dry ingredients well. Drizzle in the melted butter and process or blend until the dry ingredients are well moistened. Press the mixture firmly into a 9-inch pie pan, pressing another pan on top to distribute the mixture evenly. Freeze for at least 1 hour, or until ready for use.

2. Make the filling: Whip the heavy cream until it holds soft peaks. Set aside.

3. In a large mixing bowl, beat the cream cheese until smooth. Add

the sugar and mix well. Add the peanut butter and vanilla and mix well, scraping the sides of the bowl. Fold in the whipped cream.

4. Place the batter into the frozen pie shell and put it back in the freezer for 1 hour.

5. Make the chocolate sauce: In a heavy saucepan, slowly bring the heavy cream to a boil. Turn off the heat, add the chocolate, and cover the saucepan, leaving it on the stove. After 10 minutes, stir the mixture until the chocolate is completely melted. Cool slightly (room temperature is best).

6. Pour the chocolate sauce on top of the pie, place it in the refrigerator for 30 minutes, and serve chilled.

Chocolate Pecan Pie

◆ ◆

3 ounces unsweetened baking
   chocolate
2 tablespoons unsalted butter
1 cup light corn syrup
1 cup sugar
4 eggs
1 teaspoon vanilla
1 cup pecans

This is another pie that combines two of my favorite ingredients, in this case chocolate and pecans. While it is not as "pure" as a traditional Southern pecan pie, it is a little less sweet—which means you can eat more of it. ◆ *One 9" pie*

1. Preheat the oven to 350°F.

2. Melt the chocolate and butter together in a double boiler over gently simmering water, then set aside.

3. Combine the corn syrup and sugar in a saucepan and bring to a boil, stirring constantly. When the mixture boils, let it simmer until the sugar is completely dissolved, about 2 minutes. Remove from the heat and set aside.

4. Lightly beat together the eggs and vanilla in a large bowl. Combine the sugar syrup and the chocolate mixture, stir well, and pour ¾ cup of this mixture into the eggs, stirring constantly. Pour it slowly back into the chocolate mixture, again stirring constantly. Stir in the pecans and pour into a frozen pie shell (recipe follows).

5. Bake for 1 hour. The pie will rise and crack as it bakes.

Pie Dough

1 cup all-purpose flour
½ teaspoon salt
2 tablespoons butter, chilled
1 tablespoon shortening
4 tablespoons cold water

For one 9" pie

1. Sift together the flour and salt. Cut the butter into the flour mixture with a fork until it is the consistency of meal. Cut in the shortening.

2. Add the cold water gradually and mix just long enough to fully incorporate it. Knead gently until the dough is smooth.

3. On a floured surface, roll the dough out to a 10-inch-diameter circle, lift it into a pie pan, and trim the edges. Let it rest before baking. For this recipe, it is actually best to freeze the pie shell 1 hour before baking.

Whistle While You Work: Refreshing Beverages

◆ ◆

Sometimes when you're outside grilling, the temperature just seems to keep on climbing. Some say that if you can't stand the heat, you should get out of the kitchen. Since you're already out of the kitchen, I say, "If you can't stand the heat, have a cool drink." Here is a selection of beverages that by reason of history, geography, or just plain good taste seem to go well with grilled foods and good times.

East Coast Grill Lemonade

1 cup granulated sugar
½ cup water
2 cups freshly squeezed lemon
   juice (about 8 lemons)
1 quart cold water
Mint sprigs for garnish

1. In a small saucepot, combine the sugar and the ½ cup of water. Bring to a boil, stirring frequently, and let them boil for 1 minute to dissolve the sugar. Let the mixture cool.

2. When the sugar mixture is cool, add the lemon juice and the quart of cold water and mix well.

3. Pour over crushed ice. Garnish with mint sprigs.

When was the last time you had a big, ice-filled glass of real lemonade? It's easy to make, exceptionally refreshing, and looks dazzling in a big pitcher with slices of lemon and sprigs of mint. This drink is a good alternative for your friends who prefer nonalcoholic beverages, and for those who don't—float a touch of dark rum on the top. ◆ *About ½ gallon*

Mint Julep

1 teaspoon sugar
10 fresh mint leaves
5 to 6 ice cubes
2 ounces (1 jigger) bourbon

1. Put the sugar and mint leaves in the bottom of a glass.

Fights, facts, fiction, and folklore regarding the mint julep, its heritage and its preparation, are as intense as those surrounding barbecue. As to origin, the only real difference is the size of the geographic area participating in the dispute; most of the South lays claim to barbecue, whereas the argument over

2. Wrap the ice cubes in a towel and smash them a couple of times with a hammer or a frying pan. It is crucial that the ice be cracked—not crushed, not cubed, but cracked into pieces about the diameter of a die (that's half a set of dice).

3. Fill the glass to the top with the cracked ice.

4. Take a spoon and muddle (bruise) the mint and sugar in the bottom of the glass for 10 seconds or so.

5. Drop in the bourbon and stir. I prefer straight bourbon to sour mash, and the brand I particularly recommend is Southern Gentleman.

the mint julep is pretty much limited to Virginia and Kentucky. I can solve that argument once and for all: It was created in Tidewater, Virginia, where I just happened to grow up.

Even the way the drink is served is controversial. Some purists refuse to recognize any drink as a julep unless it's served in a silver cup. Personally, I've drunk it out of many things, including a silver cup, and I can't see where it makes much difference.

The following preparation is completely authentic, and from my numerous hours of research on the subject I can testify that it is real tasty. Whether you're watching your horse pull up lame in the Kentucky Derby or just passing time on a sunny afternoon, this is the appropriate drink for a hot summer's day. ◆ *Serves 1 Southern belle or gentleman*

Grandma's Lemon Iced Tea

◆◆◆

1 pitcher water (1 quart plus 1 pint)
4 tea bags
8 fluid ounces frozen lemonade
Mint sprigs for garnish (optional)

Do what Grandma did. A few sprigs of mint add a nice, cooling effect.

Every summer when we visited Grandma Wetzler, she would make this drink. Each morning when we got up there would be a big pitcher of water, with tea bags floating in it, sitting on the kitchen windowsill where the sun would hit it. By midafternoon it was good, strong tea, and Grandma would throw in frozen lemonade, give it a few stirs, and pour it out into tall glasses full of ice. This drink has been with me ever since. I particularly love it because its appearance is one of the first harbingers of summer. ◆ *About ½ gallon*

Daiquiris

◆◆◆◆◆◆◆◆◆◆◆◆◆◆◆◆◆◆◆◆◆◆◆◆◆◆◆◆◆◆◆◆◆◆◆◆◆◆

My close personal relationship with tropical climates has caused me to acquire many new tastes. One of the earliest was an appreciation of rum, a characteristic Caribbean liquor made from the sap of sugarcane, which is boiled down to molasses, which in turn is fermented and distilled.

Originally this was simply a budgetary decision, as rum is the least expensive liquor in island regions. Through the years, however, I have come to enjoy this fine liquor and its character in the same way other folks enjoy wine. In the West Indies, where rum is the drink of choice for most of the population, its subtle characteristics change from island to island.

One of the tastiest and most refreshing ways to enjoy rum is in combination with fresh fruit, and that is the basic concept of the daiquiri. This drink appears to have originated in Cuba around the turn of the century, but it was perfected and popularized in Havana in the twenties and thirties. During this period bartending in Cuba was raised to an art form, displaying a professionalism and creativity unequaled in the annals of the trade.

The daiquiri has changed over the years, but its essential components remain rum, lime juice, and sugar, and in this simple but elegant combination, the character of the rum is featured. Adding fresh tropical fruits mellows the drink a bit. Here are a couple of versions of this rum classic.

Your Basic Daiquiri

◆ ◆

2 ounces amber rum
2 tablespoons lime juice (about
   1 lime)
2 teaspoons sugar (superfine if
   you have it)

Fill a glass with ice, pour the rum over the ice, add the lime juice and sugar, and stir vigorously. That's the classic, and that's all there is to it.

As close to the original as you can get. I recommend that you use an amber rum such as Barbancourt from Haiti or St. James from Martinique. The brandylike quality of these has a more distinct character than that of the ubiquitous white rums. ◆ *1 drink*

Pineapple-Mango Daiquiri

◆ ◆

1 whole pineapple
2 mangoes
1 whole vanilla bean
Zest from 3 limes
½ cup sugar
1 quart amber rum (such as
   Cockspur *or* Ron del
   Barrilito)
1 pint dark rum (such as
   Myers's *or* Goslings)
1 pint white rum

Lime quarters for garnish

1. Slice off the top and bottom of the pineapple and cut it into quarters, leaving the skin on. Peel the mangoes, but leave the pits in.

A daiquiri may not be the first thing that comes to your mind when you think of drinks of the American Southwest, but it was in Santa Fe, New Mexico, that I enjoyed one of the most memorable daiquiris of my life.

I was sitting at the bar in Mark Miller's Coyote Cafe with a couple of friends. Facing us was a huge glass container stuffed with a darkish liquid, whole pineapple quarters, and what we later found out were vanilla beans. This concoction was listed on the menu as Brazilian Daiquiri, and I had to give it a try. It was superb. The straight rum had been mellowed and flavored by the pineapple, and the vanilla provided a smooth finish, yet the rum retained its strong character. A truly outstanding cocktail.

2. Put the pineapple, mangoes, vanilla bean, lime zest, and sugar into a wide-mouthed, one-gallon glass container. Pour the 3 types of rum into the container and seal it. (Most such containers have screw-on lids. If yours does not, seal it tightly with plastic wrap and cover that with tinfoil.)

3. Shake the container gently to dissolve the sugar. Set it aside and allow it to stand unrefrigerated for 3 weeks.

4. Strain it, discard the solids, and refrigerate the liquid. Serve over ice, garnished with a lime quarter.

Upon returning home, I was eager to develop my own version, and this is it. I've added mango to Mr. Miller's original recipe to smooth it out just a bit more. This might seem like a large amount to make, but if you are a rum drinker, this could be the best drink you have come across in years. ◆ *½ gallon or about 10 drinks*

Basic Fruit-Flavored Frozen Daiquiri Strategy

◆◆

5 ice cubes
2 ounces rum of your choice
2 teaspoons sugar
2 tablespoons lime juice (about 1 lime)
½ cup chopped fruit of your choice

Put it all into the blender, turn it on, and blend until smooth. Pour it out into a glass, lie back, and relax.

It's summertime and the livin' is easy. Time to slip on the baggy shorts and whip out the blender. There are thousands of different varieties of fruit-flavored frozen daiquiris, so here are some general rules and proportions that will let you make use of whatever fruits you prefer.

Approach the blender with some of the same principles in mind as when you approach the stove. The best results come from using the freshest, highest-quality ingredients and doing as little damage to them as possible. So the fruit you choose needs to be at its peak or even slightly overripe. I also like to have a bottle of very dark rum around—like Demerara from Guyana or Myers's—so I can float a touch on top of the finished drink. ◆ *1 drink*

The Last Resort

1 12-ounce can papaya juice
2 12-ounce cans guava juice
1¼ cups pineapple juice
1¼ cups orange juice
1 8-ounce can Coco Lopez
½ cup grenadine
1 jigger (2 ounces) golden rum
   per regular drink
1 splash dark rum per drink

1 slice mango *or* papaya per
   drink for garnish

1. Combine all the ingredients except the rums in a large container and mix well.

2. Fill a 16-ounce glass with ice, and add one shot (2 ounces) of golden rum such as Mount Gay or Ron del Barrilito.

3. Fill the glass to the top of the ice level with the Last Resort mixture and pour the contents of the glass into a blender.

4. Blend until completely combined (about 1 minute), pour into a fancy glass, and garnish with a slice of papaya or mango.

5. Float a splash of dark rum such as Myers's or Goslings on top.

One day the word came down from the top that the East Coast Grill needed to create a drink; everyone seemed to be doing it, and the Blue Margarita had run its course, calling for a successor. Answering the call of duty, we all got together one night after work for an R&D session at the bar. This is the result of that long, arduous night. This drink is something like a frozen Planter's Punch or Mai Tai, is as refreshing as a trade wind, and the addition of a tropical fruit garnish like mango or papaya completes the scene. ◆ *4 huge or 8 regular drinks*

Herman's Margarita Number Three

◆◆

5 ice cubes
2 ounces white *or* golden tequila
2 tablespoons lime juice (about
   1 lime)
1 ounce Cointreau
Kosher salt

1. Place all the ingredients except the salt in a shaker and mix well.

2. Rub the rim of an oversized martini glass (or other substantial glass) with the lime, just to wet it, and dip it in salt. You just want to coat the rim lightly here, so don't overdo it.

3. Strain the liquid into the glass.

Back in the fifties, the margarita introduced America to tequila, a powerful spirit of Mexican origin that is distilled from the sap of the agave cactus. My traveling buddy Herman "Tex" Burke, who considers himself somewhat of a margarita genius, has generously agreed for the first time to part in print with what he calls one of his "top 3 or 4" margarita renditions. The taste is strong and very tart, with a hint of orange, and light salt on the rim of the glass completes the concoction. ◆ *1 drink*

Planter's Punch

1 ounce amber rum
1 ounce bourbon
2 tablespoons lime juice (about
  1 lime)
2 tablespoons orange juice
2 teaspoons sugar
¼ ounce grenadine

No need to spend a lot of time fussing about: Mix all the ingredients together in a large glass with plenty of ice, stir well, and drink up.

Punches were very big in the Colonial South, with recipes handed down for generations, the ingredients and proportions closely guarded secrets. Today Planter's Punch has come to mean any combination of fruit juice and alcohol, usually containing grenadine. The addition of bourbon in this version may seem unusual, but I assure you it is authentic—early settlers of the South not only liked mixing spirits and fruit juice, they also were partial to mixing spirits with spirits. ◆ *1 drink*

Your Basic Pantry

◆◆

Part of the fun of grilling is using new and unusual foods, particularly staples from warm-weather climates where grilling is the predominant method of cooking. To make this easier for you, I have included this Pantry. It is divided into three sections: the Pantry of Processes describes techniques used to create recipe ingredients, such as braised garlic and roasted red peppers, which are either unavailable pre-prepared or markedly superior when made at home; the Pantry of Products lists pre-prepared ingredients you should have on hand, including such standards as kosher salt, hoisin sauce, and canned chipotles; and the Pantry of Produce describes the less-well-known fresh fruits and vegetables, and the chile peppers, used in this book.

This Pantry includes all of the somewhat unusual ingredients you will need in order to make some of the recipes in this book, but it is only the tip of the proverbial iceberg when it comes to ethnic ingredients. I strongly recommend that you take up what I have come to think of as Urban Foraging. Basically, this means that you get out there, find out what unfamiliar ingredients are available in your area, and learn to use them. Search out ethnic neighborhoods, walk into the food shops, and look for foods you have never seen before. The salespeople are always happy to let you know how they are used, and then you can take them home and build a dish or even a meal around them. In the same way, go to your local specialty stores—butcher shops, cheese stores, bakeries, fishmongers—and find out what the owner recommends as particularly fresh or of unusually high quality that day. This way, the whole process of creating the meal becomes as exciting as eating the final dish, and what you once may have thought of as a chore becomes fun.

The Pantry of Processes
◆◆◆◆◆◆◆◆◆◆◆◆◆◆◆◆◆◆◆◆◆◆◆◆

To Braise Garlic:

A head of garlic will yield about 4 tablespoons (2 ounces) of braised garlic. To prepare it, place the whole, unpeeled head of garlic in the center of a foot-long sheet of tinfoil, pour about 3 tablespoons of virgin olive oil over the entire bulb of garlic, and wrap it up very tightly. Roast in a 300°F oven for about 1 hour, or until the individual garlic cloves are soft to the touch. Remove the bulb from the oven and allow it to cool to room temperature, which will take about ½ hour. If necessary, you can refrigerate the bulb at this point and remove the pulp later, but it is much easier to do while the cloves are still warm. In either case, be sure you reserve the oil in which the garlic has roasted.

To remove the pulp, simply break the individual cloves of garlic from the bulb and squeeze out the inner meat. (There is no need to cut open each clove, since it will break when you separate it from the bulb.) When all the cloves have been squeezed, add the reserved oil to the meat. The oil has a deep garlic flavor and will prolong the shelf life of the braised garlic. With the oil, braised garlic can be stored, covered and refrigerated, about 2 weeks; without the oil it lasts only 1 week.

To Roast Red Bell Peppers:

Roasting a bell pepper removes the skin and adds a rich, smoky flavor. It might seem like an odd technique the first time you do it, but sprinkle the resulting peppers with salt and pepper and a little olive oil, splash them with balsamic vinegar, and you'll be torching these babies every time the grill is out.

With the fire at high heat, take 5 red bell peppers and whip them on the grill. Now, I know that this goes against your better instincts, but you're going to burn them until they are completely black. It is theoretically possible to burn them too much, but if you kind of roll them around until they are completely dark and the skin is well blistered, you've got it right. Remove the peppers from the grill, pop them into a brown paper bag, tie the bag shut, and allow the peppers to cool in the bag for 1 hour. This facilitates the removal of the burned skins.

After 1 hour, remove the peppers from the bag and sort of fondle them in your hands, caressing the skins into falling off. Tear the peppers in half, remove the inner cores and seeds, and run the peppers gently under cold water to remove any remaining charred pieces of skin. That's it. Put them in a small container, cover with olive oil, cover the container, and refrigerate. They will keep up to 2 weeks stored in this manner. If you wish, a fresh herb such as basil or rosemary and a little chopped garlic can be added to complement the flavor of the peppers.

To Make Coconut Milk:

Do not confuse this staple of Indonesian cooking with the liquid in the center of a coconut, often mistakenly referred to by the same name. The following procedure will yield about 2 cups of milk.

Remove the outer husk of a 1½-pound coconut by throwing it repeatedly at a brick wall or the sidewalk—or you can smash it with a hammer. This should render the coconut into 4 to 6 smaller, more manageable pieces. With a blunt object such as a potato peeler, pry off the outer husk from each piece. The thinner brown inner skin can be left on. Put the husked coconut pieces into a food processor or blender and purée until it is very fine, with no large chunks. Turn off the food processor or blender, add 2 cups of boiling water, then blend for about 10 seconds. Remove the mixture from the food processor or blender and strain it through a fine sieve or cheesecloth. Reserve the liquid (the "milk") and discard the solids. The milk will keep in the refrigerator, covered, up to 10 days.

If you live near an Asian, Indian, or Caribbean market, you will be able to find canned coconut milk, which is a good product. Do not confuse this with Coco Lopez, a sweetened coconut-flavored cream.

To Reconstitute Sun-dried Tomatoes:

You can buy sun-dried tomatoes either dry or packed in oil. The dried version are much less expensive, so I recommend that you buy them and follow these directions to prepare them for use. You should be also aware that sun-drieds vary widely in quality, so make sure to find ones that are not brittle. Avoid ones that are cracked or very dry to the touch—they are either too old or mass-produced or both.

To bring back about 20 sun-dried tomatoes, heat 1 cup of virgin olive oil over medium heat until it is hot but not smoking, about 5 minutes. (When the oil is too hot to keep your finger in, it is ready.) Turn off the heat and stir the tomatoes and 2 peeled garlic cloves into the oil. Allow to cool to room temperature, then place them in a tightly covered jar and refrigerate. As long as they are in oil, the tomatoes will keep, covered and refrigerated, for up to 6 weeks.

Pantry of Products
◆ ◆ ◆ ◆ ◆ ◆ ◆ ◆ ◆ ◆ ◆ ◆ ◆ ◆ ◆ ◆

ACHIOTE: The Spanish name for the seed from a small tropical tree. It is used in Latin America primarily to color lard, either in seed form or ground up and made into a paste. It does not have a very pronounced flavor and paprika is an acceptable substitute. (Also see page 375.)

CHIPOTLES: Dried, smoked jalapeño chile peppers, available dried or canned. I prefer canned. If chipotles are unavailable, you may substitute a mixture of Liquid Smoke, 2 to 3 puréed fresh chile peppers of your choice, and 3 tablespoons ketchup.

GUAVA PASTE: This Brazilian product is just what its name says it is—a paste made of guava. It has a supersweet concentrated guava taste and is found in 1-pound cans in Latin markets.

HOISIN: A Chinese sauce made from soy sauce, yellow beans, sugar, vinegar, and spices, hoisin is used both in conjunction with other sauces and by itself. It is found in all Asian markets and some supermarkets in cans and jars.

KOSHER SALT: This coarse-grained sea salt containing natural iodine is the only type that I use. I like it in soups and relishes because it dissolves more quickly than iodized salt, and on meat and fish because it has a better flavor than the free-flowing variety. Besides, it just feels better when you are sprinkling it on with your fingers. Try it and you'll agree.

MISO (aka fermented bean paste): This Japanese staple is the result of injecting mold into boiled soybeans. The addition of wheat, rice, or barley produces varying strengths, colors, and flavors. In Japanese cooking, miso is used in everything from salad dressings to soup to condiments for grilled foods, and its versatility and adaptability make it a wonderful item with which to experiment.

OILS: You should keep at least three types of oil handy. First, an inexpensive vegetable oil to coat foods before grilling. There's no point in using a better or tastier oil, since the flavor is lost during grilling anyway, and the oil is used only to prevent sticking. Second, a low- to medium-quality olive oil for use in relishes and dressings. The taste of the oil does come through somewhat in these preparations, but it is usually dominated by the other ingredients. Finally, a very fine, expensive, extra virgin olive oil. I would keep this stashed away and break it out only for those dishes in which the olive oil is really going to stand out—those late-summer tomatoes eaten with basil, salt, pepper, and a drizzle of olive oil, for example, or Grilled Pompano with Lime and Olive Oil (page 95) or Grilled Figs with Prosciutto and Provolone (page 178).

PEPPER, FRESHLY CRACKED, BLACK OR WHITE: The difference between pre-ground and freshly cracked pepper is enormous. Pepper is used in almost every recipe in this book, and I can't emphasize strongly enough how important it is that you use freshly cracked. It has a strong impact on a dish. For many of my simple meat, fish, or vegetable dishes, the only seasonings used are salt and pepper, so you might as well use the best. In my house a small dish of kosher salt and a small dish of freshly cracked black pepper are permanent fixtures next to the grill and on the dining room table.

There are a couple of ways to crack peppercorns. In the East Coast Grill, a part of each cook's daily routine is to crack a bowlful of black and white peppercorns by placing them on a cutting board or other hard surface and rolling the edge of a sauté pan over them (see the diagram). This is a good technique, and you can quickly crack enough to last you a week or so, which is how long cracked pepper will retain its intensity. On the other hand, the pepper mill is also a perfectly acceptable tool for cracking pepper. If you use a mill, though, I recommend that you set it to its coarsest grind.

In many of my seafood and Asian-inspired recipes, I suggest using white pepper. This is because I find the more aromatic, less robust nature of this pepper to be more appropriate for these rather delicate dishes.

PICKLED GINGER (aka *gari*) (also see Homemade Pickled Ginger, page 191): A traditional Japanese raw fish accompaniment, this very thinly sliced, vinegared ginger has a natural affinity for grilled food. It is available in Japanese markets or in the Japanese sections of Asian markets in 1-pound plastic containers. It will keep indefinitely in your refrigerator, covered, in its liquid.

SESAME OIL: Made from sesame seeds, this oil has a very pronounced, nutty/ burned flavor and is used more for flavoring than for straight cooking.

TOMATILLO: This Latin American staple looks like a small, unripe tomato with a brown husk. It is cooked and used in sauces and salsas in Latin cuisines, and is widely available in the United States canned as well as fresh.

VINEGARS: Vinegars, along with citrus juices, are high-acid liquids that stimulate the sour taste buds on the tongue. As such, they are excellent flavor balancers, helping to bring other strong tastes into harmony. I use many kinds in my recipes—red wine, cider, white, rice wine, and balsamic. Rice wine vinegar is a beautifully delicate vinegar, its subtle sweetness being its major characteristic. My personal favorite, however, is the balsamic vinegar of Italy. The process of making this intensely flavored vinegar includes lengthy aging in charred oak barrels, and it may be this period of close proximity to charred wood that explains its phenomenal compatibility with grilled foods. A sprinkle of balsamic will bring a simple piece of grilled meat or poultry to life, drawing out its innate flavor. If I could have only three seasonings with me at the grill, balsamic vinegar would be there, along with kosher salt and freshly cracked pepper.

WASABI (aka Japanese horseradish): A traditional Japanese accompaniment to raw fish, this root is more aromatic but less powerful than the white root we know as horseradish. In the United States it is available as paste or as powder that you mix with water yourself to form a paste. I find the powder to be far superior to the premade paste, for it better conveys the floral, nasal heat that is characteristic of horseradish.

Pantry of Produce

BONIATO (aka batata or Cuban sweet potato): This is basically a white sweet potato. Originally a New World product, it is widely used in Asia as well as in the Caribbean and South America. In the United States, it is found mostly in Latin markets.

BREADFRUIT: Why was there a mutiny on the *Bounty*? Well, one of the reasons was because Captain Bligh cut the crew's water ration. Why did he do that? To keep the breadfruit trees alive. The mission of the H.M.S. *Bounty*, after all, was to retrieve breadfruit seedlings from the South Seas and transport them to the West Indies to be planted as inexpensive food for slaves in the sugarcane fields. Breadfruit now grows on almost every Caribbean island and also on the mainland of South America as far south as Brazil.

The breadfruit tree is a prolific producer of its fruit, which is actually a vegetable. When mature, the fruit ranges in size from 5 to 8 inches in diameter and has a yellowish-greenish-brown skin. As with a number of other tropical fruits and vegetables, it is eaten in its green, ripe, and overripe stages. The flesh is fibrous but is prepared in the same manner as a potato. Breadfruit is sold all year long in West Indian markets.

JICAMA: This tuber, with a taste that lies somewhere between an apple and a potato, originated in Mexico or the Amazon basin or both, depending upon whom you ask. It was spread by the Spanish to the Philippines and eventually throughout the Pacific Rim. In the United States, its crunchy texture and slightly sweet taste have become increasingly familiar as part of the Southwestern food trend. Peel its skin off with a knife, cover it with water, and jicama will keep covered in the refrigerator for up to 2 days. Jicama can be found in Latin and Asian markets and some supermarkets.

LEMONGRASS: It is this grass, grown in tropical areas around the world, that produces the characteristic flavor of Thai and Vietnamese cuisines. Its distinctive taste illustrates aromaticity better than any other herb or spice with which I am familiar. The inedible, tough upper stems are excellent for infusing stocks and soups, and are used in many parts of the world to make tea, while the bottom section can be chopped fine and used directly in recipes. To prepare lemongrass, remove the stems above the bottom third (the bulb) and reserve them for use in broths, soups, or teas. Remove the outer leaves from the bottom third, and inside you will find a tender core. Mince this core very fine as you would ginger or garlic, and add to dishes as directed. It is found in Asian and specialty markets. Although not as aromatic, dried lemongrass makes a decent substitute.

MALANGA (aka yautia): This Caribbean root vegetable is very similar in appearance to the taro of the Pacific. Mealy and starchy, it has a more dynamic flavor than its many brother tubers, its distinct, earthy flavor hinting of beans or nuts. Like many other tubers, it is prepared in the same way as potatoes. Available in West Indian markets.

MANGO: Along with the watermelon, this is one of my very favorite fruits. It originated somewhere in Southeast Asia, perhaps Burma, but today the largest crops are grown in India, where it is considered the "king of fruits." It is also a cash crop throughout Mexico, Central and South America, and the Caribbean. Like the papaya, the mango is used in its green state as a vegetable, either cooked or added raw to salads. The flesh is somewhat difficult to get at, but well worth the effort, since the person who does the job gets to suck and gnaw on the pit. If that sounds strange to you, it's okay by me—I'll peel all the mangoes I can get my hands on. In urban areas, mangoes are sold in Asian markets and even many supermarkets.

PAPAYA: Used as both a fruit and a vegetable, the papaya is native to the Caribbean and is found in tropical regions throughout the world. It can grow up to twenty pounds in size. The musky-flavored fruit—also known for its ability to tenderize meat—ranges in color from greenish-yellow when underripe to bright orange and in some cases even red when fully ripe. It is used as a salad ingredient, cooked in soups, or eaten raw as a kind of snack food with just a squeeze of lime juice. Unfortunately, this fruit travels poorly, so most Americans have never had the opportunity to taste it at its peak. In urban areas, papayas are sold in Latin markets, specialty stores, and some supermarkets.

PLANTAIN (**aka green banana, cooking banana**): This tropical relative of the banana is always cooked before being eaten. In its green state, it has the starchy quality of a potato, but by the time it is ripe (the skin will be black), the starch has turned to sugar. In its ripe stage, the plantain is used in desserts or as snack food. Popular in the West Indies, Central America, Africa, and Asia, it keeps for a long time and is a wonderfully adaptable ingredient with which to experiment in stews, fritters, and desserts. In urban areas, plantains are found in Latin and West Indian markets.

TAMARIND: This fruit consists of a pod from 3 to 6 inches long covered with brown, furry skin, and containing sweetish dark brown pulp along with several seeds. It is used to flavor a number of condiments, of which Worcestershire sauce is the most familiar to Americans. In Latin cuisines, its tart flavor is sometimes substituted for lemon or lime. It is sold in a convenient-to-use paste form in Asian and Indian markets.

YUCA (**aka cassava or manioc**): This sticky, bland root vegetable originated in Brazil and was a staple of the Arawaks, pre-Columbian tropical Native Americans. Today it is widely used in Africa as well as Central and South America, and in the South Pacific it is combined with coconuts to make desserts. The yuca is generally prepared in the same way as a potato, except that it contains a main central fiber which must be removed before cooking. It is available in Latin markets.

Peppers and Chiles

I'm not sure if the pepper family (the genus *Capsicum*) is a botanist's fondest dream or worst nightmare, but it sure has changed the food of the world. Try to imagine the cuisines of North Africa, India, or Southeast Asia with no heat or spiciness except that of black and white peppercorns. It is hard to conceive of, but that's the way it was before 1492. It is no wonder that peppercorns used to be counted out one by one, and were even used as currency in some cultures.

This all changed, though, with Columbus's voyage to the New World and his discovery of *Capsicum*, which he kind of confused with pepper (as in peppercorns), which was what he was supposed to be finding. The capsicum's own rampant promiscuity took it from there, as it mated at high speed with any available member of the whole genus to produce a constant array of new species. The peppers from the New World were embraced and used heavily in cuisines throughout the world as soon as they became available. Lagging behind, North Americans only in the past few years have begun to appreciate some heat in their food.

What exactly is the source of our intense attraction to these hot, spicy little plants? Paul Rozin, a psychologist, believes that our body's reaction to the intense burning sensations caused by eating chile peppers is a danger signal, designed to make us stop eating them. However, since it is not really a dangerous situation, we can ignore our body's signals and plunge ahead. He calls this a "constrained risk" situation, and likens it to a roller coaster ride or gambling. Basically it's exciting. Some say that the brain might also be secreting its own opiates (endorphins) during the process, which gives new meaning to the term "chile pepper junkie."

In any case, peppers vary widely in heat, so you can decide for yourself just how much of a thrill you want. An individual chile pepper's heat is measured in Scoville units, which are a measurement of how many units of water it takes to neutralize one unit of capsaicin, the heat-causing substance contained in chile peppers. The familiar jalapeño checks in at 2,500 to 3,000 Scoville units. My personal favorite, the Scotch Bonnet, registers 150,000 to 300,000 Scoville units. More thrilling than Las Vegas.

The majority of the heat of a fresh chile pepper is contained in the seeds and white interior ribs, which can be removed if you want to make it milder. (If you have sensitive skin you should definitely wear gloves during the cleaning process, and avoid rubbing your eyes. I found this out the hard way and spent a very embarrassing lunch with yogurt smeared all over my face—it worked, but it looked a little silly.) You should also be aware that the heat of a particular type of chile pepper varies from field to field and even from plant to plant, so you may get an occasional surprise.

In my recipes, I have used many different chile peppers, most of which are quite readily available but which vary wildly in intensity of heat. With the exception of the Scotch Bonnet or rocotillo, you can substitute one for another without altering the recipe, so my suggestion is that you locate a particular chile pepper that you enjoy and establish a relationship with it. Then, when the honeymoon ends, step it up a level.

If you are interested in learning more about chile peppers, I highly recommend what I consider the best work on the subject, *Peppers, the Domesticated Capsicums*, by Dr. Jean Andrews (Austin: University of Texas Press, 1984). For an even closer connection, these peppers are beautiful and fun to grow at home. If you are so inclined, Dorothy L. Van Vleck, 10536 119 Avenue, North Largo, Florida 34643, is a superb source for a phenomenal range of chile pepper seeds —tomato peppers, black dollars, goat horns, rat tails, ring of fire, and yatsafusa are just a few in her arsenal.

Let me give you a brief description of each of the chile peppers used in this book, progressing from mild to mind-blowing.

ANCHO: A dried chile, this pepper has more flavor than heat. To prepare one (or more) for use in cooking, remove the seeds, toast it lightly, then place it in a bowl, add boiling water to cover, and allow it to soak for 40 minutes. Physical description: Flat; dark brown to red; 2 to 3 inches long and about 1½ inches wide.

ROCOTILLO: One of the few peppers for which I feel there is no substitute. It has all the aromaticity and flavor of the awesome Scotch Bonnet (*habañero*) with none of its heat. The fascinating rocotillo can be found in West Indian and Latin markets, but be careful—while smaller in size, it is similar in shape to the king of heat, the Scotch Bonnet. Physical description: Shaped like a wrinkled pattypan squash; red, orange, or various shades of green; very small, like a bottle cap.

CHIPOTLE: A dried, smoked jalapeño, it usually comes canned, packed in a tomato sauce. If you find dried ones, they can be reconstituted by soaking in boiling water for 40 minutes. Their strong, imposing flavor makes them my favorite dried chile. A little goes a long way, since their smoky, earthy heat is strong and forceful. I use chipotles not only in sauces and relishes, but also in salad dressings, mayonnaises, and butters. Physical description: Flat and wrinkled; dark reddish-brown; 1 to 1½ inches long.

JALAPEÑO: Probably the largest cash chile pepper crop, this is the most widely known pepper in the United States. It is easy to find and, although relatively low on the heat scale, it still packs a decent punch. Although the red variety is a bit more difficult to find than the green, I find it has a richer flavor. Physical description: Plump and bullet-shaped; either red or green, with a sleek and shiny look; about 1 to 1½ inches long.

SERRANO: Like the jalapeño, the serrano is native to Mexico, but it is less widely available in the United States. These "green bullets from hell" are one step up the heat ladder from jalapeños. Physical description: Shaped like a skinny jalapeño; either red or green; 1 to 1½ inches long and ½ inch in diameter.

TABASCO: A step hotter yet, this chile pepper was popularized by the McIlhenney Company of Louisiana in the hot sauce that bears the pepper's name. The sauce itself makes a good heat source. Physical description: Shaped like a blunt jalapeño with wrinkled skin; red, yellow, or orange; 1 to 1½ inches long.

CAYENNE: Turn it up one more notch. This chile pepper, found all over the world, is most familiar to us in its powdered form but can also be found fresh. Either is fine. The Chile de Árbol is a type of cayenne, most often found dried. Physical description: Skinny, tubular pod shape, usually starting to bend toward the tip; either red or green; 3 to 4 inches long.

SCOTCH BONNET (*Habañero*): This is it. Generally acknowledged as the hottest commercially available chile pepper in the world, this baby, with its Scoville rating of up to 300,000, will take you places you've never been before. Go ahead, laugh, but you won't be laughing after you get ahold of one of these. Mike Turk, a regular customer at the East Coast Grill and a true devotee of the pepper, is known for his legendary tolerance for hot food. On a bet one day, he ate a single Scotch Bonnet. Watching his face for the next five minutes was well worth the loss of the wager. His recovery only began some fifteen minutes after blast-off, aided by a large glass of vintage port—which I guess will now be added to the long list of heat remedies.

Grown in Belize, many of the islands of the West Indies, and the Yucatán of Mexico, this is not an easy pepper to find. Your best bet is to try West Indian or Latin markets, where it can sometimes be located. Physical description: Lantern-shaped, short, fat, and slightly wrinkled (as its West Indian name suggests, it looks somewhat like a Scotsman's bonnet); yellow, red-orange, or green; 1 to 1½ inches long and about 1 inch in diameter.

Where to Get It

Sources for Unusual Ingredients

This list of places will enable you to get some of the harder-to-find ingredients used in this book. They are listed alphabetically by city within each category, and mail-order sources are indicated by an (*). Many of these stores also have catalogues they will send you, which is fun because then you can browse through the pages of exotic foreign ingredients.

General Ingredients

These four stores have a huge selection of ingredients, both fresh and prepared, from all over the culinary map. They all have mail-order catalogues, and you can get a wide variety of ingredients from a single source if you so desire.

*Rafal Spice Company
2521 Russell Street
Detroit, MI 48207
(800) 228-4276
In Michigan: (313) 259-6373

*Balducci's
Mail-order Division
424 Sixth Avenue
New York, NY 10011
(800) 247-2450
In New York: 212-673-2600

*Dean & DeLuca
560 Broadway
New York, NY 10012
(800) 221-7714
In New York: 212-431-1691

*G. B. Ratto, International Grocers
821 Washington Street
Oakland, CA 94607
(800) 325-3483
In California: (800) 228-3515

Mexican/Latin American/Caribbean Ingredients

India Tea and Spice, Inc.
453 Common Street
Belmont, MA 02178
(617) 484-3737

Tropical Foods, Inc.
2101 Washington Street
Boston, MA 02119
(617) 442-7439

El Coloso Market
102 Columbia Street
Cambridge, MA 02139
(617) 491-1361

La Casa del Pueblo
1810 South Blue Island
Chicago, IL 60608
(312) 421-4640

El Original Supermercado Cardenas
3922 North Sheridan Road
Chicago, IL 60607
(312) 525-5610

*La Preferida, Inc.
3400 West 35th Street
Chicago, IL 60632
(312) 254-7200

Hernandez Mexican Foods
2120 Alamo Street
Dallas, TX 75202
(214) 742-2533

Johnnie's Market
2030 Larimer Street
Denver, CO 80205
(303) 297-0155

Algo Especial
2628 Bagley Street
Detroit, MI 48216
(313) 963-9013

La Colmena
2443 Bagley Street
Detroit, MI 48216
(313) 237-0295

Hi-Lo Market
415 Centre Street
Jamaica Plain, MA 02130
(617) 522-6364

The Grand Central Market
317 South Broadway
Los Angeles, CA 90013
(213) 622-1763

International Groceries and Meat Market
5219 Ninth Avenue (39th and 40th Streets)
New York, NY 10018
(212) 279-5514

Latin American Products
142 West 46th Street
New York, NY 10036
(212) 302-4323

Casa Sanchez
2778 24th Street
San Francisco, CA 94110
(415) 282-2400

Americana Grocery
1813 Columbia Road N.W.
Washington, DC 20009
(202) 265-7455

Casa Peña
1636 17th Street N.W.
Washington, DC 20009
(202) 462-2222

Asian Ingredients

Ming's Market
85-91 Essex Street
Boston, MA 02111
(617) 482-8805

*New England Food
225 Harrison Avenue
Boston, MA 02111
(617) 426-8592

Sun Sun Company
18 Oxford Street
Boston, MA 02111
(617) 426-6494

*Star Market
3349 North Clark Street
Chicago, IL 60657
(312) 472-0599

Tan Viet Market
10332 Ferguson Road
Dallas, TX 75228
(214) 324-5160

*Bangkok Market, Inc.
4804-6 Melrose Avenue
Los Angeles, CA 90029
(213) 662-9705

Yee Sing Chong Company, Inc.
977 North Broadway
Los Angeles, CA 90012
(213) 626-9619

Keesan Imports
9252 Bird Road
Miami, FL 33165
(305) 551-9591

*Southeastern Food Supply
400 N.E. 67th Street
Miami, FL 33431
(305) 758-1432

*Kam Kuo Food Corporation
7 Mott Street
New York, NY 10013
(212) 349-3097

*Kam Man Food Products
200 Canal Street
New York, NY 10013
(212) 571-0330

*Katagari & Company, Inc.
(large Japanese selection)
224 East 59th Street
New York, NY 10022
(212) 755-3566

*The Chinese Grocer
209 Post Street at Grant Avenue
San Francisco, CA 94108
(415) 982-0125 or (800) 227-3320

*Da Hua Market
623 H Street N.W.
Washington, DC 20001
(202) 371-8880

Greek and Middle Eastern Ingredients

*Sahadi Importing Company, Inc.
187 Atlantic Avenue
Brooklyn, NY 11201
(718) 624-4550

*C & K Importing Company
2771 West Pico Boulevard
Los Angeles, CA 90006
(213) 737-2970

Indian Ingredients and Exotic Spices

Indian Tea & Spices
453 Common Street
Belmont, MA 02178
(617) 484-3737

*Bazaar of India
1810 University Avenue
Berkeley, CA 94703
(415) 548-4110

*International Grocer
3411 Woodward
Detroit, MI 48201
(313) 831-5480

*House of Spices
76–17 Broadway
Jackson Heights, NY 11373
(718) 476-1577

Market Spices
85A Pike Place Market
Seattle, Washington 98101
(206) 622-6340

Miscellaneous Ingredients

GENUINE SMITHFIELD HAMS:
*Gwaltney, Inc.
P.O. Box 489
Smithfield, VA 23430
(804) 399-0417

A VARIETY OF HARDWOODS AND HARDWOOD CHARCOALS:
*Don Hysko
People's Woods
55 Mill Street
Cumberland, RI 02864
(401) 725-2700

HOT CHILE PEPPERS TO GROW YOURSELF:
The Pepper Gal, Dorothy L. Van Vleck
10536 119th Avenue North
Largo, FL 34643

Roswell Seed Co.
115-117 South Main
P.O. Box 725
Roswell, N.M. 88201
(505) 622-7701

LATIN VEGETABLES TO GROW YOURSELF:
J. A. Mako Horticultural Experience
P.O. Box 34082
Dallas, TX 75234

ASIAN VEGETABLES TO GROW YOURSELF:
Mellinger's
2310 West South Range Road
North Lima, OH 44452
(216) 549-9861

FOR INNER BEAUTY HOT SAUCE:
Le Saucier
632 Hyde Park Avenue
Boston, MA 02131
(800) EAT-SAUC

*Dean & DeLuca
560 Broadway
New York, NY 10012
(800) 221-7714
In New York: 212-431-1691

East Coast Grill
(617) 491-6568

The Pottery Barn's catalog

Index

About the Authors

♦ ♦

Chris Schlesinger grew up in Virginia and, at age eighteen, dropped out of school to wash dishes. He soon graduated to fry cook, went on to receive his formal training at the Culinary Institute of America, and subsequently cooked in restaurants ranging from Hawaiian burger joints to New England's finest dining rooms. In 1985, he and partner Cary Wheaton opened the East Coast Grill in Cambridge, Massachusetts, and in 1987, they opened Jake and Earl's Dixie Barbecue next door.

John Willoughby was born and raised in Iowa, and graduated from Harvard University in 1970. He has worked as a community organizer, legal services advocate, health administrator, and free-lance writer in the Boston area, and for three years worked part-time with Chris Schlesinger in the kitchen of the East Coast Grill. He has published articles about food in several national magazines and is the feature writer for *Cook's* magazine.